Law and Philosophy Library

Volume 127

The Law and Philosophy Library, which has been in existence since 1985, aims to publish cutting edge works in the philosophy of law, and has a special history of publishing books that focus on legal reasoning and argumentation, including those that may involve somewhat formal methodologies. The series has published numerous important books on law and logic, law and artificial intelligence, law and language, and law and rhetoric. While continuing to stress these areas, the series has more recently expanded to include books on the intersection between law and the Continental philosophical tradition, consistent with the traditional openness of the series to books in the Continental jurisprudential tradition. The series is proud of the geographic diversity of its authors, and many have come from Latin America, Spain, Italy, the Netherlands, Germany, and Eastern Europe, as well, more obviously for an English-language series, from the United Kingdom, the United States, Australia, and Canada.

More information about this series at http://www.springer.com/series/6210

Izabela Skoczeń

Implicatures within Legal Language

Springer

Izabela Skoczeń
Department of Legal Theory and Jagiellonian
Centre for Law, Language and Philosophy
Jagiellonian University
Kraków, Poland

ISSN 1572-4395 ISSN 2215-0315 (electronic)
Law and Philosophy Library
ISBN 978-3-030-12531-8 ISBN 978-3-030-12532-5 (eBook)
https://doi.org/10.1007/978-3-030-12532-5

Library of Congress Control Number: 2019931925

This Springer imprint is published by the registered company Springer Nature Switzerland AG.
The registered company address is: Gewerbestrasse 11, 6330 Cham, Switzerland

Acknowledgments

This research was funded by the Polish Ministry of Science and Higher Education (grant number DI2012 019042). I would like to warmly thank Prof. Tomasz Gizbert-Studnicki and Prof. Katarzyna Kijania-Placek for their invaluable comments. I would also like to thank Prof. Francois Recanati for our helpful discussion during my stay at the Institut Jean Nicod. My heartfelt thanks are also extended to professors Stephen Neale, Francesca Poggi, Marcin Matczak, Jeffrey Goldsworthy and many others for the insights and inspiration gained during conferences. I am also very grateful to my colleagues from the Department of Legal Theory as well as Krzysztof Posłajko and Paweł Banaś from the Institute of Philosophy at the Jagiellonian University for their input. Finally, I would like to thank Jerzy Gabriel Wróbel, Ewa Grzęda, Magda Brewczyńska, Agnieszka Staszek, Maria Turbasa and Anika Zemowska for their help in unearthing interesting case law.

Contents

Chapter 1
Introduction

1.1 A Roadmap

In 1975 Paul Grice, the famous British philosopher, published his seminal work 'Logic and Conversation'. This work was a milestone in his effort to delimit the fields of interest of semantics and pragmatics. Grice noticed that people usually convey much more than just the amalgam of the meanings of the words they utter; he labeled this surplus of meaning a conversational implicature. For instance, consider the following conversation:

A: Are you hungry?
B: I have just had breakfast.

What B has said is that he has just had breakfast, but he has also conveyed something else, something that makes the two seemingly unconnected utterances very closely related. What B has implicated is simply that he is not hungry. According to Grice, hearers calculate 'what is implicated' with the use of some special rules called maxims of conversation and the conversational principle. Grice also created an internalist theory of meaning, claiming that it is the speaker's intention that determines the meaning to be conveyed.

The purpose of the present study is to propose an analytical or explanatory[1] theory of legal discourse in a modified Gricean paradigm. This study adopts a chronological order, meaning that it first considers implicatures as defined by Paul Grice before considering the neo-Gricean theories of implicatures and other pragmatic effects. By 'other pragmatic effects' I mean pragmatic enrichments, which are pragmatic developments of the notion of 'what is said'. Neo-Griceans point out that quite often a part of a proposition decoded on the basis of what is said is not decoded

[1] I purposefully refrain from using the word 'descriptive' since I want to avoid associations with the descriptive-normative opposition. This is because I am tackling issues related to linguistic meaning in the book and I want to avoid questions raised in the debate of whether meaning is normative as this would require a separate book. I thank an anonymous reviewer for pointing this out to me.

I. Skoczeń, *Implicatures within Legal Language*, Law and Philosophy Library 127, https://doi.org/10.1007/978-3-030-12532-5_1

solely on the basis of the syntax or semantics of the sentence. Consider the following example:

A: Are you hungry?
B: I have had a very large breakfast [today].

What B has said is 'I have had a very large breakfast', *tout court.* Clearly, there is a pragmatic enrichment of this with the word 'today' because it would be quite absurd if B's answer meant that he had had a very large breakfast sometime once in his life. Consequently, the full truth-apt proposition decoded on the basis of B's answer is 'I have had a very large breakfast today'. By contrast, the proposition conveyed by B in the conversational implicature is 'I am not hungry'. This proposition is independently truth-evaluable.

Through 'legal discourse', one can mean several types of discourse, for instance:

1. An exchange within a legislative body
2. An exchange between a legislature and courts
3. An exchange between a court and parties
4. An exchange between parties
5. Contracts and other legal declarations of intent (F. Poggi calls them acts of private autonomy: 'the acts with which the individuals regulate their own relations through singular norms that produce effects which are both recognized and guaranteed by the legal system (ex. contracts, wills, other unilateral acts)' (Poggi 2011, p. 37))

This study concentrates on the second type of legal discourse, namely the exchange between legislatures and courts. It will build an analytical or explanatory theory—a theory intended to explain the mechanisms behind courts' decisions—rather than a normative theory that would state how these mechanisms should work.

Two elements will be preserved from the Gricean ideas used in sketching the theory. The first is the treatment of linguistic exchanges as communication; the second is that there are strong pragmatic effects in language that take the form of conversational implicatures. However, important modifications to the Gricean way of thinking will need to be introduced. Firstly, the sketched theory will adopt different notions of 'what is said' and different content of maxims of conversation (different assumptions about what rules your interlocutor is following). Secondly, the Gricean theory of meaning will be rejected.

The theory outlined here will rely on a modified Gricean idea, updated with all the corrections brought to the classical Gricean theory by neo-Gricean theorists. The theory will add a novel, second-order strategic framework to the picture. Let me now provide a roadmap of the construction of the aforementioned analytical or explanatory theory of legal discourse.

This study consists of six chapters, including the introduction. In the second chapter, I give an outline of the classical Gricean theory and suggest that it is not directly applicable to the legal realm and needs substantial modification. I also sketch a novel theory that includes the strategic framework. In the third chapter, I question Grice's ideas on the number of maxims of conversations and their content. In the fourth chapter, I question Grice's views on the notion of 'what is said'. Next, in the fifth chapter I show that the Gricean notion of meaning is not applicable to the legal realm. The last chapter contains examples of pragmatic processes from the Polish legal system and an explanation of these processes through the lens of the theory sketched in this study.

Let me now provide a slightly more detailed roadmap. In the first chapter, I give an outline of the classical Gricean theory of implicatures, outlining the points in which it is not applicable to the legal realm. Next, I give an account of theories that have tried to modify the Gricean picture to fit it to the legal realm. The most important of them is Andrei Marmor's account of 'strategic speech'. I try to illustrate how Marmor's account has some weak points that require modification so as to form a fully fledged, explanatory theory of the legal discourse. Finally, I propose a second-order, strategic framework that explains linguistic exchanges in the realm of law.

In the second chapter, I deal with certain influential neo-Gricean theories. These are theories that discuss Paul Grice's idea of the maxims of conversation. I show how the four Gricean maxims can be reduced to fewer rules of this type: the Q and R principles proposed by L. Horn. I also argue that some theories that reduce the number of maxims, such as Relevance Theory, cannot be applied to the legal realm. Finally, I show that the theory I sketched in the second chapter is applicable regardless of the content or number of maxims we postulate at the 'first' level.

In the third chapter, I question the Gricean notion of 'what is said'. I give an outline of arguments supporting the thesis that there are more pragmatic elements of the 'what is said' notion than just disambiguation and reference assignments. These additional elements are referred to as 'pragmatic enrichments' by neo-Griceans and are distinguished by them from conversational implicatures.[2] I argue that such pragmatic enrichments are subject to the same strategic framework as strong pragmatic effects such as conversational implicatures.

In the fourth chapter, I begin with an outline of the theory of meaning provided by Paul Grice. This is an inherently internalist theory, which means that meaning is determined by the speaker's intention. I show that legal language needs an externalist theory of meaning. Thus, I argue that while the internalist may have a point in explaining what is going on in everyday linguistic exchanges, the externalist is in a much better position to give a coherent account of legal language. In other words, I postulate an internalist theory of everyday language and an externalist theory of legal parlance. I also argue that the Gricean theory of implicatures can be separated from his theory of meaning.

In these four chapters, I discuss some famous cases that appear often in the literature. Most of these cases are from common law systems. In order to demonstrate that the theory that I propose is generally applicable, I have added a sixth chapter in which I provide examples of pragmatic effects in the law in the Polish legal system (a continental system). I select examples from civil and criminal law and hope that this shows how the strategic framework is a universal mechanism that is not restricted to any particular type of legal system.

---

[2] Note that this is neo-Gricean terminology, since Grice himself would have called any pragmatic effect different from disambiguation and reference assignment a conversational implicature.

Before proceeding, it is crucial to note that both the Gricean theory and any neo-Gricean version are by definition theories of communication and conversation. Thus, in order to analyze the legal discourse in modified-Gricean terms, one assumption is necessary: the assumption that the linguistic exchange between legislatures and courts is a certain form of—even very loosely understood—communication and conversation. Nevertheless, this element must be present.

Now, much of the debate in jurisprudence has been fueled by the argument between the claims of Herbert Hart presented in his 'The Concept of Law' and the critique of Hart's theory developed by Ronald Dworkin in 'Law's Empire' and his subsequent works. Crucially, these theorists seem to have exactly opposing views on the question of the communicative nature of the legal–linguistic exchange. I would like to briefly present their views below and claim that the theory sketched in the present study is a third solution between the two stances that should reconcile them because it requires only a counterfactual assumption of the communicative nature of the exchange at a first level. The theory also has a second level which can operate in non-conversational contexts. Let us now have a look at Hart and Dworkin's opinions.

1.2 Hart and Dworkin on Communication in Law

In Chap. 7, entitled 'Formalism and rule-skepticism', of his book 'The Concept of Law', Herbert Hart claims that the exchange between legislatures and courts has a communicational and conversational nature:

'If it were not possible to communicate general standards of conduct, which multitudes of individuals could understand, without further direction, as requiring from them certain conduct when occasion arose, nothing that we now recognize as law could exist.' (Hart 2012). Later Hart discusses his famous example[3] of a rule prohibiting any vehicle from entering a park. He considers the indeterminacy of the word vehicle and the hypothetical exceptions that could arise. He notes that the communicational nature of law may take on a conversational character since the courts may be called upon to answer the legislative speaker:

> Faced with the question whether the rule prohibiting the use of vehicles in the park is applicable to some combination of circumstances in which it appears indeterminate, all that **the person called upon to answer** can do is to consider (as does one who makes use of a precedent) whether the present case resembles the plain case "sufficiently" in "relevant" respects. [emphasis mine] (Hart 2012)

In a subchapter on 'interpretive concepts' from the book 'Law's Empire', Dworkin questions this communicational and conversational picture provided by Hart. Dworkin claims that interpretation cannot be a matter of communication or

[3]The example originally comes from 'Positivism and the Separation of Law and Morals' (Hart 1958).

conversation. He treats legal interpretation as a form of 'creative interpretation', which he contrasts with conversational interpretation:

> I shall capitalize on that similarity between artistic interpretation and the interpretation of social practice; I shall call them both forms of "creative" interpretation to distinguish them from conversational and scientific interpretation. (Dworkin 1995)

According to Dworkin, legal interpretation is 'constructive' rather than 'conversational':

> Interpretation of works of art and social practices (...) is indeed essentially concerned with purpose not cause. But the purposes in play are not (fundamentally) those of some author but of the interpreter. Roughly, constructive interpretation is a matter of imposing purpose on an object or practice in order to make of it the best possible example of the form or genre to which it is taken to belong. (Dworkin 1995)

However, this construction is not completely free and the interpreter has various constraints: 'It does not follow, even from that rough account, that an interpreter can make of a practice or work of art anything he would have wanted it to be (...) For the history or shape of a practice or object constrains the available interpretations of it, though the character of that constraint needs careful accounting. (...) Creative interpretation, on the constructive view, is a matter of interaction between purpose and object.' (Dworkin 1995)

For Dworkin, legal interpretation is not about duly discovering the intention of the speaker. Rather, it is a decision on ascribing a purpose to an object: 'an interpretation is by nature the report of a purpose; it proposes a way of seeing what is interpreted – a social practice or tradition as much as a text or painting – as if this were the product of a decision to pursue one set of themes or visions or purposes, one "point," rather than another.' (Dworkin 1995).

Dworkin backs his argument with the observation that legislators are usually collective entities and the practice of the courts is not a conversation with the entity, but rather an interpretation of what this entity does. He uses the example of courtesy as a similar, collective social practice:

> Conversational interpretation is inappropriate because the practice being interpreted sets the conditions of interpretation: courtesy insists that interpreting courtesy is not just a matter of discovering what any particular person thinks about it. So even if we assume that the community is a distinct person with opinions and convictions of its own, a group consciousness of some sort, that assumption only adds to the story a further person whose opinions an interpreter must judge and contest, not simply discover and report. (Dworkin 1995)

Dworkin emphasizes that collective actions are even more in need of interpretation since there is no single person with whom conversation would be possible: 'He [the interpreter] must still distinguish, that is, between the opinion the group consciousness has about what courtesy requires, which he thinks he can discover by reflecting on its distinct motives and purposes, and what he, the interpreter, thinks courtesy really requires. He still needs a kind of interpretive method he can use to test that entity's judgment once discovered, and this method cannot be a matter of conversation with that entity or anything else.' (Dworkin 1995).

The theory proposed in this study is a path between Hart's argumentation for a communicational nature for legal language and a Dworkinian anti-communicational approach.[4] This is because the strategic framework built in this study involves a two-step procedure. The first step is a counterfactual assumption of conversation. This step limits the range of possible interpretive alternatives and is more Hartian in nature. By contrast, the second step of the theory has a Dworkinian flavor; it consists of a strategic and purposive choice among the possible interpretive alternatives identified through the first step.[5]

Before proceeding directly to the considerations described above, let me give a brief account of how the field of pragmatics evolved before the revolution brought about by the works of Paul Grice.

1.3 The History of Linguistic Pragmatics

What is pragmatics? In 1980, in an introduction to the book 'Speech Act Theory and Pragmatics', Searle, Kiefer and Bierwisch wrote:

> Pragmatics is one of those words (societal and cognitive are others) that give the impression that something quite specific and technical is being talked about when often in fact it has no clear meaning. (Searle et al. 1980)

The reader may think that starting a dissertation with this kind of provocative quote is sheer madness. However, as we shall soon see, pragmatics can mean very different things and it is extremely difficult to formulate a single, coherent definition.

The lexicon of analytical philosophy defines pragmatics as an aspect of language crucial to the analysis of speech acts, contextual dependence, the speaker's meaning and the structure of discursive speech (Prechtl 2009). The reason that this definition is an enumeration of diverse elements is probably the long and diverse history of the pragmatic field of inquiry. The term 'Pragmatics' was first used in 1930 by Charles Morris in his book entitled 'Foundations of the Theory of Signs' (Morris 1938). Morris' aim was to define the borders of semiotic inquiry, which he divided into three main fields. The first, syntax, was the study of 'the formal relation of signs to one another'. Secondly there was semantics, the study of 'the relations of signs to

[4]Another extremely interesting solution that falls between the Hartian and Dworkinian claims was provided by Scott Shapiro in his book entitled 'Legality'. This scholar builds a theory of interpretation as creation, choice of, or fulfillment of plans that can also be created in a bottom-up manner. The level of discretion granted to an agent in the system depends on the allocation of trust in the system (Shapiro 2011).

[5]An anonymous reviewer objected that Dworkin would reject the strategic maxim formulated in the present study as a maxim for judges. However, I am proposing a 'third way' that need not be in line with the classical Hartian or Dworkinian ideas. Through the expression 'Dworkinian flavor' I meant only that Dworkin's judge Hercules always knows what is just and what fulfills the public good. For this reason, in this limited sense, Hercules always has a strategic goal to pursue.

the objects to which the signs are applicable' (their designata). Thirdly, there was pragmatics, the study of 'the relation of signs to interpreters' (Morris 1938; Levinson 1983). Moreover, within each of the fields, Morris distinguished two approaches: meta-linguistic and descriptive. The inquiry of this study lies somewhere on the border between semantics and pragmatics and touches upon both approaches. As Morris remained a declared behaviorist, he believed that the study of pragmatics should also involve psycholinguistics, sociolinguistics or neuro-linguistics. Therefore, he anticipated the modern turn of research interests toward a better understanding of what is going on in the human brain when it processes language. Nevertheless, such a definition would definitely be too broad for the present considerations.

Rudolf Carnap provided a narrower definition of pragmatics. He claimed that pragmatics are the considerations that pertain directly to a language user (Carnap 2007). He also formulated a notion of pure pragmatics as one that deals with notions such as '*belief*, *utterance* and *intension* and their logical interrelations' (Levinson 1983).

In his famous textbook 'Pragmatics' (1983), Stephen Levinson emphasized that for philosophers such as Bar-Hillel, Kalish or Montague, a central notion for defining pragmatics is the study of deictic or indexical expressions. Roughly speaking, indexicals are expressions whose meaning is highly context dependent. The theory of indexicals depends on the chosen theory of meaning. Some examples are expressions such as 'I, you, him, that, there etc.' David Kaplan provided the most influential account of indexicals: he created a list of expressions that he believed were paradigmatically indexical (Kaplan 1979). Kaplan views indexicals as functions that are labeled 'characters'. A character is a function from context to content (Kaplan 1979).

To sum up, for the aforementioned philosophers to fall within the scope of interests of the pragmatic field of inquiry, it was sufficient that a language, whether natural or artificial, contained an indexical expression (Levinson 1983).

Chronologically speaking, the next milestone was the invention of generative semantics. This idea relied upon the Carnapian understanding of pragmatics as a field related to the study of language users, but with a slight modification. As a result, the definition could be summarized as 'those linguistic investigations that make necessary reference to aspects of the context' (Levinson 1983). Within such a framework, context was defined as 'the identities of participants, the temporal and spatial parameters of a speech event, and (…) the beliefs, knowledge and intentions of the participants in that speech event, and no doubt much besides.' (Levinson 1983).[6]

[6] Generative semantics must not be confused with the generative grammar project developed by Noam Chomsky. His principal claim was 'nativism'—the idea that children dispose of an innate module that enables them to easily grasp and use complicated linguistic structures at an early stage of development. It was grounded on observations that relatively scarce linguistic input (the very limited number of utterances that children hear from adults) enabled them to generate sentences which they had never heard before (Cowie 2017).

The program of linguistic pragmatics emerged as a legacy of the above theories. The principle goal was to show that it made no sense to analyze language abstracted from context. Only specific tokens of type sentences or concrete utterances in some context were to be viewed as fully fledged objects of interest to a linguistic inquiry. This lead to a gradual shift of interest from semantic toward pragmatic inquiries. Semantics increasingly seemed to be predestined for formal calculus rather than characterizing natural language.

Thus, one of the possible definitions provided by Levinson is that 'pragmatics is the study of those principles that account for why a certain set of sentences are anomalous, or not possible utterances' (Levinson 1983). The problem with this definition is the variety of contexts that can render any anomalous utterance perfectly fit and understandable. However, such an approach is far from being the only possibility. Various other definitions were proposed, each with pros and cons. Taken together they give an adequate and fine-grained picture of what the study of pragmatics consists of.

The functional approach claims that the linguistic structure reflects some extra-linguistic causes. However, one could formulate the counter-claim that a linguistic theory should mainly be concerned with rules governing language use itself and not a structure grounded in different fields; otherwise, delimiting a separate field of pragmatic inquiry would be extremely difficult. As a result, pragmatics should be concerned with performance principles of language use rather than linguistic competence (Levinson 1983).

To provide a clear delimitation between pragmatics and other fields such as sociolinguistics or psycholinguistics, Levinson advances the following definition: 'Pragmatics is the study of those relations between language and context that are grammaticalized, or encoded in the structure of a language.' (Levinson 1983). The beauty of this formulation is that it embraces elements such as deixis, presuppositions or speech acts. However, this definition would be absolutely unacceptable for the present considerations because it excludes strong pragmatic inferences from its scope which are not grounded in the grammatical structure of any language—or conversational implicatures in other words (Levinson 1983). Even though much of the debate nowadays concentrates on the borders between semantics and pragmatics, as they cause controversy, the core of pragmatic occurrences is still conversational implicatures. Moreover, even though they are conceptually less questionable than pragmatic enrichments as far as a theory of natural language is concerned, they still trigger heated debate within the theory of legal language.

To sum up, in formulating a definition of pragmatics we must strike a balance between an overinclusive treatment of linguistic phenomena and an over-restrictive boundary that excludes crucial features of the field from the scope of inquiry. We need criteria that enable discrimination between relevant elements of a pragmatic theory and some accidental patterns which remain genuinely beyond the scope of our interest. Levinson proposes the following criteria for 'a feature of the context to be linguistically encoded':

(a) it must be intentionally communicated,
(b) it must be conventionally associated with the linguistic form in question,
(c) the encoding form must be a member of a contrast set, the other members of which encode different features,
(d) the linguistic form must be subject to regular grammatical processes. (Levinson 1983)

Requiring a feature of context to fulfill all the above criteria would again lead to an over-restrictive definition of the pragmatic field of inquiry. Therefore, the fulfillment of at least one of them should be sufficient.

In light of the above, it seems that the only fairly uncontroversial formulation is that pragmatics describes those aspects of meaning that are outside the scope of a semantic theory (Levinson 1983). The problem with such a negative formulation is that while it probably raises relatively few objections, it does not supply us with much information because, on this account, the scope of pragmatics is utterly dependent on the scope of the chosen theory of semantics.

In 1983, Levinson enumerated the following elements that needed classification on either the semantic or the pragmatic side:

(1) truth conditions or entailments
(2) conventional implicatures
(3) presuppositions
(4) felicity conditions
(5) conversational implicature – generalized
(6) conversational implicature – particularized
(7) inferences based on conversational structure. (Levinson 1983)

While considering the current trends and principal scopes of interests of research, unarticulated constituents or pragmatic enrichments must be added to the above list (Borg 2006; Recanati 2004).

Apart from arguments concerning which linguistic elements should be analyzed by pragmatics, researchers also disagree over some of the more primary assumptions of this field of inquiry, such as intentions or context itself.

First, as has already been mentioned, they quarrel over whether it is necessary to postulate the existence of a speaker's intentions at all. Grice treated intention as a necessary element of his theory of meaning. However, there are numerous theories—such as the research program developed by Ruth Millikan—which are undoubtedly research programs in pragmatics, but which deny the necessity of postulating speaker intentions. The anti-intentionalist approach is labeled as externalist with respect to meaning (Millikan 1987, 2005; Matczak 2016).

Second, the adopted definition of context could also influence the scope of pragmatic inquiry. Consider another definition: 'Pragmatics is the study of the relations between language and content that are basic to an account of language understanding.' (Levinson 1983).

Two conclusions loom from such a formulation. First, understanding in language must involve more than just knowledge about the meaning of words and grammatical structures. Second, the ability to draw correct inferences from context and linguistic data is vital.

The concept of context itself is controversial. For the purposes of this chapter, let us restrict the considerations to the influence of the preferred definition of context to the scope of the pragmatic inquiry.

Following Lyons, Levinson enumerates the elements of the context of utterance: '(i) knowledge of role and status (where role covers both role in the speech event, as speaker or addressee, and social role, and status covers notions of relative social standing), (ii) knowledge of spatial and temporal location, (iii) knowledge of formality level, (iv) knowledge of the medium (roughly the code or style appropriate to a channel, like the distinction between spoken and written varieties of a language), (v) knowledge of appropriate subject matter, (vi) knowledge of appropriate province (or domain determining the register of a language).' (Levinson 1983)

Such a list is far from exhaustive. A sharp definition of context is extremely difficult if not impossible to formulate; for this reason, most philosophical conceptions rely instead on an approximation which is sufficient to ground their preferred conclusions.

To sum up, researchers adopt very different conceptions of both intentions and context. Therefore, attempts to define pragmatics should involve a more stable element. For instance, proponents of the Austinian legacy speak of appropriateness or felicity: 'Pragmatics is the study of the ability of language users to pair sentences with the contexts in which they would be appropriate.' (Levinson 1983).

On this account, semantics is the study of truth conditions, or of what it takes for a sentence to be true, while pragmatics is the study of felicity conditions and formulates a class of contexts in which a sentence could be used. Nevertheless, this definition takes us back to the initial issue; moreover, the notion of felicity conditions is just as underdetermined as the notion of context itself, as it is quite a challenge to foresee *in abstracto* what they will be in different contexts (Levinson 1983).

Therefore, as central notions in pragmatic theories are contestable notions, the only fairly uncontroversial version we are left with is the negative definition. The most reasonable move is to give up the idea of formulating an exact overarching definition. Each theory that aspires to be pragmatic must formulate an enumerative definition of what constitutes its research core; in other words, it must formulate an ostensive definition. For instance, Levinson formulates it as follows:

> Pragmatics is the study of deixis (at least in part), implicature, presupposition, speech acts, and aspects of discourse structure. (Levinson 1983)

To conclude, the adopted definition of pragmatics is dependent upon the adopted definition of semantics and the preferred conception of meaning. Moreover, if a pragmatic theory is a theory of communication, then it must take a clear stance on the existence and functioning of intentions as well as on the notion of context. Additionally, any pragmatic inquiry must not neglect the findings of other research areas such as neurolinguistics or sociolinguistics. Any convincing philosophical enterprise must build upon different fields by giving a coherent picture that does not contradict empirical results. Finally, a theory of communication cannot abstract itself from the pragmatic legacy and thus it should take a stance toward the most debated issues in the field, such as speech acts, presuppositions, indexicals or implicatures.

1.4 Some Remarks Concerning Current Interdisciplinary Approaches to Philosophy of Language, Law and Mind

When Paul Grice formed the backbone of a theory of strong pragmatic inferences such as conversational implicatures in the 1970s, he probably never suspected that his ideas would become much more than just an enterprise in the philosophy of language. In fact, his theory has been an inspiration over recent decades not only for the philosophy of mind or cognitive studies, but also for linguistic or sociological enterprises. Dan Sperber and Deirdre Wilson's 'Relevance Theory', which was coined in the 1980s, contributed to this shift from Gricean philosophy of language toward cognitive inquiries. Today, fields such as experimental pragmatics or cognitive linguistics are blossoming. All of these scientific investigations are usually underpinned by the assumption that what we need to know is how exactly meaning is formed in the mind; in other words, the mental processes used and how they lead to the fact that we can communicate with language. Therefore, giving an account of the mental processing of language is seen as uncontroversial and trivially necessary. The initial Gricean goal of creating a theory that provided an account of a step-by-step semi-formalized reasoning that grounded the linguistic inferences seems to be viewed as an obsolete program because it creates artificial theories that do not reflect the functioning of the brain. But does this mean that there is no place within philosophical inquiry for theories a la early Grice? This seems not to be the case for two main reasons.

Firstly, such an inquiry is useful in explaining phenomena pertaining to special types of natural language, such as the language of law. This is because it is inherent in the job of, for instance, a judge, that he must depict his line of reasoning in an intelligible way. If this can be done step by step, analogously to formal operations and on the basis of some fixed rules such as the Gricean maxims, then it is simply convincing for a larger audience.

Secondly, Gricean-type theories can be modified. Yet the aim of the modification is not for the theory to fit the human cognitive architecture, but to give a more adequate account of, for example, the nature of interpreting legal provisions. This is because even if the first grasp of a provision by a judge is fully reliant on the effort and effect interplay of 'Relevance Theory' (maximum effect with minimum effort), it is rarely the case that this first attempt prevails. Judicial reasoning is not an automatic, subconscious process; on the contrary, it is reflexive in the sense that it is a conscious process of reflection upon the pro and con arguments available. Even if it is underpinned at some lower level of description by various neuron-firings and effort–effect tradeoffs, this is not really the kind of explanation that we are searching for in legal theory. What a legal theorist wants to find out is what makes legal reasoning so special or different. Various scholars from diverse legal systems have developed folk theories of the phenomenology of judicial reasoning. Even if these folk theories differ, they must have one common point, namely that legal reasoning is transmitted through natural language. Consequently, a theory of communication within the realm of law based on duly describable inferences in natural language could claim to be global. The Gricean framework seems to be about duly describable inferences in natural language. Therefore, an explanatory theory of communication in law created by means of a modified Gricean picture is construed in this study.

The key challenge is to take a stance on the occurrence of strong forms of pragmatic reasoning in legal inferences such as Gricean implicatures. If the theories we choose remain Gricean in spirit, the next step is to provide some arguments as to which types of implicatures are most common in the legal realm. Consequently, while sticking to the Gricean terminology of the conventional and conversational, both generalized and particularized implicatures will be considered. However, as the balance tilts toward some neo-Gricean versions, the typology alters and thus—in order to choose the best-fitting theory of implicatures—I will also have to relate to a certain extent to the pragmatic foundations of the theory: the weaker pragmatic inferences such as unarticulated constituents as well as the semantic–pragmatic interface.

This study brings together an account of the Gricean and Neo-Gricean ideas so as to enable the author to pick out the most adequate projects. In other words, those which fit the legal picture in the most elegant way. The aim of creating such a *compte rendu* of the pragmatic inquiries is to flesh out the points where the chosen best-fitting theory requires modifications to the legal realm.

Authors who have written in the field so far have mostly focused on verifying whether natural language theories would fit the legal realm. I intend to overturn the trend in the sense that I believe it is precisely the differences and not the similarities that render an inquiry into legal language interesting. Therefore, the study is oriented towards finding differences between the natural language account and the legal language account, but this does not mean that I will build an entirely new and different account. Legal language remains a specialized variety of natural language, therefore most of the linguistic mechanisms found in everyday communication apply to the legal realm.

Before we identify the main elements that require rethinking, we must bear in mind the difficulty that legal language is used in several types of linguistic exchanges between different agents. I have argued elsewhere (Skoczeń 2013) that at least five main types can be identified:

- Communication within a legislative body
- Exchanges between legislatures and courts—it is controversial whether or not this is a kind of communication at all
- Communication between participants of some legal proceedings in court
- Communication between a legislature and the laymen for whom the content communicated is supposed to be action-guiding
- Contracts and other legal declarations of intent

Let us now turn to the identification of the main elements of the Gricean-style linguistic–pragmatic theories that require rethinking. The list is not supposed to be exhaustive but is only a guide to the controversial issues that have already triggered a wealth of philosophical considerations by legal theorists.

First, comes the question of intentions. For Paul Grice, the intentions of speakers were crucial (Grice 1989). This was probably the direct result of an Austinian legacy: speech acts did involve speakers' intentions[7] and perlocutionary effects rely on the recognition of intentions. Therefore, any fully fledged theory of legal interpretation must take a stance on the existence (or absence) of some collective intentionality within legislative bodies. As a result, when analyzing existing pragmatic theories of natural language, the task is to pick the one that fulfills one of two possibilities: it either provides a direct solution to the question of whether we need intention-based reasoning at all, or it does not contradict an out-of-the-theory solution.

Moreover, it would be ideal if the theory accounted for whether or not there can be collective intentionality, or whether public institutions can have some sort of intentions. However, these are features more of a social than a linguistic theory. Thus, an idea of a language that would leave room for such notions would be sufficient. I will tackle the intention issue in Chap. 5.

Second, most if not all neo-Gricean theories enable the hearer to grasp the pragmatic elements of speech through rule-guided inferences. In the standard Gricean version they are labeled maxims of communication. The content of the maxims in such special non-standard communication may need revision and, therefore, the required theory has to show some flexibility as to both the content and the number of maxims. However, the theory sketched in this study is analytical or explanatory rather than normative.

Third, another primary feature of a theory of pragmatic communication is the reliance on some principle of cooperation. In building a theory of communication within the law, this element needs thorough revision for two main reasons. First, if an exchange by use of legal texts between a legislature and courts is no communication at all, then we need no cooperative principle (CP). Although holding such a stance may seem counter-intuitive, Mark Greenberg argues for such a thesis: 'On my view, enacting a statute is a way of changing our obligations, rather than a way of communicating them, and moral or other normative considerations determine what difference to our obligations the enactment of a statute makes.' (Greenberg 2011).

If it is a form of communication, then an extremely liberal version of CP will probably be necessary. Additionally, in courtroom interactions the parties do not entertain a standard communication directed at conveying as much information as they can. On the contrary, they often aim to fool their opponents through a myriad of pragmatic tricks such as ambiguous expressions or indeterminate implications.

Fourth and final, another central notion of a pragmatic theory is the context and many definitions of what it is and of what it consists. Therefore, the task will be to find a definition that is closest to the idea of the numerous legal cases to which a single provision must be repeatedly applied. I will tackle the problems of the content of the maxims and of the content of the CP and context in Chaps. 2–4.

---

[7] There also exists an externalist tradition of reading Austin, presented among others by Sbisa (2012).

As a result, we are left with at least four elements that must be analyzed from our best-fitting neo-Gricean pragmatic theory:

1. The intention issue
2. The maxim issue
3. The cooperation issue
4. The context issue.

This enumeration is by no means intended to be exhaustive.

To conclude, the primary hypothesis at stake is that although approaches to language which aim to discover the functioning of the brain are slowly coming to dominate scientific inquiry, there still remains a place for pragmatic-style analysis in fields such as the legal communicative realm

References

Borg E (2006) Minimal semantics. Clarendon, Oxford

Carnap R (2007) Pisma semantyczne [Essays on semantics]. Fundacja Aletheia, Warszawa

Cowie F (2017) Innateness and language. Stanford Encyclopedia of Philosophy

Dworkin RM (1995) Law's empire, 9. print. Belknap Press of Harvard University Press, Cambridge

Greenberg M (2011) Legislation as communication? Legal interpretation and the study of linguistic communication? In: Marmor A, Soames S (eds) Philosophical foundations of language in the law. Oxford University Press, USA, Oxford

Grice HP (1989) Studies in the way of words. Harvard University Press, Cambridge

Hart HLA (1958) Positivism and the separation of law and morals. Harv Law Rev 71:593. https://doi.org/10.2307/1338225

Hart HLA (2012) The concept of law, 3rd edn. Oxford University Press, Oxford

Kaplan D (1979) Dthat. In: Uehling T, Wettstein H (eds) Contemporary perspectives in the philosophy of language. University of Minnesota Press, Minneapolis, pp 383–400

Levinson SC (1983) Pragmatics, nineteenth printing 2008. Cambridge University Press, Cambridge

Matczak M (2016) Does legal interpretation need Paul Grice? Reflections on Lepore and Stone imagination and convention. Polish J Philos 10(1):67–87

Millikan RG (1987) Language, thought, and other biological categories new foundations for realism. MIT Press, Cambridge

Millikan RG (2005) Language: a biological model. Clarendon Press/Oxford University Press, Oxford/New York

Morris CW (1938) Foundations of the theory of signs. In: Neurath O, Carnap R, Morris C (eds) International encyclopedia of unified science. University of Chicago Press, Chicago, pp 77–138

Poggi F (2011) Law and conversational implicatures. Int J Semiotics Law - Revue internationale de Semiotique juridique 24(1):21–40. https://doi.org/10.1007/s11196-010-9201-x

Prechtl P (2009) Leksykon pojęć filozofii analitycznej [Dictionary of concepts from analytical philosophy]. Wydawnictwo WAM, Kraków

Recanati F (2004) Literal meaning. Cambridge University Press, Cambridge

Sbisa M (2012) Austin on meaning and use. Lodz Papers Pragmatics 8:5–16. https://doi.org/10.1515/lpp-2012-0002

Searle J, Kiefer R, Bierwisch M (1980) Speech act theory and pragmatics. Reidel, Dordrecht

Shapiro S (2011) Legality. Harvard University Press, Cambridge

Skoczeń I (2013) Why do pragmatics matter in the legal framework? Argumentation 2013 International Conference on Alternative Methods of Argumentation in Law Conference Proceedings

Chapter 2
The Strategic Principle and the Maxim of Selectivity

This study aims to outline the functioning of legal language through a modified Gricean paradigm. Thus, I will first present the Gricean and the neo-Gricean ideas as well as where they cannot fit the picture of legal language. Secondly, I will try to alter some Gricean ideas so as to give an adequate account of the legal realm. The hypothesis is that there is a folk theory of how legal language should function in a democratic society. Moreover, this folk theory is close to the classic Gricean picture. Nevertheless, the actual way in which legal language functions is quite different and I will try to show why this is the case and in what respect.

In chapter I, the term 'legal discourse' is often employed. Under this term, one could mean the following linguistic exchanges that occur within the realm of law:

1. An exchange within a legislative body
2. An exchange between a legislature and courts
3. An exchange between court and parties
4. An exchange between parties
5. Contracts and other legal declarations of intent

This study concentrates on the second type of legal discourse—the exchange between legislatures and courts. My purpose is to develop an explanatory theory.

2.1 Outline of the Classical Gricean Project

In 1975 Paul Grice published the article 'Logic and conversation' (Grice 1975). At its outset he claims that he wants to stay away from the debate over formalism vs. anti-formalism, which is understood as a debate of whether we should construct an ideal language or instead analyze the ways in which natural language actually works. He claims:

I. Skoczeń, *Implicatures within Legal Language*, Law and Philosophy Library 127, https://doi.org/10.1007/978-3-030-12532-5_2

> I wish, rather, to maintain that the common assumption of the contestants that the divergences [between the 'ideal' language of logic and natural language] do in fact exist is (broadly speaking) a common mistake, and that the mistake arises from an inadequate attention to the nature and importance of the conditions governing conversation. (Grice 1975)

Thus, it is possible to give an account of the different uses of language or the different language games we play with the use of some at least quasi-logical rules which enable inferences about what someone is intending to communicate.

Grice's idea was that people engage in all sorts of rational and purposive behavior governed by rules, and that one variety of such behavior is communication. Grice is more specific because he uses the word 'talking' (Grice 1975). The main purpose is 'giving and receiving information, influencing and being influenced by others' (Grice 1975), because this is what enables humans to achieve further goals.

Grice claims that the analysis of an uttered sentence leads to the distinguishing of two contents that are propositional (that are truth-apt): what is said and what is implicated. Both are complex. To grasp what a speaker has said in Grice's sense one needs more than just knowledge of the English language (even if the utterance is in standard English and is uttered literally). Thus, it is necessary to have knowledge of the 'circumstances of the utterance'. Grice understands such circumstances fairly broadly; he believes they encompass, for instance, the referents of indexicals, parameters such as the time of utterance, and information allowing for disambiguation.[1] (Grice 1975).

2.2 The Cooperative Principle and the Maxims

According to Grice, to grasp what is implicated the hearer needs first to assume that the speaker follows the general 'cooperative principle' (CP), which can be formulated as follows: 'make your conversational contribution such as is required, at the stage at which it occurs, by the accepted purpose or direction of talk exchange in which you are engaged' (Grice 1975). Second, the hearer must carry out an inferential reasoning based on a set of rules called the maxims of conversation. Four of them are essential:

[1] Suppose someone uttered the sentence *He is in the grip of a vice*. Given knowledge of the English language, but no knowledge of the circumstances of the utterance, one would know something about what the speaker has said on the assumption that he was speaking standard English and speaking literally. One would know that he had talked about some particular male person or animal x, that at the time of the utterance (whenever that was), either (1) x was unable to rid himself of a certain kind of a bad character trait or (2) some part of x's person was caught in a certain kind of tool or instrument (approximate account, of course). However, for a full identification of what the speaker said, one would need to know (a) the identity of x, (b) the time of the utterance, and (c) the meaning, on the particular occasion of utterance, of the phrase 'in the grip of a vice' [a decision between (1) and (2)] (Grice 1975).

1. Quantity
   a. Make your contribution as informative as is required (for the current purposes of the exchange).
   b. Do not make your contribution more informative than is required.[2]
2. Quality
   a. Do not say what you believe to be false.
   b. Do not say that for which you lack adequate evidence.
3. Relation: be relevant.
4. Manner: be perspicuous:
   a. Avoid obscurity of expression.
   b. Avoid ambiguity.
   c. Be brief (avoid unnecessary prolixity).
   d. Be orderly (Grice 1975).

The enumeration above is not exhaustive. 'There are (…) all sorts of other maxims (aesthetic, social, or moral in character), such as 'Be polite', that are also normally observed by participants in talk exchanges.' [emphasis mine] (Grice 1975).

Thus, we follow all these rules (not only in communication) in order to cooperate with others in society. The nature and source of the rules is twofold. First, their existence and general observance by people is a social, empirical fact: 'it is just a well-recognized empirical fact that people usually DO behave in these ways; they have learned to do so in childhood and not lost the habit of doing so; and, indeed, it would involve a good deal of effort to make a radical departure from the habit. It is much easier, for example, to tell the truth than to invent lies.' (Grice 1975) Here Grice gives way to the skeptics: instead of claiming that it is just a fact, he admits that it is only highly probable that we behave just as we have been taught to behave. We have developed some habits and it is easy and convenient to follow them. Therefore, it is not absolutely sure, but very highly probable that we will follow them, and the same goes for our interlocutors. There will be cases in which we will not follow the maxims. Nevertheless, they are minority cases, and this is what makes communication possible and effective.

Moreover, we have reasons to follow the maxims and we 'should not abandon them'. Observing the maxims is called a 'quasi-contractual matter' that leads to 'cooperative transactions' (Grice 1975).

The second sub-maxim of Quantity ('do not make your contribution more informative than is required') is proof of an interesting pragmatic effect. This effect is referred to by J. Goldsworthy an 'implicit assumption' (Goldsworthy 1994). Implicit assumptions are 'assumptions which supplement or qualify the express meanings of

[2] Grice concludes that disobeying this maxim would result in wasting time. However, in the legal realm the consequences could be worse. Consider situations in which you must adopt a strategy in the sense that you cannot reveal some information that could for instance incriminate your client. Moreover, if you are part of an institution that drafts a statute, you cannot be overspecific or casuistic in the statute. You need to formulate more general indications.

utterances. These assumptions are not expressly stated because speakers take them for granted; they may not consciously resort to them at all, or if they do, they expect their hearers to take them for granted too. In either case it seems inapt to think of them as being communicated by speakers to their audiences through the medium of their utterances. It therefore seems better to describe them as being implicit in rather than implied by those utterances.' (Goldsworthy 1994).

Thus, implicit assumptions are obvious assumptions which we take for granted in communication—they are a part of our concept of rationality. This idea is based on John Searle's notions of 'background' and 'network'. Searle gives the following example: 'imagine you enter a restaurant and say "give me a hamburger, medium rare, with ketchup and mustard, but easy on the relish", and being brought a hamburger encased in a cube of solid, lucite plastic, which can only be opened by a jackhammer.' (Searle 1978) Would this comply with the order? In a sense it would, because the order did not specify that the hamburger should not be encased in solid plastic. Yet Goldsworthy points to the fact that most people would consider this as implicit in the order that the hamburger should be easily accessible by anyone who orders it and ready to be eaten without great difficulty (Goldsworthy 1994). Thus, everything we communicate is based on rationality assumptions that we take as 'obvious'. In fact, they are so obvious that their expression is simply not required. 'Our understanding of meanings is in this respect similar to the way in which our understanding of what we see when we focus on something depends on our surroundings, which our peripheral vision registers even when we are only dimly aware of them, or do not consciously notice them at all.' (Goldsworthy 1994).

'Searle goes further, and insists that his order stated exactly and literally what he wanted, but that its exact and literal meaning was 'relative to a set of assumptions which are not and for the most part could not be realized in the semantic structure of the sentence' (Searle 1978) However, it seems doubtful that the hamburger order did state exactly and literally what he wanted because, if so, it is difficult to preserve any meaningful distinction between what is implied and what is expressed. It seems more plausible to conclude that the assumptions were implicit in the order. Searle objects that if this is so, then it is never possible for us to state exactly and literally what we mean or want, because no matter how many absurd possible misinterpretations we expressly rule out, there will always be others of which we have not thought. But that indeed appears to be the case.' (Goldsworthy 1994).

Thus, implicit assumptions are so 'obvious' that agents usually do not consciously think of them; instead, these are unconscious pieces of our general beliefs about the world that encircles us. This is what Searle labels 'the background', and the folk term for this seems to be 'common sense'.

The problem with this type of pragmatic effect is there can be borderline cases of obviousness arising from competing theories of rationality (Sbisà 2017). The threshold between what is obvious and non-obvious is hard to delimit. Nevertheless, some cases are blatant and uncontroversial: they are clearly implicit assumptions, just as in the hamburger case.

Coming back to Grice, there are various ways of failing to fulfill the maxims that generate different consequences:

1. Violation—quiet and unostentatious, the speaker is liable to mislead.
2. Opt out—the speaker indicates that he does not abide to the CP and maxims.
3. Clash—the speaker is unable to fulfill all maxims at once. Thus, he needs to stop following one of them.
4. Flout—the speaker blatantly fails to fulfill a maxim. This often gives rise to conversational implicatures and, when it does, Grice calls it 'exploiting' (Grice 1975).

2.3 Conversational vs. Conventional Implicatures

The CP and maxims build a normative framework which constitutes the basis for inferences that lead to what this theory purports to explain: conversational implicatures. So, what is a conversational implicature?

Consider the following example of a conversation before noon:

I. A: Are you hungry?
II. B: I have had breakfast.

What B is trying to convey through uttering (II) is that he is not hungry. Therefore, by saying that he has had breakfast, B implicates that he is not hungry. The proposition that B is not hungry is the content of a conversational implicature, but how exactly is the implicature generated? How exactly does this reasoning proceed? Grice provides the following answer:

> A man who, by (in, when) saying (or making as if to say) that p has implicated that q, may be said to have conversationally implicated that q, PROVIDED THAT (1) he is to be presumed to be observing the conversational maxims, or at least the cooperative principle; (2) the supposition that he is aware that, or thinks that, q is required in order to make his saying or making as if to say p (or doing so in THOSE terms) consistent with this presumption; and (3) the speaker thinks (and would expect the hearer to think that the speaker thinks) that it is within the competence of the hearer to work out, or grasp intuitively, that the supposition mentioned in (2) IS required. (Grice 1975)

Consequently, the generation of an implicature requires, amongst others, that condition (1) is fulfilled and that there is at least a CP in operation. The goals or aims of a conversation based on the Gricean CP may vary: it may have the goal of transmitting information or it might be the goal of guiding action. Nevertheless, all these goals and aims are cooperative.

According to Grice, there exist two basic types of implicatures in language: conversational and conventional. The definition of the latter is controversial and has come under considerable criticism. Nevertheless, this dispute is irrelevant for the considerations laid out in this study and I will not discuss it. A conversational implicature requires reasoning based on the context of an utterance; in contrast, a conventional implicature is supposed to be intuitively grasped without reference to the context. For instance:

I. Even philosophers are boring.
II. John is a philosopher, but he is boring.

In (I) 'even' suggests that there is a probability scale on which philosophers are the least probable to be boring. However, even if this scale is false and philosophers are the most probable ones to be boring, then claiming that the utterance (I) is false would be an overstatement. In (II) there is an implicated contrast between being a philosopher and being boring. This contrast is not reflected by the truth conditions of the statement because even if being a philosopher did not entail usually being an interesting person, this would not affect the truth conditions of sentence (II). Thus, for (II) to be true it would still be sufficient that John was a philosopher and John was boring. Nothing else would be required. In other words, the sole fact that the contrast does not hold cannot make (II) false. Because of this independence between the truth of the contrast of 'but' (or the scale in 'even') and the truth of the said statement, Grice concluded that this contrast (or scale) must be conventionally implicated.[3]

By contrast, a conversational implicature is not intuitively grasped but can be worked out on the basis of the following data:

> (1) the conventional meaning of the words used, together with the identity of any references that may be involved; (2) the CP and its maxims; (3) the context, *linguistic* or otherwise, of the utterance; (4) *other items of background knowledge*; and (S) the fact (or supposed fact) that all relevant items falling under the previous headings are available to both participants and both participants know or assume this to be the case. [emphasis mine] (Grice 1975)

Grice's understanding of context is broad: he defines it as any background knowledge, including linguistic. Therefore, other linguistic items such as previous utterances will also be included in the context.

There are two mechanisms for generating conversational implicatures. The first involves the observance of the maxims while the second requires a clash or an exploitation of a maxim (a blatant flouting). The following procedure reflects the first mechanism:

> He has said that p; there is no reason to suppose that he is not observing the maxims, or at least the CP; he could not be doing this unless he thought that q; he knows (and knows that I know that he knows) that I can see that the supposition that he thinks that q IS required; he has done nothing to stop me thinking that q; he **intends** me to think, or is at least **willing** to allow me to think, that q; and so he has implicated that q. [emphasis mine] (Grice 1975)

An instance of a concrete reasoning based on the first mechanism of implicature generation could be as follows:

[3] Kent Bach criticized this view. According to him, a separate category such as conventional implicatures is not worth distinguishing because some of them are parts of what is said and some of them are second-order speech acts. This criticism relies on the observation that we can convey several truth-apt propositions with only one utterance (Bach 1999). Whatever their exact nature, they are closely related to what we call the semantics of language. Nevertheless, let me repeat that this issue is irrelevant for the considerations carried in the present study.

> A is standing by an obviously immobilized car and is approached by B; the following exchange occurs:
>
> I. A: I am out of petrol
>
> B: There is a garage around the corner. (Gloss: B would be infringing the maxim 'be relevant' unless he thinks, or thinks it possible, that the garage is open, and has petrol to sell; so he implicates that the garage is, or at least may be open etc.). (Grice 1975)

By contrast, Grice presents a second type of the first mechanism involving a clash as follows:

> A is planning with B an itinerary for a holiday in France. Both know that A wants to see his friend C, if to do so would not involve a prolongation of his journey:
>
> II. A: Where does C live?
>
> B: Somewhere in the South of France. (Gloss: There is no reason to suppose that B is opting out; his answer is, as he well knows, less informative than is required to meet A's needs. This infringement of the first maxim of Quantity can be explained only by the supposition that B is aware that to be more informative would be to say something that would infringe the maxim of Quality, "Don't say what you lack adequate evidence for", so B implicates he does not know in which town C lives.)' (Grice 1975)

Finally, Grice gives the following example of the second mechanism of implicature generation, which involves a blatant flouting of a maxim: Imagine a professor writing a recommendation for a student who is a candidate for a philosophy job. The professor includes in the letter the following statement: 'My student has an excellent command of the English language and is never late for class'. Grice illustrates the inference in the following way: 'The professor cannot be opting out, since if he wished to be uncooperative, why write at all? He cannot be unable, through ignorance, to say more, since the man is his pupil; moreover, he knows that more information than this is wanted. He must therefore be wishing to impart information that he is reluctant to write down. This supposition is tenable only on the assumption that he thinks Mr. X is no good at philosophy. This then is what he is implicating.' (Grice 1975).

2.4 Intention

The assumption that the interlocutor has an intention to convey some content is necessary to carry out a correct inference of the implicature. Without this assumption it makes no sense to seek out implicated content. In other words, intention is the reason for which we try to figure out what someone is trying to implicate. More than that, we try to guess what someone is thinking, what someone knows, and finally what someone intends to convey.

Paul Grice is mostly known for his theory of implicatures. However, he also created an internalist theory of meaning which treats the speaker's intention as a necessary component of meaning (Grice 1989). By contrast, externalists about meaning do not treat the speaker's intention as a necessary component of meaning (Matczak 2016).

There are two ways of viewing the relation between the two theories Grice created: his theory of meaning and his theory of implicature. The first way is to see both theories as metaphysical theories. In other words, both theories aim to answer the question of what metaphysically constitutes meaning. On this reading of the relation between the two theories, the existence of a speaker's intention to implicate is necessary for the implicature's existence.

However, one may actually wonder whether it is genuinely necessary that there exists a real intention—a mental state in the head of the speaker. After all, it seems sufficient just to assume that there is one. In other words, it is possible to view Paul Grice's implicature theory as a purely epistemological theory. This modified theory is a theory that aims to depict how hearers infer implicatures. On this view, it is sufficient that a hearer is able to infer an implicature in a context. The actual existence of the speaker's intention is not a necessary condition of implicature. This reading treats the Gricean internal theory of meaning as a theory that aims to answer a different question than the theory of implicature. To sum up, the stance is that the implicature theory answers the epistemological question, and the theory of meaning answers the metaphysical question. Since the theories purport to answer different questions, they are independent of one another.

Consequently, regardless of whether one is an internalist or an externalist about meaning, one can simultaneously accept the Gricean implicature theory without any incoherence arising.

I will assume the second stance on the relation between the Gricean theory of meaning and the theory of implicatures. Thus, I will claim that both theories are independent and purport to answer different questions. Consequently, the theory of implicatures aims to answer the epistemological question. In this way one could infer an implicature on the basis of all the data that one has (context, CP, maxims etc.). Even if the intention did not in fact exist, the implicature would be formed. However, imagine the following situation: a computer is generating random sentences which by luck happen to be true and generate a true implicature on the basis of context, CP, maxims etc. It would be weird to say that the computer has implicated something, precisely because we know that it has done so unintentionally as no intention can be ascribed to a computer. It did not want to implicate something, and it did not want you to understand that it had implicated something. Consequently, if you know that there is no intention behind an utterance, you do not feel fully warranted to carry out the inference leading to the decoding of an implicature. If you were not aware that the utterance is a random product of a computer, you would probably assume the existence of intention and infer the implicature. Nevertheless, as soon as you learnt that it was just a computer generating random sentences, you would consider it to be a matter of luck or coincidence rather than real communication.[4] Computers do not have semantics in the sense that humans do.[5] Thus, while communicating we make a general prima facie assumption that the speaker has a communicative intention and we stick to this assumption until we encounter arguments to the contrary.

Another argument for the importance of intentions in communication is the case of miscommunicating. Take the example:

A: Smith does not seem to have a girlfriend these days.
B: He has been paying a lot of visits to New York lately (Grice 1975).

Most probably you would infer that Smith has a girlfriend in New York. But imagine that B in fact intended to implicate that Smith travels so often that he has no time to meet someone. As soon as you learn what B's true intention was (because, for example, B explicitly tells you what he wanted to implicate), things change. You cannot uphold anymore that, in the Gricean sense, there was an implicature about Smith having a girlfriend in New York even if he indeed has one in New York. In other words, B did not want to allow you to think that Smith has a girlfriend in New York, but rather he intended you to think that Smith lacks time to meet one. Therefore, any indirect information about the speaker's state of mind is relevant for your inference. Of course, you can never be sure what the speaker REALLY thought. However, you will take into account any indirect evidence of his mental state.

What the above arguments attempt to show is that, for Grice, intention is crucial. Decoding the implicature requires reasoning about the mental state of the agent. Moreover, if you have information that there is no such mental state, or the mental state is different than you assumed, you cannot conclude that there was an implicature in the Gricean sense.

Finally, there is one more reason for the hearer postulating some intentional mental state of the speaker (at least until the hearer finds out that there is no intention or there is a different one than he thought on the basis of some additional evidence). It is the possibility that a speaker can be lying, deceiving, or telling only a part of the relevant information that he knows etc. To understand the argument, let us have a look at the core claims of John L. Austin's theory of speech acts (Austin 1962).

Austin noticed that people genuinely do things with words. They perform all sorts of actions such as requesting, commanding, promising, congratulating,

---

[4] According to Grice, there are two kinds of conversational implicatures: generalized and particularized. The latter require context to occur. Since a computer generates text out of context, it cannot generate a particularized implicature. Whether a computer could generate a generalized conversational implicature remains an open question.

[5] I believe Searle's Chinese room argument illustrates this point neatly: 'Imagine a native English speaker who knows no Chinese locked in a room full of boxes of Chinese symbols (a database) together with a book of instructions for manipulating the symbols (a program). Imagine that people outside the room send in other Chinese symbols, which, unknown to the person in the room, are questions in Chinese (the input). And imagine that by following the instructions in the program the man in the room is able to pass out Chinese symbols, which are correct answers to the questions (the output). The program enables the person in the room to pass the Turing Test for understanding Chinese but he does not understand a word of Chinese.' (Searle 1999a).

pronouncing, convincing etc. through making utterances. More specifically, he claimed that through an utterance a three-element act can be performed. These three elements are labeled locutionary, illocutionary and perlocutionary.

The locutionary act is 'the production of an utterance that can be classified by its phonetic, grammatical, and lexical characteristics, up to sentence meaning (the phatic act). It is also the performance of an act that can be classified by its content (the rhetic act)—a feature distinctively of acts of speech. If I promise that I'll be home for dinner and then promise that I'll work late, my actions are instances of two different locutionary acts: one with the content that I'll be home for dinner, and one with the content that I'll work late.' (Austin 1962; Longworth 2017).

The illocutionary act is 'an act classifiable not only by its content—as with the locutionary act—but also by its force (stating, warning, promising, etc.). If I promise that I will be home for dinner and later state that I will be home for dinner, my actions are instances of the same locutionary act: both actions involve the content that I will be home for dinner. However, my actions are instances of different illocutionary acts: one has the force of a promise, while the other has the force of a statement' (Austin 1962; Longworth 2017).

The perlocutionary act is classifiable through its ' … consequential effects upon the feelings, thoughts, or actions of the audience, or of the speaker, or of other persons …' (Austin 1962) 'If I warn that the ice is thin, and so perform one illocutionary act, I may thereby perform a variety of perlocutionary acts: I may persuade someone to avoid it, or encourage someone to take a risk, and so forth.' (Longworth 2017).

If as a hearer you do not postulate or assume some perlocutionary intentions of the speaker you are listening to, you cannot really hold anyone responsible for lying. This is because the sole illocutionary intention only allows one to state that someone has uttered a false statement. To discriminate between making a false statement and lying, a perlocutionary intention to deceive the interlocutor is needed. This deception consists of making (or wanting to make) your interlocutor believe a false proposition. Without perlocutionary intentions, the very existence of lies is challenged and the fact that there are no lies seems deeply counterfactual. Since any theory of natural language needs to explain lies, perlocutionary intentions are an important element of every such theory. Nevertheless, in further parts of this study I will concentrate on locutionary and illocutionary intentions because they are what Grice analyzed and labeled 'communicative intentions'.

Thus, my claim is as follows: a hearer must assume some intention on the part of the speaker, yet he may never know whether there was in fact any intention. However, if he does not make the assumption, communication (or lying) would hardly be possible.[6] If one does not assume an intention on the part of the speaker, it is just a random coincidence that relevant and true content happens to be conveyed.

[6] Unless you adopt a behavioral theory that treats intention and meaning as unnecessary.

2.5 Generalized and Particularized Conversational Implicatures

According to Grice, conversational implicatures are of two types. First, there are particularized conversational implicatures (PCI): 'cases in which an implicature is carried by saying that p on a particular occasion in virtue of special features of the context, cases in which there is no room for the idea that an implicature of this sort is normally carried by saying that p.' (Grice 1975) Second, there are generalized conversational implicatures (GCI), which are formed when 'the use of certain words in an utterance would normally (in the absence of special circumstances) carry such and such an implicature or type of implicature.' (Grice 1975).

To grasp what a GCI is, let us look at the following examples:

(I) Could you pass me some sugar?
(II) Would it be possible to open the window?

In standard casual conversation (I) implicates a polite request to pass the sugar bowl. This implicature is a GCI as it does not require a special context for its existence. It is just a feature of how we usually use such phrases. Even though what is said is an inquiry into the ability to pass the sugar or open the window, what is meant is more than just an inquiry—it is a polite request to actually do so. A mere answer 'yes' to both (I) and (II) without actually passing the sugar or opening the window would be considered to be a communicative failure.

There are numerous competing explanations of the generalization of implicatures. For instance, in a book entitled 'Presumptive Meanings', Stephen Levinson claims that we have default, preferred (presumptive) pragmatic interpretations (Levinson 2000). Dan Sperber and Deidre Wilson explain GCI in terms of their Relevance Theory, claiming that GCI interpretations are the result of the interplay of cognitive effort and effect (Sperber and Wilson 2006). I will return to this idea in further parts of this study.

By contrast, to grasp what a PCI is let us have a look at the following set of sentences:

(I) The dog is looking very happy.
(II) Perhaps the dog has eaten the roast beef.
(III) A: What on earth has happened to the roast beef?
B: The dog is looking very happy (Levinson 1983).

The uttering of (I) will be taken as implicating (II) only if it is located in a specific contextual setting of (III) (Levinson 1983).

2.6 Some Features of Conversational Implicatures

Conversational implicatures possess certain characteristic features. First, implicatures are cancelable either explicitly or contextually. An explicit cancellation of a GCI could be:

I. They got married and had kids, but not necessarily in that order.

The proposition 'they got married and had kids' contains the conjunction 'and', which can semantically be ascribed a truth-value in two contexts. First, in a context in which they first had kids and subsequently got married. Second, in a context in which they first got married and subsequently had kids. However, the pragmatic reasoning leading to a GCI makes us choose the second interpretation on the basis of the maxims of conversation. The second part of (I), 'but not necessarily in that order', cancels the GCI that they first got married and subsequently had kids. The mechanism is explicit because the speaker utters more content.

A contextual cancellation of a GCI does not require the speaker to produce a longer utterance and/or additional content. The GCI is cancelled in virtue of the special elements of the context of utterance. Take an example: A has had a serious injury to both his right and left hands. B asks A, 'could you pass me the salt?'. B is literally inquiring about whether A is able to pass him the salt, rather than asking A to pass him the salt.

Second, conversational implicatures are nondetachable because the use of synonymous expressions or sentences (but in the exact-same context! (Gizbert-Studnicki 1983)) does not result in the loss of the implicature:

I. Could you pass me the salt?
II. Would you be able to hand me the salt?
III. I need some salt.

Third, 'conversational implicata are not part of the meaning of the expressions to the employment of which they attach' (Grice 1975). If you tell me that you have run out of petrol and I reply that there is a gas station around the corner, nothing in the meaning of the words I have uttered contains any content about the station being open.

Fourth, it is possible that the proposition decoded on the basis of what is said is true, while the implicature is false, or vice versa. Take the example:

A: Are you hungry?
B: I have had breakfast.

Even if I have not had breakfast, I still may not be hungry. Thus, the content of what is said may be false, while the implicature is true. By contrast, it is perfectly possible that I have had a very modest breakfast and I am still hungry. Therefore, it is possible that the content of what is said is true, but the implicature is false. In other words, what is said and what is implicated convey two distinct propositions that can be evaluated independently of one another in terms of truth or falsity.

Finally, conversational implicatures are often indeterminate. There may be a ‘disjunction’ of the implicature’s possible explanation and the choice of only one explanation might require additional contextual information. Recall the example of Smith, who made so many visits to New York lately. Was it because of a woman, or just because of his job? Take another example:

A: The new manager is really annoying.
B: The weather is extremely sunny today.

B could be implicating very different contents: that the manager is approaching and can hear the conversation, or B strongly disagrees with A but does not want to quarrel over it, etc. Unless we get some additional contextual information, we will not be able to decide which possible explanation the speaker could have had in mind.

Having established the overall picture of the Gricean idea, let us proceed to the question that this study purports to answer: is a theory of conversational implicatures useful for the theory of law? Does this theory enable us to explain some features of legal discourse? Finally, if the answer is positive, which version of the theory best fits the purposes of legal theory?

2.7 Applying the Classical Gricean Project to the Legal Realm

An exhaustive and detailed account of the points where the classical Gricean picture may not be straightforwardly applicable to the legal realm has been provided by Marcin Matczak in his ‘Does legal interpretation need Paul Grice? Reflections on Lepore and Stone’s Imagination and Convention’ (Matczak 2016). The analysis below will be carried out along similar lines.[7]

Grice advances the idea that communication is usually about ‘giving and receiving information, influencing and being influenced by others’ (Grice 1975). First, there is a sense in which the members of any collective law-creating institution want to influence each other to take one decision rather than another. Second, legislative institutions want to inform subjects of the laws they create which guide them on what they should do and, in a sense, influence them so that they will do it. There is also a sense in which a legislative institution informs and influences judges as to the verdicts they should issue. A discussion in a courtroom also aims to disclose some information and influence the judge or the other party to act in some way. Nevertheless, Grice uses such words as ‘talking’ or ‘conversation’. On closer inspection, these labels do not fully fit legal discourse. For instance, what a legislative body conveys to the law’s subjects seems closer to a monologue, on the assumption that it is a form of communication at all. Analogously, the courtroom situation

[7]A description of the specificity of legal pragmatics can also be found in Skoczeń (2011, 2012, 2013, 2015a).

is an argument—a form of war between the parties—and war is intrinsically uncooperative.

The Gricean 'circumstances of utterance' are also problematic in some legal situations (Smolak 2012). Consider the task of the judge: even if she treats the text of a statute as the legislator's utterance (which is already controversial), which 'circumstances of utterance' should she take into consideration? The circumstances of the law's enactment or the circumstances at the moment of the trial?

In 'Logic and conversation' Grice also formulates a statement that is of crucial importance to the legal theorist: 'But while some such quasi-contractual basis as this [meaning CP and maxims] may apply to some cases, there are too many types of exchange, *like quarreling and letter writing, that it fails to fit comfortably.*' [emphasis mine] (Grice 1975).

Grice does not give a precise delimitation of the applicability of his theory. He gives only two examples for which his theory is not applicable, yet he does not rule out the possibility that there are more such examples. The two exclusions permit us to infer that his theory was supposed to apply to a direct, immediate communicative exchange which aims to exchange information.

Quarreling, which was mentioned in the above citation, is a typical courtroom situation. Moreover, drafting a statute by a legislative institution that is directed at the judges and the law's subjects does in some respects resemble letter writing. Thus, if the above framework does not fit these situations (there is no quasi-contractual consent to cooperate), we need to seek a different explanation for utterances in the realm of law.

Even if we accept the applicability of CP and maxims in legal discourse, there remains the question of interactions between the maxims. Is it possible to violate, opt out, clash or flout maxims in legal discourse? At first sight, violation seems out of the question because there is no sense in which one could say that the legislature is lying by enacting a text.[8] One is also precluded from saying that a court is lying in its verdict. Moreover, if a party lies during a trial, she would be accused of perjury. As far as the opt out is concerned, only refusing to testify could be viewed as some form of opt out in the legal realm. It could be that the clash and flout mechanisms operate within the law. However, the content of the maxims in the legal realm needs to be discussed. It could be that the maxims that clash or are flouted in the legal realm differ in content from the standard Gricean maxims.

Summing up, as far as giving an account of the legal realm in terms of the Gricean paradigm is concerned, there are several options. First, one can claim that in legal situations no one abides by the CP and maxims. Consequently, the agents behave just as if there had been an opt out. Second, one can claim that some CP and maxims are in force, but the content of the maxims may be either identical to the one given by Grice, or different. Third, one can claim that in the law some additional normative framework containing principles and maxims is in force.

[8] With some exceptions, such as the common law doctrine of 'legislative illicit motive'. For more on 'legislative illicit motive' see Sadurski (2014).

In conclusion, if one wants to claim that implicatures occur in the legal realm, one has to assume CP is in force. The question of intentions in the legal realm is more complex because the legal world is full of institutions constituted by groups of people. It is controversial whether we can treat them as speakers, or collective speakers, or even whether we can treat the decisions, texts or other actions and artifacts that they produce as collective speech. Finally, the most controversial matter seems to be whether we can speak of anything like collective intentionality, a matter I elaborate on further in the chapter entitled 'The Meaning of Law'.

2.7.1 *The Cooperative Principle in Law*

First, to speak of implicatures, Grice requires that the CP is in force. However, the purpose of the linguistic exchange assumed by CP seems different in law. Moreover, the maxims in the legal framework may have different contents than the standard ones and may be governed by different mechanisms. There could also be an additional normative framework in the law. Nevertheless, to speak of such strong pragmatic phenomena in language as implicatures, there must be a normative framework that allows the inference leading to the content of the implicature to be made. Thus, the total 'opt-out' option is ruled out as an explanation of implicatures.

Some researchers, such as Andrei Marmor or Stefan Goltzberg, have been trying to apply this classical Gricean framework to the legal realm. I will now briefly present what this has resulted in and argue that their account does not fully explain certain important phenomena in legal discourse and how it could be modified to fit the legal picture better.

2.7.2 *Strategic Speech*

In his book, 'The Language of Law', Andrei Marmor refers to the legal modification of CP and maxims as 'strategic speech'. The idea is as follows: there are some linguistic exchanges that are not directed at exchanging information. Grice gives an example politeness. The normative framework of politeness, according to Marmor, may require telling lies. For instance, if a host asks you if you enjoyed your dinner, you may feel required to answer in the positive (Marmor 2014). That may be true, but I fear that the label 'lies' can generate some confusion. Marmor's stance is similar to the stance adopted by G. Leech, who claims that there is an overarching principle of tact, a principle that can even override the CP. This principle can sometimes license lying (Leech 1983), but it is worth noting that such polite lies often consist of a false implicature, rather than the utterance of a false proposition. In natural everyday language, some theorists claim that falsely implicating is lying, see for instance (Antas 2008). Nevertheless, in the realm of law we should be more cautious about making speakers responsible for their statements because the outcome might be severe and thus it might be more sensible to hold people responsible for a more limited amount of propositional content, namely the content uttered. Pragmatic reasoning such as implicature inference is defeasible. Consequently, we should be more cautious in ascribing responsibility where the externalized evidence of any mental state might be substantially weaker.

The purpose of a lie in the realm of law should be strictly viewed as conveying a false proposition, but the purpose of politeness is different. To be polite is to act in a way that does not hurt the feelings of your interlocutor and has much more to do with emotions than making someone believe false content. Lies could be categorized as a violation of the maxim of quality (say only what you believe to be true). By contrast, Grice explicitly states that politeness is an additional maxim rather than a violation of the maxim of quality; therefore, Marmor uses the notion of lying in a different sense than Grice.

According to Marmor, while polite conversations are still cooperative, the kind of exchange that we encounter in the law is not fully cooperative. In other words, on a scale between fully cooperative and fully uncooperative behavior, the legal case would be somewhere in between. Moreover, 'the limiting case of non-cooperative implicature is manipulation'. Marmor defines it as 'cases in which a speaker asserts something true while deliberately trying to implicate something that he knows to be false'. He gives the example of Smith, a philosophy doctor, who presents himself to a nurse in a hospital as a doctor *tout court*. Manipulation is 'possible because the hearer wrongly assumes that the speaker adheres to the ordinary Gricean conversational maxims' (Marmor 2014).

So, as Marmor claims, lawyers are not manipulative, yet they are not fully cooperative. Such a formulation seems suspicious. According to the above definitions, if you are manipulative, then your hearer wrongly assumes that you are abiding to standard maxims, but in fact there is lack of cooperation on your part. By contrast, if your hearer knows that you are not abiding to standard maxims, then it is partial cooperation (as the hearer is warned that the inferences he carries about the content you want to convey may prove false or deceptive). Thus, the difference lies in the awareness of the hearer. It is in his knowledge about the speaker's actual normative framework, understood as observance of the standard maxims (including their clash and obvious floutings). Now, if the hearer knows that you, as a speaker, are not fully abiding by standard maxims, then he can never be sure when you are implicating something according to standard maxims, when you are implicating something that departs from the standard maxims, or when you are not implicating anything at all. This is the mechanism that is supposed to guarantee to the speaker the possibility to say 'I have never implicated this content!' Marmor calls this 'strategic speech' and claims that 'what makes a speech strategic is the fact that the speaker aims to **gain some advantage** by implicating certain content that he would not be willing to express or acknowledge explicitly.' (Marmor 2014) Yet this is an insufficient definition. Recall the example of the professor writing a recommendation letter for his student for a philosophy job. This example also falls within the scope of this definition, yet the situation is cooperative. Thus, Marmor adds two requirements. First, it must be uncertain whether a maxim applies at all. Second, the level of compliance with the maxim also needs to be unknown.

However, this seems an extremely unstable idea of communication. In such circumstances the hearer can never be sure whether there is an implicature and the most reasonable thing to do would be to ignore all implications completely and focus solely on the 'what is said' content. Yet we know that strategic hearers do not act this way. Strategic hearers—understood as hearers that want to attain some precise strategic goal (by which someone must win and the other must loose)—do not ignore all implicatures completely (see the numerous examples below).

Strategic hearers select implicatures when they fit their preferred reasoning and reject those that do not. Thus, I do not think that there is an uncertainty, but rather there is a fixed strategic normative framework that is more complicated in content than the standard one. It is a framework in which the linguistic exchange has a strategic purpose or goal. In this framework, interlocutors make the counterfactual assumption that the CP is in force, derive implicatures, and then select among them. Thus, the purpose is not cooperative. This framework, I shall claim, contains a strategic super-maxim of selectivity: select only the implicatures you need or accept for your purpose. To sum up, I believe this has much more to do with the selective hearing of implicated content.

Take the example of the famous American supreme court case, *Smith vs U.S*. The facts were roughly the following: Smith exchanged firearms for drugs. There was a statute in force (Title 18 U.S.C. 924(c)(1)) requiring the imposition of specified penalties if the defendant 'during and in relation to . . . [a] drug trafficking crime uses . . . a firearm'.

The interpretive question was whether 'using a firearm' implicates using it strictly 'as a weapon' or rather no such implicature (pragmatic enrichment) occurs.

In light of neo-Gricean theories, this would not be an implicature but a pragmatic enrichment. Moreover, this would entail that it is part of 'what is said' or 'explicature' or 'impliciture' rather than 'implicature'. I will come back to this typology in detail in the next chapters. Nevertheless, the maxim (including selectivity) applies also to pragmatic enrichments. Therefore, the introduction of a more fine-grained distinction than the one between 'what is said' and 'what is implicated' will not change the conclusions presented in the present chapter.

A hearer in a standard situation would have probably understood the phrase 'using a firearm' as carrying the implicature 'as a weapon' because it is the most stereotypical one. This can be illustrated along the lines of the following reasoning: Since the default interpretation is to use a firearm 'as a weapon', the second submaxim of quantity—do not make your contribution more informative than is required—leads to this default understanding. Finally, the maxim of manner—be brief—makes the phrase 'as a weapon' redundant.[9] Nevertheless, this is where the

[9] Note that this passes all three tests for implicature: cancelability, reinforceability and calculability. This is because it is possible to cancel the implicature by saying, 'use a firearm, but not only as a weapon'. It is possible to reinforce the implicature by saying, 'use a firearm only as a weapon'. Finally, reasoning on the basis of the maxims in the text is proof of the calculability requirement being satisfied.

strategic super-maxim of selectivity comes in. Consequently, the judicial hearer can decide to ignore the 'as a weapon' implicature. In other words, she can claim that the legislative speaker, when asked if she intended this implicature, would have replied 'not at all!' In fact, the court ruled that a barter transaction was also an instance of 'using a firearm'. This can be illustrated by the following reasoning: The first sub-maxim of quantity—make your contribution as informative as required—leads to the conclusion that the speaker was not required to provide more information than she provided. She was not required to restrict use of the firearm to use as a weapon. The sub-maxim of manner—avoid obscurity of expression—indicates that the speaker is supposed to avoid obscurity whenever she can. Thus, she must have been unable to avoid the obscurity this time. Since the obscurity was unavoidable, then it had to be used with all of its consequences. In other words, this formulation is deliberately such so as to allow all kinds of uses of firearms.[10] Thus, the court took the above provision to implicate that a barter transaction involving firearms should fall within its scope. Only Justice Scalia dissented.

Marmor's analysis of legal language is quite narrow as it is confined to legislation and the exchange between legislatures and courts. His claim is that 'legislation is not a form of manipulative speech. But it is not fully cooperative either' (Marmor 2014). He labels this in-between solution 'strategic speech'. Recall that the defining element of strategic speech is 'the fact that the speaker aims to gain some advantage by implicating certain content that he would not be willing to express or acknowledge explicitly.' (Marmor 2014) Moreover, 'there is a certain level of uncertainty about the normative framework that governs the conversation' (Marmor 2014). This uncertainty is of two kinds. It is either 'not clear whether a given maxim applies or not' or 'the level of compliance with a given maxim' is different than in standard speech (Marmor 2014). The first kind occurs, for instance, when your host asks you whether you liked the food and you are somehow expected not to tell the truth (I have already stated my objections to viewing Gricean politeness this way). The second kind is the following:

> Consider, for example, a stipulation in some commercial contract saying "X will not issue A without Y's proof of B." In an ordinary conversation, a hearer would have inferred that proof of B is the only condition for X to issue A; otherwise, the speaker would have flouted the maxim of quantity (do not say too little). But in the context of commercial negotiations, this would be a very insecure inference. X might want to be able to claim that stating one condition does not necessarily preclude others, and Y might be expected to know this, to some extent, and to know that this might be what X presumes in the conversational context. But if it is obvious to both parties that the maxim of quantity does not apply here, then X would not have been able to gain any advantage in implicating less than would otherwise follow from his utterance; if a strategic move is possible here, it is only because the maxim of quantity is not entirely flouted but not entirely complied with either. (Marmor 2014)

[10] This shows that the implicature passes the test of calculability. Yet it also passes two further tests of cancelability and reinforceability. This is because you can cancel the implicature by saying 'use a firearm yet only as a weapon'. Moreover, you can reinforce the implicature by saying 'use a firearm but not only as a weapon'.

This is a case in which it is not clear what the parties collectively intended to implicate through the provision in their contract. The lack of sufficiently rich contextual cues makes the content of the implicature indeterminate. The state between flouting and compliance with a maxim described by Marmor is weird. Flouting is an overt non-compliance with a maxim. Therefore, if you comply with a maxim, you cannot be flouting it. I do not believe that there can be something between those two contradictory phenomena; rather, the hearer can decide whether he will take under consideration the implicature that the list of requirements is exhaustive, or will ignore it.

The crucial thing about Marmor's strategic speech is that it is not only the speaker who is interested in maintaining the uncertainty about the normative framework; it is also the hearer that is interested in 'maintaining some plausible deniability of the uptake of the implication, acting as if he did not grasp or hear it.' (Marmor 2014).

I believe that this is guaranteed by the additional strategic super-maxim of selectivity. The speaker can deny his commitment to an implicature and the hearer can also ignore an implicature. A strategic speaker, when asked 'have you implicated this content?', can reply through an explicit denial, 'I have never implicated this!' Analogously, a strategic hearer, when asked whether he grasped implicature_1 and implicature_2 from the utterance can reply, 'I have grasped implicature_1 but not implicature_2'. Moreover, even when they do not state it explicitly, such replies can be inferred from their subsequent linguistic and non-linguistic behavior.

Marmor characterizes two types of linguistic exchange as strategic: those inside a legislative body and those occurring between a legislature and courts. According to him, in these contexts it is not only unclear whether a maxim applies, but it also remains unclear what the level of conformity with the maxim is. It is also the uncertainty of who counts as the relevant party and what counts as a relevant contribution to the conversation (Marmor 2014). Consequently, it is unclear whether and to what extent one is supposed to take into account legislative history, records of disputes within specialized agencies or the legislative body, the opinions of the majority party, social campaigns, etc. In this picture, every element of the theory is blurred, and no sharp distinctions and definitions can be formulated.

To sum up, in Marmor's book we get a complex picture: we do not know who the speaker is or what he is saying, and on what basis we could infer the conveyed content. This picture is so skeptical that it raises doubts over whether these phenomena can be labeled communication at all. They seem almost completely random, while it would be useful to have an approach that would guarantee a higher probability of (at least partially) stable content being conveyed. This is why I believe it is a better conceptualization of this situation to claim that there is a fixed normative framework consisting of an additional, second-order strategic super-maxim of selectivity as to the implicated content. Both speaker and hearer can select implicatures formed in speech according to the standard maxims as abiding or not abiding to their communicative goal.

2.7.3 *The Strategic Super-Maxim of Selectivity*

Consequently, I agree with Marmor's observation that the result of strategic behavior is a selective acceptance of implicated content. I only disagree with the claim that it is completely uncertain which implicatures the speaker or hearer will uphold because it will be the implicatures that fit the speaker's or hearer's current argumentative goal. If admitting that one has implicated something could impede the achieving of one's goal, then one would most probably deny having meant the implicature. If taking into account an implicature could prevent one from achieving a strategic goal, then it might be reasonable to deny having inferred the implicature. Consequently, if a speaker knows the strategic goal of the hearer, she can foresee which of her implicatures the hearer will ignore. The hearer will ignore exactly those implicatures that do not conform to her own goal. Analogously, if the hearer knows more or less what the strategic goal of the speaker is (or could be), she can foresee which implicatures the speaker may deny having meant. She will deny precisely those implicatures whose content does not conform with her strategic goal. Moreover, she will not make an explicit cancellation of the implicatures she wants to deny because this generates a higher level of responsibility over an additional explicit proposition expressed by the implicature. The less explicit propositions generating responsibility, the better. Context may always evolve and new data may appear that forces the agents to modify their strategies.

Consider again the content of Grice's CP: 'make your conversational contribution such as is required, at the stage at which it occurs, by the accepted purpose or direction of talk exchange in which you are engaged'. Grice clearly discussed cases in which the 'purpose or direction of talk exchange' was to convey some information. However, this is not the only purpose of talk exchange that humans have—in fact, they may have very different purposes. The maxims of conversation are just rules that make it possible to achieve these different purposes: 'technical rules (or directives) that indicate a means to reach a certain goal, aiming not at directing the will of the receivers but at indicating to them that their will is conditioned: in other words, that if they want to reach a certain goal, then they must maintain certain behavior' (Poggi 2011). Thus, the Gricean CP enables us to attain all kinds of very different cooperative goals with the use of the Gricean maxims. These goals not only convey information, but also achieve a cooperative purpose; for instance, setting the address of a meeting.

However, humans also use linguistic communication to achieve all kinds of non-cooperative goals. These are goals when one must win and the other must lose, and I label them strategic goals. The standard Gricean CP and maxims are insufficient to achieve non-cooperative and strategic goals and, as already mentioned, an additional normative framework is required.

I would like to emphasize that the Gricean definition of 'cooperation' and the definition of 'strategic' speech or interlocutors provided by Marmor and modified in this chapter are slightly divergent from the notions of 'cooperative' and 'strategic' games used in game theory. Let me now briefly describe the differences in the definitions of these identically spelled terms and establish the relations between these definitions.

Game theory is a branch of rational choice theory, which is a branch of mathematics that can be divided into three parts: decision theory, social choice theory and game theory. Game theory is 'devoted to the study of strategic interactions, i.e. interactions which involve more than one agent and in which the effects of each agent's decision depend not only on her decision but also on the decisions of the other agents so that what each agent does depends on what she thinks the other agents will do.' (Załuski 2013) Game theory can be further subdivided into classical and non-classical (evolutionary) theory: the former consists of cooperative and non-cooperative game theory, while the latter 'analyzes non-cooperative games, i.e. games in which joint action agreements between agents are not enforceable (binding).' (Załuski 2013) By contrast, cooperative games are 'games in which joint-action agreements are enforceable (binding)' (Załuski 2013).

What is crucial is that 'the terms 'cooperative' and 'non-cooperative' refer not to the nature of the outcomes of the game, but to the way in which the player's actions are implemented: collectively in the former case and individually in the latter. Thus, it is not the case (contrary to what the names of the games might suggest) that cooperation cannot be the result of non-cooperative games, and that cooperative games are free from competition between players.' (Załuski 2013) Thus, both cooperative and uncooperative strategic games in the game-theoretical sense can lead to outcomes that are cooperative in the Gricean sense. It is not the purpose of this study to provide an account of the Gricean theory in terms of game theory; this has already been well explained by Robin Clark in his book 'Meaningful games': 'Grice's maxims fit into the game-theoretic framework; we can encode their effects using utilities.' (Clark 2012) Utilities are functions that are 'a numeric reflection of preference: an agent strictly prefers x to y just when the utility of x is greater than the utility of y.' (Clark 2012).

Note that in my framework the word 'strategic' is used in a different sense than the game-theoretic one. In game theory, practically all language games are labeled 'strategic' (in the game-theoretical sense). By contrast; I label a subset of human goals 'strategic'. These are goals that can be achieved only when one wins and others lose the game, thus I am trying to describe games in which the Nash equilibrium is rarely the outcome. Consequently, in terms of outcome, strategic games in game theory and in the present chapter are quite different. Yet, in terms of the process and not the outcome, the definitions of cooperative and non-cooperative games are very close to the intuitions described in the present chapter. In fact, game theory claims four mains possibilities:

(a) cooperative games with a cooperative outcome
(b) cooperative games with a non-cooperative outcome
(c) non-cooperative games with a cooperative outcome
(d) non-cooperative games with a non-cooperative outcome

Consequently, what I label 'strategic' is mostly (c) 'uncooperative strategic games (in terms of game theory) with a cooperative outcome' because the joint action (of linguistic cooperation in inferring the pragmatic phenomena) is not enforceable as the agent can always ignore some implicature. Thus, the process of selecting pragmatic phenomena is uncooperative in the game theoretical sense. However, the outcome of games in the law is cooperative in the sense that legal decisions settle various issues and create a more stable society.

You could object that the communication between legislatures and courts is not strategic since it is not the case that one wins and the other loses. I agree that it is not strategic in simple cases. However, the theory sketched in this study is an explanatory rather than a normative theory and needs to be applied to hard cases, which are relatively hard to come by. In these cases, judges need to decide whether they should uphold the legislative interpretation or diverge from it. In other words, the legislative interpretation can either win (be upheld) or lose (be ignored). When it is ignored, we face the well described in the literature occurrence of judicial activism. In this case, the legislature is not successful (loses the game) in implicating the content it wanted to implicate; in other words, it is not successful in achieving the goal it wanted to achieve.

The divergence in goals can happen, for example, because the moment of enactment of a statute and the moment of judicial interpretation are distinct points on a timeline. As a consequence, the context at the moment of the application of the rule is richer than the context of enactment. This can result in the legislative goal being obsolete and contrary to the judicial goal. Take the example of the rule from the American constitution that all men are equal. The founding fathers of the constitution understood this as 'all white men are equal', whereas the courts encompassed Black Americans and women under this label before the introduction of the thirteenth amendment. Another example is the fact that the courts can have a different interpretations of constitutional values. For instance, an element of the principle of proportionality is effectiveness, and in the context of a concrete case this element often takes a distinct form from the one assumed *in abstracto* by the legislator.

Moreover, we sometimes face situations in which the court loses the game, while the legislature wins because it ignores the ruling of the court. An example of this would be the current relations between the legislator and the constitutional court in Poland. The legislator enacted statutes which were proclaimed unconstitutional by the Polish constitutional tribunal. Next, the executive power refused to publish the rulings of the Polish constitutional tribunal, which prevented the rulings from entering into force. As a result, the legislature kept ignoring the rulings of the Polish constitutional tribunal (for a detailed description of the situation see (Matczak 2017)). I am not claiming that the aforementioned situations are positive or normatively good, I am just claiming that they happen, and our explanatory theories should take them into account.[11]

[11] An anonymous reviewer suggested that 'a legal system is in a pathological state and has to some extent abandoned the rule of law if the courts do not cooperate with the legislature.' However, I believe that in extreme cases when the legislature deviates from democratic behavior or neglects the rule of law, it is precisely the role of the judiciary to stick to the rule of law even if this means less cooperation with the legislature.

The strategic purpose or direction understood as the will to achieve one's goal is common and widespread and occurs not only in legal discourse situations but also in everyday life. Our linguistic exchanges are most often a mixture of the two purposes: the cooperative (including informative) and the strategic. The cooperative (informative) purpose is made more precise (and made possible to infer by the hearer) through the four Gricean maxims of quantity, quality, relation and manner. By contrast, the strategic purpose is precisified through different maxims:

1. The strategic maxim—pursue your goal (independently of your interlocutor's ultimate goal).
2. The selectivity maxim—deny implicated content that does not conform to your goal.
    a. Maxim of selectivity for speaker—deny the implicated content formed on the basis of standard maxims if it does not conform to your goal (admit only the implicatures you want to admit)
    b. Maxim of selectivity for the hearer—take into account only the content that does conform with your goal (hear only what you want to hear)
3. The anticipation maxim—anticipate the goal of your interlocutor and anticipate the content he may wish to deny
4. The persuasion maxim—model your strategic contribution so as to convince the hearer to adopt your goal.

If the speaker or hearer knows or suspects—at least roughly—what the strategic goal of the other party of the linguistic exchange is, he can make a substantial prediction on the basis of this normative framework. The picture we receive is a two-stage procedure, with the first being the counterfactual assumption of the CP and standard maxims and the inferring of all possible implicatures. The second stage is the application of the strategic principle and the strategic maxims, and it aims to choose the implicatures that conform to one's goal while ignoring others.

Note that the strategic maxim claims that you should pursue your goal independently of your interlocutor's *ultimate* rather than immediate goal. This is because parties modify their goals depending on the goal of their opponent. However, they modify only their immediate goals, rather than their ultimate goals. The ultimate goal consists usually of the need to protect the interests of the party independently of the interests of the other party. Take the example of a divorce: even though the immediate goals of the parties can vary depending on the immediate goals of their opponent (for instance, if one wants financial compensation, the other wants to minimize it; or, if one wants exclusive custody over the children, the opponent will argue for a different distribution), the ultimate goal of the parties will be convergent or divergent (to get a divorce or not) independent of the goal of the other.

Analogously, legislators and courts have different immediate goals because they operate in different contexts, while they have a common ultimate goal of maintaining a well-functioning society, doing what is just and serves the public good, and they have this goal independently of whether the other power has it.[12]

How can a legislator choose the content he wants to implicate? The legislator can indicate what content he wishes to implicate through various contextual cues at the moment of the law's enactment. For instance, he can indicate this in a preamble to the enacted text, in a document issued by a legislative committee, through a social campaign etc. Moreover, it is true that the legislator cannot deny an implicature at the moment of the *in concreto* interpretation.[13] However, he can do so by enacting a subsequent new statute or amending the statute to preclude an implicature previously attributed to him.[14]

One might well wonder why judges have to anticipate the legislative goals if they decide who wins the game. It is true that it is the judges who decide who wins in a concrete case. However, if the judicial powers start deciding cases in a way that does not conform to the legislator's goals, the legislator can enact a new statute or modify the old one and preclude judges from deciding future cases in the old manner. In this case, their judicial efforts will prove pointless for future cases.

Another point that requires clarification is why judges should convince legislators to adopt their goals. It may transpire that an enacted rule leads to absurd or inefficient or blatantly unjust consequences, yet this can be seen only in the context of a concrete case. If this happens, the judicial powers should create a stable interpretive line that mitigates these consequences to signal the legislative powers that they should amend the rule or enact a new rule. In other words, since judges encounter a broader range of problematic contexts, they should convince legislators to take them into account. Take the example of the famous 'Riggs versus Palmer' case described by Dworkin (1978). The facts were the following: Elmer Palmer murdered his grandfather to inherit his fortune. At the time, there existed no legal rule that would prohibit him from inheriting, yet the court ruled that Palmer could not inherit since no one should profit from his wrongdoing. Later, the legislator introduced a rule to the system that prohibited inheriting in such situations. In other words, the court convinced the legislator to adopt the court's goal.

Thus, a legislature adopts judicial goals through the enactment of a statute. As mentioned above, the enacted rule can lead to absurd or inefficient or blatantly unjust consequences. If the judicial powers create a line of cases containing a coherent/efficient/just interpretation, they can convince the legislator to introduce an amendment or a new rule that conforms to the judicial interpretation. Take the example of the case of Polish MP, Beata Sawicka. She was accused of taking a bribe, but the offer was made by a 'secret agent' in a sting-type operation. At the

---

[12] I thank Francesca Poggi for this remark.

[13] It is true that the *in concreto* interpretation is rather one-sided. However, if we take a broader view, we can notice that the interaction between the legislature and courts is more complex. Namely, the way judges interpret the law does influence the legal texts enacted, and vice versa. Judges can prompt the legislator to amend a rule or enact a new statute. Moreover, judges are directly influenced by legislators through the texts they enact.

[14] I thank Marcin Matczak for a helpful discussion on this point.

time, there was no provision in the code of penal procedure that explicitly precluded the admission of evidence obtained through a crime in a trial. Yet the highest court ruled that the secret agent's deeds were illegal and subsequently, in 2014, the court dismissed the evidence and found B. Sawicka innocent. Later, in 2015, the legislator amended the code of penal procedure by adding article 168a, which prohibited the admission of evidence obtained through a crime in court proceedings. This amendment was motivated by B. Sawicka's case and other similar cases.[15]

Such a two-stage procedure is hardly a new idea in philosophy. In the first chapter of 'Communication and the evolution of society' Jurgen Habermas claims that 'Coming to an understanding is the process of bringing about an agreement on the presupposed basis of validity claims that can be mutually recognized. In everyday life we start from a background consensus pertaining to the interpretations taken for granted among participants. As soon as this consensus is shaken, and the presupposition that certain validity claims are satisfied (or could be vindicated) is suspended, the task of mutual interpretation is to achieve a new definition of the situation which all participants can share. If their attempt fails, communicative action cannot be continued. One is then basically confronted with the *alternatives of switching to strategic action*, breaking off communication altogether, or recommencing action oriented to reaching an understanding on a different level, the level of argumentative speech.' (Habermas 1979).

I hope that the maxims listed above depict clearly that, contrary to what Marmor claims, the selectivity of pragmatic phenomena is far from being completely random and unpredictable. I believe people are quite adept at predicting the strategic goals of their interlocutors. Moreover, I am positive that lawyers are the true masters of this pragmatic ability. Lawyers predict very well which implicatures their opponents will want to deny having meant because such implicatures do not conform to their goals.

If the language found in statutes or legal rules results in the underdeterminacy of the content expressed, the judge also has to choose from a range of possible implicatures. Sometimes the goals of the legislature and of the judiciary conform. However, it may be that the legislative and judiciary powers have different immediate goals, even though they have one common goal (of doing what is just and serves the public good). In other words, it is not necessary that the legislative and judicial powers have conforming strategic goals. Poggi notes that:

> The first feature is the conflicting nature of legal practice, as typically emerges in legal trials. The parties in litigation are not interested in understanding legislative norms, but in winning the case, and, likewise, judges are not interested in understanding legislative norms but in settling the specific case in the way they think to be (legally and/or morally) right (…). (Poggi 2016)

There thus arises the question as to what is the theory's power of prediction since it is hard to identify a judge's sense of justice. However, even if this is a challenge, it is not impossible. A judge's sense of justice can be identified by observing his

[15] See http://www.rp.pl/artykul/1324444-Dowody-zdobyte-z-przekroczeniem-granic-prowokacji-sa-nielegalne%2D%2D-wyrok-Sadu-Apelacyjnego-we-Wroclawiu.html#ap-1.

decisions in previous cases. Moreover, I do not claim that the proposed theory will always yield a single prediction in every case; rather, I claim that there will be multiple predictions based on the multiple possible goals identified in each case. Take the example of the Smith vs. US case. The proposed theory yields two main predictions. First, if the courts' goal is to solely protect the interests of the defendant, then the chosen enrichment will be 'use a firearm {as a weapon}'. Second, if the court's goal is to avoid the mixing of guns and drugs in the same place and at the same time because this increases the probability of further crimes being committed, then the chosen enrichment will be 'use a firearm {in any possible way}'.

The distinctive feature of strategic speech is that it is built upon cooperative speech. By this I mean that to select an implicature that conforms to your goal you must first have a range of possible implicatures from which you can select the one convenient for you. In other words, you need to first carry out the inference in the Gricean sense; only then can you choose which implicature you want to accept or claim to have meant through your utterance. Thus, strategic speech is *parasitic upon* cooperative speech. Consequently, strategic speech seems to be based on a different 'strategic' principle:

I. **Strategic principle (SP)—assume that the speech is cooperative, infer all the implicatures, and then apply the second-order strategic maxims to the inferred implicatures (anticipate which implicatures your hearer/speaker will choose/ignore)**

The crucial maxims in strategic speech are the first two: the strategic maxim and the selectivity maxim. The selectivity maxim is the instrument of achieving the strategic purpose of conversation because in strategic speech the strategic purpose is most often achieved by ignoring some implicatures while preserving others. The selectivity maxim is best illustrated when the implicated content in a context is indeterminate. This usually happens when some features of the context are not known or are questionable. Consider the following example. A and B are representatives of opposing parties in a courtroom. A is C's defendant. C lives in Chicago and is suspected of murdering D in New York. C is also suspected of having an affair with D's wife in New York (it is the purported motive). The following exchange occurs in front of a judge:

A: C does not seem to have a girlfriend these days.
B: He has been paying a lot of visits to New York lately.

Recall that B's answer gives rise to a range of possible implicatures. At least two implicatures can be inferred from B's answer. First, the implicature that B has a girlfriend (or lover—D's wife) in New York. Second, the implicature that B does too much travelling to be in a relationship. Clearly, A's goal (as a defendant of C) is to deny the first implicature and uphold the second. By contrast, B's goal as a prosecutor is to uphold the first implicature and deny the second.

Take another example that is more related to the realm of law. Imagine that the claimant argues that he lent the respondent a substantial sum and the respondent did not return the loan. In response to this, the respondent argues that it was not a loan but a donation and thus he did not need to return the money to the claimant. The judge asks the respondent the following question:

J: Did you borrow money from the claimant?
R: I received a bank transfer from the claimant.

Now, the respondent will be interested in denying that her answer implicates that she took a loan. By contrast, the claimant will be interested in viewing the answer as proof for the implicature that there indeed was a loan.[16]

Andrei Marmor also provides examples of cases in which the legal rule and context were indeterminate because numerous contradictory implicatures could be inferred. In these cases, all the possible inferred implicatures were equally 'reasonable'. According to Marmor, in these cases the judge has a large discretion and it is very difficult to foresee the outcome of the interpretive process (Marmor 2016). I believe that the strategic framework provides a mechanism for a higher predictability of judicial outcomes. The decisions are not arbitrary, they are strategic in the sense described in this chapter. The examples provided by Marmor occur in contexts in which 'an inference to implicated content comes into conflict with a salient contextual fact presumed to be common knowledge between speaker and hearer' (Marmor 2016). This happens because a 'superseding premise demonstrates that the usual or the typical fails to obtain in the particular case' (Marmor 2016). Consider the examples below:

[16] Take another example: a legislature enacts the provision 'No vehicles in the park'. Imagine, the legislature wants this to implicate that ABSOLUTELY and without exception no vehicle can enter the park. In other words, the legislature believes that ecology is the implicated value. The enactment of the statute is accompanied by a huge ecological campaign by the 'green' party. However, the judicial powers are faced with the decision whether or not to convict an ambulance driver for breaching the statute. Imagine that the court's goal is to promote human health. The court believes that the value of saving someone's life should prevail over ecology, yet the court is faced with the following legislative implicature: since the legislator is truthful (maxim of quality), according to the second sub-maxim of quantity, 'say no more than you must', combined with the huge ecological social campaign, the legislator wants me to understand that the aim of the provision is to protect ecology rather than any other value. This is backed by the sub-maxim of manner: be brief. This reasoning need to assume a form of hybrid expressivism about values because this stance allows values to be conversationally implicated (see Barker 2000; Finlay 2005; Fletcher 2014). Thus, the court will have to ignore the legislative implicature and will state that this statute implicates that an ambulance can enter the park if someone's life is endangered. This usually takes the form of the following reasoning: had the legislators been in the judicial shoes (or in the context of the case) they simply could not have wanted to imply that ecology is more important than human life or health! Thus, they must have implied that human life or health is more important than ecology. The reasoning would take the following form: since the legislator must be truthful (maxim of quality), according to the second sub-maxim of quantity (say as much as you can) she must have been unable to say more on the values she wished to promote. Since the sub-maxim of manner (avoid obscurity) has not been respected, then there may be exceptions to the promotion of ecological values. A very similar selection situation can occur within a legislative body. Some members of parliament (MPs) might wish that a discussed statute implicates one thing, while others might wish that it implicates quite another. This often results in what Marmor calls legislative compromises. The legislative body votes on and enacts a statute, but without indicating whether by provision X it wants to implicate that Y or that Z (Marmor 2014). For more examples see Skoczeń (2015b, 2016).

1. Senator McCain and the Republicans voted against the bill.
   - McCain is a Republican
2. John and Mary went to Paris last summer.
   - John and Mary divorced last spring.
3. All the graduate students who passed the exams went to the party last night.
   - All the students passed the exam.' (Marmor 2016)

In all three examples, the sentences carry conversational implicatures which are contradicted by features of the context cited below. For instance, in the first example, the implicated content is that McCain is not a Republican. Yet it is common knowledge that this is not a true proposition. Therefore, 'the speaker must have had a different reason to single out McCain'. Since this reason is unknown, the implicated content is indeterminate (Marmor 2016). The second example suggests that John and Mary went to Paris together, which conflicts with the divorce statement. Finally, the third example suggests that some of the students did not pass the exam, which contradicts the statement that all did. Marmor sees an analogy between these cases and two legal cases (*FDA vs Brown and Williamson* and *West Virginia University Hospitals v. Casey*) in which the same sort of indeterminacy was at stake. These are cases in which 'conflicting reasons are on a par with each other' and they have 'roughly equal weight or incommensurability', which leads to an indeterminate conclusion (Marmor 2016). Marmor's first example is the *FDA vs Brown and Williamson Tobacco Corp.* case. The facts were the following: In 1938 the Food, Drug and Cosmetic Act was enacted. In 1965, Congress amended the act and the Food and Drug Administration (FDA) was given the authority to regulate, in the relevant section, any 'articles (other than food) intended to affect the structure or any function of the body'. Until 1996 the FDA was explicitly denied authority over tobacco products. In 1996 the new director of the FDA decided that the wording 'suggested a complete prohibition of tobacco products'. In the meantime, between 1965 and 1996 Congress enacted statutes such as one prohibiting the sale of tobacco to minors. This implicated that adults could freely buy tobacco products. Nevertheless, during this period, there was also an attempt to pass an act that would prohibit tobacco sales entirely. Consequently, contradictory implications could be drawn of such a context. The implicature was indeterminate (Marmor 2016). To sum up, the context was such that it could provide reasonable arguments that backed both implicatures:

1. The FDA cannot prohibit the sale of tobacco because it is legal.
2. The FDA has the authority to prohibit the sale of tobacco entirely.

However, does this mean that the court's decision was completely arbitrary? What was the mechanism for taking this decision? Similar issues arise from the second example: *West Virginia University Hospitals v. Casey*. The question was whether expert fees were included in the expression of a federal statute allowing the court to award 'a reasonable attorney's fee'. In the ruling, the chief argument was that expert fees were explicitly mentioned in many acts enacted by the American Congress. Thus, if the formulation of the statute at stake was such that only attorney fees were mentioned, expert fees should be excluded. By contrast, the dissenting opinion stated that 'the purpose of the legislative provision was to make sure that a plaintiff in a civil lawsuit who prevails in trial can recover its reasonable litigation costs from the losing party.' (Marmor 2016) This again meant that the context provided reasonable arguments for both implicatures of the following content:

1. A reasonable attorney's fee includes expert fees.
2. A reasonable attorney's fee does not include expert fees.[17]

As a judge, you cannot ask the legislature for clarifications, thus indeterminacy is inquiry resistant. Does this mean that in the case of an indeterminate hard case it is impossible to predict the judgment? Is the choice of contradictory implicatures or enrichments completely arbitrary? Is there not a mechanism that explains what will happen?

I think that the second-order strategic framework that I sketch in the present study can answer these questions. I believe that this strategic framework can also explain an example from Italian law provided by F. Poggi. She cites the following legal rule:

> In applying the statute no other meaning can be attributed to it than the one made evident by the meaning of the words, (…), and by the legislator's intention.[18] (Poggi 2016)

Poggi gives the following commentary to the rule: 'Does this provision implicate, by virtue of the fourth maxim of manner ("Be orderly"), a sort of priority of literal meaning on the meaning based on legislative intention? That is to say, does the conjunction "and" implicate "and then"? Well, sometimes Italian judges have argued in favor of this priority, and sometimes against. So, for instance, many courts have claimed that, according to this provision, there is "a primacy of the literal canon" (e.g. Cass. civ. sen. n. 7279/1991; Cass, civ. sen. n. 4000/1982), by virtue of which "when the text is clear, it is not permitted to inquire whether the legislator's intention was possibly different from the one manifestly expressed" (Commissione tributaria regionale di Perugia, Sez. VI, sen. n. 364 del 9/11-23/11/1999; in the same direction cf., e.g., Cass. civ. sen. n. 2663/1986; Cass. civ. sen. n. 13817 del 23.06.2011; T.A.R. del Lazio sen. n. 89 del 7/01/2013). On the contrary, judges have argued on other occasions that there is no such a priority (Cass. civ., sen. n. 4909 del 12.11.1977; Cass. pen., sez. un., sen. n. 5385 del 26.11.2009) and, more often, judges have directly applied arguments based on the legislative intention to a plain [statutory] text (see, e.g., Corte Cost. Sen. n. 347 del 1998; Cass. Civ., sez. I, sen. n.

[17] In light of neo-Gricean theories this would be seen as a pragmatic enrichment rather than an implicature. However, since I have adopted a chronological order in the present study, I treat as implicature in the present chapter anything that Grice would have labeled an implicature, since Grice did not dispose of the notion of pragmatic enrichment.

[18] Par. 12 disp. prel. c.c. (Statutory Interpretation):

2315/1999) without taking a position on the interpretation of the par. 12 disp. prel. c.c.' (Poggi 2016).

I think that what happened in these cases can be explained within the strategic framework. The cited rule carries the implicature that the literal meaning of a rule should be considered first, and the intentional interpretation can only be considered second. Courts select this implicature when it conforms to their interpretive goal. When the implicature does not conform to their goal, they simply ignore it and accord a privileged position to the intentional interpretation.

The examples above, I believe, are cases of selecting an implicature (while ignoring others). Moreover, this is a typical case of selecting some contextual elements while ignoring others.

To sum up, the entire strategic framework can be summarized in one super maxim (based on the strategic principle):

- **The strategic maxim—pursue your goal through selecting conforming implicatures.**[19]

Thus, I believe that when there is a strategic purpose in play, the content of the implicatures inferred on the basis of the four standard maxims is further selected on the basis of the strategic principle and the strategic maxims that precisify it.

Let us take stock. I believe following the Gricean CP and maxims is sufficient to achieve all sorts of cooperative goals and purposes. However, when strategic goals are at stake (goals when one wins and the other loses—a decision must be taken), the classic CP and maxims are insufficient. Achieving strategic goals requires a set of second-order maxims that are a precisification of a strategic principle. Thus, taking part in an argument in a courtroom requires following the strategic principle and the strategic maxims because it is inherently uncooperative (and strategic).

Marmor highlights the fact that the content of the maxims partly depends on the normative (i.e. the moral or political) understanding of the role of legislation in a legal system, and partly on the interpretive practices that the courts actually follow.' (Marmor 2014) 'Over time, the norms of statutory interpretation that are actually followed by the courts may partly determine some conversational maxims of legislation. (…) the courts could create some kind of Gricean maxims for the legislative context. (…) if the courts do not consistently adhere to the relevant interpretive practices, the legislators would not have clear signals about what would count as a relevant contribution to the conversation between them and the courts and, therefore, inevitably, even between the legislators themselves.' (Marmor 2014).

Robyn Carston believes (Carston 2013) the courts do form such Gricean maxims, labeled canons of construction or interpretive principles (or named in a different

[19] I believe that this clarifies F. Poggi's observation: 'the jurist's common experience shows that, in legal interpretation, not everybody is willing to follow the maxims, and, above all, there is not a general expectation that everyone follows them. This is a fact, simply a fact: and this is how things work'. I think that while observing legal practice one can have the impression that the maxims are not followed because of the selectivity of pragmatic phenomena due to a choice of phenomena conforming to one's goal.

sense depending on the legal system). The canons can work just like standard Gricean maxims because, when enacting a statute, the Parliament already knows the canons and can predict what implicatures the courts will draw. Analogously, the courts carry out the pragmatic inferences from the statutes through the canons of construction instead of standard maxims. Moreover, some of the canons of construction can sometimes give contradictory results just as when standard Gricean maxims clash with one another. For instance the canon 'ubi lex voluit dixit, ubi noluit tacuit', which precludes a judge from seeking implicatures, can clash with the canon 'lex minus dixit quam voluit', which causes the judge to seek implicatures (Poggi 2011). Or the canon 'expressio unius est exclusio alterius' and 'eiusdem generis' can also clash.[20] (Carston 2013).

This idea of a stable interpretive practice is also reflected in the Polish system, which contains an act issued by the prime minister called a 'rozporządzenie' that contains rules or guidelines on drafting legal texts.[21] It is a collection of directives on drafting legal texts which mirrors some of the canons of construction employed by the Polish courts. This is the consequence of a jurisprudential guideline of a civil law system: if the guidelines on drafting statutes mirror the guidelines (canons) of interpreting them, then the system is predictable. When drafting a statute, the legislature knows how the court will interpret what it has written down. Moreover, while performing her interpretive task the judge has clear signals as to what the legislature could have meant by using one wording rather than another (Wronkowska 2012; Wronkowska and Zieliński 1985).

As far as the guidelines for drafting statutes are concerned, Francesca Poggi reformulated the Gricean maxims so as to form rules for legislators clarifying how to draft normative texts:

> Quality (pseudo-maxim): Do not issue norms you do not want to be obeyed.
>
> Quantity: Issue norms that satisfactorily specify the recipients' behaviors (i.e. as is required for the current purposes of the communicative exchange in which you are engaged), and in particular:

[20] B. Slocum seems to claim that the canons expressio unius est exclusio alterius and eiusdem generis are applicable only to lists (Slocum 2016). However, the canons ubi lex voluit dixit, ubi noluit tacuit and lex minus dixit quam voluit have almost identical purposes and were not created to explain the interpretation of enumerations. Moreover, expressio… and eiusdem… seem to create coherent interpretations of rules that do not contain enumerations. Thus, the burden of showing the problem is on those that question their applicability to rules that do not contain an enumeration. Recently, in a conference discussion, Marcin Matczak applied the eiusdem generis canon to a rule that did not contain an enumeration. The rule states in the first sentence that some X represents Poland. In the second sentence, it states that this representation does not encompass the representation in the UN Security Council. Since the legislator usually speaks about a uniform subject, the general rule from the first sentence needs to be of the same kind as the exception. This means that the first sentence cannot be read as allowing X to represent Poland in a football match, since this would be absurd.

[21] See rozporządzenie Prezesa Rady Ministrów z dnia 20 czerwca 2002r., w sprawie zasad techniki prawodawczej Dz.U. Nr 100 poz. 908.

1. indicate clearly whether you intend to permit, or to prohibit or compel;
2. issue definite norms: i.e. do not issue (unclearly) defeasible norms;
3. be exhaustive when you indicate the behavior(s) permitted, forbidden or somehow required;
4. do not issue simple stereotypical norms to prescribe anomalous, not stereotypical, not simple behavior, and vice versa.' (Poggi 2016)

The idea is again that the courts should take such guidelines into consideration when interpreting a legal text; nevertheless, it is a fact that no system is perfectly stable in this regard. The legislature cannot predict what new contexts will appear in the future. The courts are often faced with cases in which the canons do not generate a clear result or generate more than one (contradictory) result. Finally, there are cases in which courts just manifestly ignore what the legislature could have meant. For these reasons, we need an additional explanation; we need a theory that explains why, even in systems in which there are stable guidelines of drafting statutes mirrored by interpretive guidelines for the courts, the decisions taken are not always cooperative. We need a theory that provides descriptive mechanisms of these uncooperative, strategic decisions (under which one interpretation wins and the other loses).

Agents acting in the law not only want to convey information but also to pursue their concrete, strategic goals. Thus, even if the basic, informative content is derived through standard Gricean maxims or through canons of constructions,[22] the strategic super-maxim explains how to choose among implicatures (derived from standard maxims or canons of construction) in strategic contexts. Finally, legal discourse is usually a mix of cooperative and strategic purposes.

Strategic selectivity works for both speaker and hearer; as a result, in strategic contexts the speaker has the basis on which to predict what the hearer will select, and the hearer knows on which basis the speaker selects.

The idea of a maxim of selectivity seems to conform with Marmor's idea: 'I am not denying the possibility that some implicatures in law would work, or that some canons of construction, if consistently applied, would amount to a kind of Gricean maxim of conversation.' (Marmor 2014).

Generally speaking, Marmor's conception accepts that all kinds of Gricean implicatures can occur both in legislation and in the exchange between legislatures and courts, it is just that implicatures are sometimes ignored:

> Consider first this familiar example of implicature in legislative speech: suppose that the law asserts, "All Xs ought to q unless X is an F, a G or an H." (…) Now, this kind of utterance would normally implicate that the mentioned exceptions are exhaustive – namely, that all Xs who are not (F or G or H) ought to q. Note that this implicature is cancelable; the legislature can easily indicate that it does not consider the exceptions to be exhaustive. However, absent such indication, it would be natural to assume that the legislature has implicated that F, G and H are the only permissible exceptions to the requirements of Xs to q. (This is an instance of a generalized conversational implicature.) Every first-year law student learns, however, that courts are not very consistent in applying such implicatures. Judges tend to be skeptical, and perhaps rightly so, of the legislature's ability to determine

[22] In the next chapter I will argue why the content of maxims mirrors the content of certain canons of construction.

> in advance all the possible justified exceptions to the rules they enact. Sometimes, therefore – but crucially, not always – courts simply ignore the implicature (…) (Marmor 2014)

I believe that the above case is precisely the result of the application of the strategic super-maxim of selectivity. The court has chosen to ignore the GCI because it does not fit the goal it wishes to achieve.

The case described by Marmor in the example is termed 'defeasibility' by logicians (Brożek 2008). The term was introduced by H.L.A. Hart in his work 'The ascription of responsibility and rights':

> When the student has learnt that in English law there are positive conditions required for the existence of a valid contract, his understanding of the legal concept of a contract is still incomplete. These conditions, although necessary, are not always sufficient and he has still to learn what can defeat a claim that there is a valid contract, even though all these conditions are satisfied. The student has still to learn what can follow on the word "unless", which should accompany the statement of these conditions. This characteristic of legal concepts is one for which no word exists in ordinary English. The words "conditional" and "negative" have the wrong implications, but the law has a word which with some hesitation I borrow and extend: this is the word "defeasible", used of a legal interest in property which is subject to termination or defeat in a number of different contingencies but remains intact if no such contingencies mature. In this sense, then, contract is a defeasible concept. (Hart 1948)

The defeasible concept of a contract is based on a defeasible rule. Linguists treat defeasibility as an analogous phenomenon to the aforementioned cancelability, which is a property of conversational implicatures.[23] (Levinson 1983) The simplest definition of the term—shared by linguists and logicians—is that 'An inference from A to B is cancellable or defeasible if one can assert A and deny B without contradicting oneself'. Take the example of the scalar term 'some':

(I) Mike likes some of his drawings.
  Implicates that: Mike does not like all of his drawings.
(II) Mike likes some of his drawings, in fact, he likes all of them.
(III) Mike likes some of his drawings. Maybe he likes all of them.

Sentences (II) and (III) contain a cancellation of the standard scalar implicature. This is a classic example of defeasible inference.

The definition can be further developed into two varieties of more specific definitions, where each deals with a different subset of phenomena. The first definition claims that 'A cognitive rule is defeasible if and only if there are situations in which its antecedent is fulfilled but its consequent does not follow'. The second definition claims that 'A cognitive rule is defeasible if and only if there are situations in which it is applied with only assuming and not proving some of the conjuncts constituting its antecedent' (Brożek 2008).

[23] Defeasibility and cancelability are only analogous; they are not synonyms since Grice wished that the implicature were calculable—he wanted this to be a quasi-inferential process. The cancelation is an additional premise to a quasi-syllogism that defeats the conclusion. By contrast, defeasibility involves a fully fledged syllogism. I thank Francesca Poggi for her comments on this point.

It is the first definition that reflects the cancelability of conversational implicatures and the defeasibility of legal rules. In other words, the implicatures carried by legal regulations can be cancelled (are defeasible) by some contextual factors. This is exactly what has happened in Marmor's example. If the two antecedents were (1) all Xs ought to q unless X is an F, a G or an H and (2) X is an E, then the consequent should be (3) X ought to q. However, this, as Marmor argues, is not always the case.

Defeasibility is not only proof for the existence of implicatures among legal inferences. It is also a challenge to the formalization of those inferences. This is because, on the grounds of first-order logic, it leads to a situation in which the formalization has nothing to do with the structure of natural (legal) language. This is solved through the application of non-monotonic logic, which does not require that if something follows logically from a given set of premises, it follows also from a superset of it (Brożek 2008)

Note that the reformulation of the principle and maxims proposed in this chapter applies to every kind of strategic behavior, not only to legal behavior. Even in a strategic exchange between a parent and child, selectivity applies. Marmor gives the example of a kid asking for chocolate and getting the reply 'you just had a bunch of candy an hour ago!', which clearly implicates that chocolate now is out of the question. The child goes ahead and gets the chocolate anyway and when asked to account for his misconduct, he says 'But Mom, you didn't say that I could not have it!" (Marmor 2014) Consequently, my point is that strategic behavior including the selectivity maxim is omnipresent in everyday life.[24]

The problem that arises with the Gricean model modified by adding the maxim of selectivity is that in the legal framework it could pose substantial threats to democracy. I will deal with the complex notion of judicial activism in detail in the third chapter.

Before proceeding further, I would like to flesh out the framework that has been created in this chapter. In other words, I would like to provide an answer to the question as to how manipulation, strategic speech and informative speech differ. This answer will be based on two criteria: being cooperative and being strategic. Being cooperative means roughly assuming a common goal with your interlocutor. Consequently, uncooperative behavior means having no common goal (and assuming no common goal). By contrast, as the strategic principle has depicted, being

[24]The fact that strategic behavior is ubiquitous in natural language and the strategic super-maxim of selectivity is often used compels me to disagree with F. Poggi. She claims that the Gricean theory cannot be applied to authoritative speech such as legislation (because it is conflictual in its very nature), while it can be applied to the interpretation of acts of private autonomy. Moreover, she claims that it can be applied to acts of private autonomy because of the bona fides (good faith) principle, which is an interpretive principle of contracts (Poggi 2011). In my framework, the issues are slightly different. I believe legislation is just as strategic as contractual negotiations. In both situations the strategic super-maxim of selectivity is widespread. However, because this strategic nature of discourse can pose threats to democracy and its basic assumptions (such as just laws) there are mechanisms that are supposed to mitigate these threats. I think the bona fides principle is just such an interpretive idea that is supposed to mitigate potential injustice such as the potential inequality of the parties.

strategic means having to (and being able to) predict the goals of your interlocutor (on the assumption that your interlocutor has different goals than you have). Finally, non-strategic games do not require the anticipation of the goals of our interlocutors (because the goals are common and our interlocutors have similar goals to ours).

In light of my theory, manipulation is both uncooperative and non-strategic because it does not enable the hearer to guess what implicatures could be ignored. The hearer cannot guess the strategic goal of the speaker. Even if there are some cases of manipulation in the legal framework, I believe they are minority cases because, as I have already stated, while people are good at guessing the strategic goals of their opponents, good lawyers are true masters of this skill. It must be so since strategic action is at the very essence of the social game or practice we call law.

Strategic speech is uncooperative and strategic for two reasons. First, the speaker and hearer have different goals. Second, such speech makes it possible to guess the goal of your interlocutor and to anticipate which implicatures he may ignore.

Finally, informative speech is cooperative and non-strategic because to be successful it does not require strategic guessing of your interlocutors' goal and anticipation of which implicatures they may ignore, because interlocutors will not ignore any of them.

When we are unable to guess or predict what goal our interlocutor has, then we are being manipulated (since strategic speakers tend to have the intention to manipulate others if possible). However, this is rare in the legal realm because lawyers are very good at anticipating the goals of their interlocutors. Communication in the legal framework is usually a mix of informative and strategic speech. In the legal realm, agents have different immediate and argumentative goals. Their ultimate goals converge (because, for instance, they both want to get a divorce or an interpretive settlement). Thus, the divergent goals I have been speaking of are immediate goals for the sake of interpreting a provision or making an argument in a debate in a courtroom. The ultimate goals are, however, convergent. The only situation in which people have completely divergent goals is war (life or death, survival or destruction). Yet the legal realm is definitely not such an extreme situation. Let me end this subsection with a quote from Searle:

> Even human conflict, in most of its forms, requires cooperation. Think of a prize fight, a football game, a legal trial, or even two philosophers engaged in an argument. For these sorts of conflict to go on, there has to be a higher level of cooperation. If one man comes up behind another in a dark alley and hits him on the head, no collective intentionality is required. But for a prize fight, a wrestling match, a duel, or even an exchange of insults at a cocktail party, a level of cooperation is required. In order to be fighting at one level, we have to be cooperating in having a fight at another level. (Searle 1999b)

This depicts why the total opt-out of cooperation in the law is an implausible hypothesis. The strategic framework must assume some minimal cooperation at a higher level, otherwise no legal system could exist and no strategic goals could ever be achieved.

This also depicts why the theory of strategic communication does not stand in contradiction with an important concept of legal positivism: Herbert Hart's internal point of view. This is because strategic speech assumes some kind of cooperation. To break rules, you need to first accept them (or internalize them as Hart would put it) at a meta-level.

2.7.4 *The Clash of the Maxims*

Marmor and Poggi are not the only theorists that rely on a modified version of the classical Gricean picture applied to the legal realm. Stefan Goltzberg perceives interpretive decisions as a result of clashing maxims. He claims that in a clash situation (when two maxims cannot be simultaneously fulfilled) the judge chooses the one that would be the least likely to be chosen in an ordinary situation. This often results in the consideration of decisions considered absurd by laypeople. 'lawyers neither fully cooperate just like laymen nor completely fail to cooperate. It looks as if lawyers happen not to cooperate because, when faced with a clash of principles, they fail to fulfill one of them since by definition in the case of a clash, the speaker is not able to fulfill all the maxims. But this is not yet a specific trait of legal discourse; indeed, most people from time to time are forced to choose between two maxims that clash with each other. If legal discourse is to be described as strategic—as opposed to cooperative—I think it means that the agent, facing a clash between two maxims, will at times choose to fulfill the maxim that was less expected to be fulfilled.' (Goltzberg 2016) I believe this works only on the assumption that implicature theory is an epistemological theory, otherwise the speaker's intention would determine which maxim is to be upheld. Thus, the idea is that in cases in which we usually favor the second sub-maxim of quantity rather than the first, the court may actually favor the first sub-maxim. Consequently, instead of claiming that 'use a firearm' implicates 'as a weapon', she may claim that there are multiple possible ways of using it.

The problem with this solution is that it does not explain cases in which there is no clash, i.e. cases in which an implicature is derived on the basis of standard maxims (or canons of construction) and yet is ignored. To explain these cases, a second-order maxim of selectivity must be added to the standard normative framework.

2.7.5 *The Strength of Implicature*

It is usually possible to infer several implicatures from one utterance. Consider the example:

> Peter: Would you drive a Mercedes?
>
> Mary: I wouldn't drive ANY expensive car.' (Sperber and Wilson 2006) empirically tested by (Sternau et al. 2015)

On the basis of Mary's utterance more than one implicature can be inferred:

> 'In trying to make Mary's utterance relevant, Peter may retrieve from his accessible world knowledge the assumption 'Mercedes is an expensive car', which will yield the very strong implicature that 'Mary wouldn't drive a Mercedes'. However, Peter may retrieve other assumptions, which will summon other implicatures. If he retrieves, for example "People who refuse to drive expensive cars disapprove of displays of wealth", it is reasonable that the inferred implicature will be "Mary disapproves of displays of wealth"'. (Sperber and Wilson 2006) This was empirically tested by (Sternau et al. 2015).

Thus, one utterance can generate several implicatures that differ in strength. Strength is a matter of degree that is dependent on how much you are warranted to infer the implicature on the basis of the contextual information that you dispose of. It often happens in legal cases that some contextual factor is questioned. Thus, an inference based on such a factor may be defeasible. Consequently, the inference could lead to a weaker implicature.

This results in another possibility for strategic speakers and hearers: they can select not only whether to ignore or to take an implicature under consideration, they can also be faced with a context in which many different implicatures can be decoded. Then, speakers and hearers select which implicature they accept and which they reject. Sometimes courts will accept very weak implicatures while ignoring quite strong ones.

Recall the *Smith vs United States* case. The interpretive decision of denying the implicature (or rather pragmatic enrichment[25]) entailed a broad scope of possible inferences on the basis of a provision taking the form of an implicature. The court chose the rather weak and defeasible implicature of rejecting the narrowing to 'as a weapon' and ruled that using a firearm in a barter transaction falls within the scope of the provision. It ignored other implicatures such as the one Justice Scalia invoked: using a firearm to scratch one's head also falls within the scope of the provision.

2.7.6 Why 'What Is Said' Is Not Always Said?

Neo-Gricean theorists usually question two elements of the standard version of the theory: the necessity of operating under all four maxims and the adequacy of the notion of 'what is said'. There are theories that rely on just one or two maxims rather than four. I will present them in detail and argue that they should also be supplemented with a second-level strategic principle with a strategic maxim. Neo-Griceans point out that quite often a part of a proposition decoded on the basis of

[25] As previously mentioned, in terms of the classical Gricean theory, the pragmatic mechanisms at stake would be labeled implicatures because Grice distinguished only implicatures versus disambiguation and reference assignment as pragmatic mechanisms influencing what is being said. However, in terms of neo-Gricean approaches, the pragmatic mechanisms discussed in this book that pertain to the Smith versus United States case are examples of pragmatic enrichments of what is said. I will elaborate on this technical difference in the next chapters.

what is said is not decoded on the basis of solely the syntax or semantics of the sentence. Consider the following example:

A: Are you hungry?
B: I have had a very large breakfast [today].

What B has said is 'I have had a very large breakfast'. *Tout court.* Clearly, there is a pragmatic enrichment of this with the word 'today' because it would be quite absurd if B's answer meant that he has had a very large breakfast sometime once in his life. Consequently, the full truth-apt proposition decoded on the basis of B's answer is 'I have had a very large breakfast today'. By contrast, the proposition conveyed by B in the conversational implicature is 'I am not hungry'. This proposition is independently truth-evaluable. François Recanati describes the process in the following way:

> In this context, my utterance conversationally implicates that I am not hungry. In order to retrieve the implicature, the interpreter must first understand what is stated: the input to the inferential process responsible for implicature generation. That input is the proposition that the speaker has had a very large breakfast . . . when? No time is specified in the sentence, which merely describes the posited event as being in the past. On the other hand, the implicature that the speaker is not hungry could not be derived if the said breakfast was not understood as having taken place on the day of the utterance. Here we arguably have a case in which something (the temporal location of the breakfast event on the day of utterance) is part of the intuitive truth conditions of the utterance yet does not correspond to anything in the sentence itself. If this is right, then the temporal location of the breakfast event is an unarticulated constituent of the statement made by uttering the sentence in that context.
>
> Such unarticulated constituents, which are part of the statement made even though they correspond to nothing in the uttered sentence, arguably result from a pragmatic process of free enrichment – 'free' in the sense of not being linguistically controlled. What triggers the contextual provision of the relevant temporal specification in example (1) is not something in the sentence but simply the fact that the utterance is meant as an answer to a question about the speaker's present state of hunger (whose state can be causally affected only by a breakfast taken on the same day). (Recanati 2002)

The fact that the Gricean notion of what is said can be further decomposed into layers of non-enriched and pragmatically enriched meaning is also relevant to the legal discussion because this gives the hearer several options. First, a strategic hearer can choose to ignore the pragmatic enrichment. Second, he may have several possibilities of enrichment and can choose the one that pleases him best, even if it does not best please the speaker.

Thus, in the following chapters I will outline the neo-Gricean solutions, choose the one that best fits the legal realm, and modify it so as to deal with possible objections. I will start with Dan Sperber's and Deirdre Wilson's 'Relevance Theory'.

To sum up, the answer advanced in this study to the question of whether implicatures occur in the realm of law is that implicatures occur in every kind of legal situation (even within the linguistic exchange between legislatures and courts). More examples will be provided in subsequent chapters. Conversational implicatures occur both as particularized conversational implicatures and generalized conversational implicatures. It is just that in strategic contexts such as legislation or exchanges between legislatures and courts, implicatures are used (or rather chosen) selectively.

References

Antas J (2008) O kłamstwie i kłamaniu [On lies and lying]. Towarzystwo Autorów i Wydawców Prac Naukowych UNIVERSITAS, Kraków

Austin JL (1962) How to do things with words: [the William James lectures delivered at Harvard University in 1955], 2nd edn. [repr.]. Harvard University Press, Cambridge

Bach K (1999) The myth of conventional implicature. Linguis Philos 22:327–366

Barker S (2000) Is value content a component of conventional implicature? Analysis 60:268–279. https://doi.org/10.1093/analys/60.3.268

Brożek B (2008) Revisability versus defeasibility. Northern Ireland Leg Q 59:139–147

Carston R (2013) Legal texts and canons of construction: a view from current pragmatic theory. In: Freeman MDA, Smith F (eds) Law and language, 1st edn. Oxford University Press, Oxford

Clark RL (2012) Meaningful games: exploring language with game theory. MIT Press, Cambridge

Dworkin R (1978) Taking rights seriously. Harvard University Press, Cambridge

Finlay S (2005) Value and implicature. Ann Arbor MI Mich Publ Univ Mich Libr 5:1–20

Fletcher G (2014) Pure versus hybrid expressivism and the Enigma of conventional implicature. In: Fletcher G, Ridge M (eds) Having it both ways: hybrid theories and modern metaethics. Oxford University Press

Gizbert-Studnicki T (1983) O sposobach formułowania dyrektyw [A few remarks on the ways of formulating norms]. Stud Semiotyczne XIII:91–109

Goldsworthy J (1994) Implications in language, law and the constitution. In: Lindell G, Zines L (eds) Future directions in Australian constitutional law: essays in honour of Professor Leslie Zines. Federation Press in association with the centre for international and public law and the law faculty. Australian National University, Sydney

Goltzberg S (2016) Cooperation in legal discourse. In: Mohammed D, Lewiński M (eds) Argumentation and reasoned action: Proceedings of the 1rst European Conference on Argumentation, Lisbon, 2015. College Publications, Londres, pp 113–128

Grice HP (1989) Studies in the way of words. Harvard University Press, Cambridge

Grice P (1975) Logic and conversation. In: Cole P, Morgan J (eds) Syntax and semantics. Academic Press, New York

Habermas J (1979) Communication and the evolution of society. Beacon Press, Boston

Hart HLA (1948) The ascription of responsibility and rights. Proc Aristot Soc 49:171–194

Leech GN (1983) Principles of pragmatics. Longman, New York

Levinson SC (1983) Pragmatics, nineteenth printing 2008. Cambridge University Press

Levinson SC (2000) Presumptive meanings: the theory of generalized conversational implicature. MIT Press, Cambridge

Longworth G (2017) John Langshaw Austin. In: Zalta EN (ed) The Stanford Encyclopedia of Philosophy (Spring 2017 Edition)

Marmor A (2014) The language of law, 1st edn. Oxford University Press, Oxford

Marmor A (2016) Defeasibility and pragmatic indeterminacy in law. In: Capone A, Poggi F (eds) Pragmatics and law. Perspectives in pragmatics, philosophy & psychology, vol 7. Springer, Cham

Matczak M (2016) Does legal interpretation need Paul Grice? Reflections on Lepore and Stone's imagination and convention. Polish J Philos 10(1):67–87. https://doi.org/10.5840/pjphil20161014

Matczak M (2017) Poland's Constitutional Tribunal under PiS control descends into legal chaos. 11 January 2017. https://verfassungsblog.de/polands-constitutional-tribunal-under-pis-control-descends-into-legal-chaos/

Poggi F (2011) Law and conversational implicatures. Int J Semiotics Law - Revue Intertnationale pour la Sémiotique Juridique 24:21–40. https://doi.org/10.1007/s11196-010-9201-x

Poggi F (2016) Grice, the law and the linguistic special case thesis. In: Capone A, Poggi F (eds) Pragmatics and law: philosophical perspectives

Recanati F (2002) Unarticulated constituents. Linguist Philos 25:299–345

Sadurski W (2014) Searching for Illicit motives: constitutional theory of freedom of speech, equal protection, and separation of state and religion. Sydndy Law School Legal Studies Research Paper 61

Sbisà M (2017) Implicitness in normative texts. In: Poggi F, Capone A (eds) Pragmatics and law. Springer, Cham, pp 23–42

Searle J (1999a) The Chinese room. In: Wilson RA, Keil FC (eds) The MIT encyclopedia of the cognitive sciences. MIT Press, Cambridge

Searle JR (1978) Literal meaning. Erkenntnis 13:207–224. https://doi.org/10.1007/BF00160894

Searle JR (1999b) Mind, language, and society: philosophy in the real world, 1st edn. Basic Books, New York

Skoczeń I (2011) Law, language and their influence on cognition. In: Argumentation 2011: International Conference on Alternative Methods of Argumentation in Law: Conference Proceedings

Skoczeń I (2012) How to reach a compromise on compromise? In: Argumentation 2012: International Conference on Alternative Methods of Argumentation in Law: Conference Proceedings

Skoczeń I (2013) Why do pragmatics matter in the legal framework? In: Argumentation 2013: International Conference on Alternative Methods of Argumentation in Law: Conference Proceedings

Skoczeń I (2015a) Implicatures within the legal context: a rule-based analysis of the possible content of conversational maxims in law. In: Araszkiewicz M, Banaś P, Gizbert-Studnicki T, Płeszka K (eds) Problems of normativity, rules and rule-following. Springer, Cham, pp 351–362

Skoczeń I (2015b) Thick concepts, implicatures and the nature of law. In: Argumentation 2015: International Conference on Alternative Methods of Argumentation in Law

Skoczeń I (2016) Czy modny i sprawiedliwy mogą mieć ze sobą coś wspólnego? – czyli kilka słów o thick terms, thick concepts oraz thick properties [Do the fashionable and the just have anything in common? a few words on thick terms, thick concepts and thick properties]. Archiwum Filozofii Prawa oraz Filozofii Społecznej 12

Slocum BG (2016) Conversational implicatures and legal texts: conversational implicatures and legal texts. Ratio Juris 29:23–43. https://doi.org/10.1111/raju.12114

Smolak M (2012) Wykładnia celowościowa z perspektywy pragmatycznej [Teleological interpretation from a pragmatic perspective]. Wolters Kluwer Polska, Warszawa

Sperber D, Wilson D (2006) Relevance theory. In: Horn LR, Ward GL (eds) The handbook of pragmatics. Blackwell, Malden

Sternau M, Ariel M, Giora R, Fein O (2015) Levels of interpretation: new tools for characterizing intended meanings. J Pragmat 84:86–101. https://doi.org/10.1016/j.pragma.2015.05.002

Wronkowska S (2012) Komentarz do zasad techniki prawodawczej: z dnia 20 czerwca 2002 r [Commentary to the rules on legislative text drafting]. Wydawnictwo Sejmowe, Warszawa

Wronkowska S, Zieliński M (1985) O korespondencji dyrektyw redagowania i interpretowania tekstu prawnego [On the correspondence of directives on drafting and interpreting legal text]. Studia Prawnicze, pp 301–327

Załuski W (2013) Game theory in jurisprudence. Copernicus Center Press, Kraków

Chapter 3
Post-Gricean Implicature Theories and Their Relevance for the Legal Realm

> *One must always take care not to clash with the subsidiary thoughts, which are however not explicitly expressed and therefore should not be reckoned in the sense.*
> Gottlob Frege, 'Sense and reference' p. 227

I concluded the previous chapter with the statement that neo-Gricean theorists usually question two elements of the standard version of the theory: the necessity of operating on all four maxims and the adequacy of the notion of 'what is said'. There are numerous theories that deserve the label neo-Gricean because they somehow reflect on or modify the works of the British philosopher, but discussing them all would require much more space than this work allows. Therefore, I will discuss only the most influential ones and the ones that can help me build a coherent picture of what is at work in the legal realm.

Among the numerous neo-Griceans, three main methodological approaches can be distinguished: the philosophical approach, the grammatical approach and the empirical-psychological theory of utterance interpretation (Perry and Korta 2015).

Paul Grice started a tradition that emphasized the primordiality of psychology over semantics. This is related to his notion of M(eaning)-intention that relied on three factors:

> (i) M(eaning)-intention is perlocutionary, that is, it is an intention that seeks a mental effect (certain belief(s) or intention(s)) on the part of the addressee; (ii) it is overt, that is, the speaker wants the addressee to recognize her communicative intention; and (iii) the satisfaction of a communicative intention consists precisely in its recognition by the addressee. (Perry and Korta 2015)

Consequently, any theory created after Grice's seminal work and which relies on a psychological root of semantics can be labeled neo-Gricean. If we want to be more precise and narrow the scope of interest to only those theories that somehow reflect the major Gricean contributions such as the CP, the maxims and the distinction between what is said and implicated, the neo-Gricean theories need to address the following:

I. Skoczeń, *Implicatures within Legal Language*, Law and Philosophy Library 127, https://doi.org/10.1007/978-3-030-12532-5_3

(I.) the fundamental distinction of what a speaker says and what she implicates;
(II.) a set of rules or principles, derived from general principles of rationality, cooperation and/or cognition, that guide, constrain or govern human linguistic communication (there are differences among neo-Griceans on the exact nature of these principles and of pragmatic reasoning generally, as we shall see);
(III.) and a notion of communicative intention (called M(eaning)-intention by Grice) A communicative intention is fulfilled if it is recognized by the addressee. (Perry and Korta 2015)

As mentioned at the outset of this chapter, neo-Griceans usually question either (I) or (II). They question either the Gricean distinction between what is said and what is implicated or the necessity of having four maxims (and their content). The ones attacking (I) are called near-side pragmatics by Korta and Perry because they are concerned with the issue of how much of what is said is actually not said (pronounced). These theories use such notions as pragmatic enrichment, pragmatic intrusion, unarticulated constituent, implicature and explicature (I will explain them in detail in the next chapter). The ones attacking (II) are labeled far-side pragmatics because they are concerned not with the notion of what is said but what is implicated. They do not deny the existence of implicatures (this is treated by philosophers of language as relatively uncontroversial), they just question the mechanisms for the derivation of implicatures—the necessity and content of the CP and the four maxims formulated by Grice.

In this chapter, I will focus on the theories that attack the set of rules or principles for deriving implicated meaning proposed by Paul Grice. In the next chapter, I will focus on the theories that attack the distinction between what a speaker says and what she implicates. Among the theories attacking the maxims formulated by Grice, the most influential ones and the ones that could potentially be useful for lawyers are Sperber and Wilson's Relevance Theory (RT), Horn's theory of the Q and R principles and Robyn Carston's theory concerning heuristics and canons of construction. I will provide a brief outline of these theories and assess whether they can be explanatorily valuable in the legal realm. Let me start with RT.

3.1 Relevance Theory

RT is based on two principles of relevance:

(I.) *the Cognitive Principle*: human cognition is geared to the maximization of relevance
(II.) *the Communicative Principle*: utterances create expectations of optimal relevance (Sperber and Wilson 2006).

This sheds more light on the Gricean claim that an essential feature of communication (both verbal and non-verbal) is the expression and recognition of intentions. In fact, the Gricean theory and all the theories that relate to it are based on the 'inferential model of communication', which claims that 'an agent provides evidence of her intention to convey a certain meaning, which is inferred by the audience on the basis of the evidence provided'. This model is opposed to the 'code model', according to which one agent codes a message and another agent receives and decodes this message. The inferential model encompasses the code model because the decoded meaning is treated as one of the inferential premises (Sperber and Wilson 2006).

The code model was created before the inferential one. The idea was simple: for communication to occur, there had to be a sender and a receiver. Both had to share a system of signs or a code, as well as a channel. The sender would encode the message and send it to the receiver through the channel. The receiver had to decode the message. If both agents shared the knowledge of the code and the channel was safe, communication was successful (Perry and Korta 2015).

Grice decided to challenge the explanatory sufficiency of this tradition. He created an inferential model that revolved around intention recognition. To recognize an intention, we need more than just the knowledge of linguistic conventions (thus conventions are still important and necessary, but they are not sufficient). We need 'ampliative reasoning about what is going on in other minds'.[1] (Perry and Korta 2015; Grice 1975)

Sperber and Wilson follow Grice's claim that the code model is insufficient, but they go somewhat further. For Grice, insufficiency applied only to the notion of 'what is implicated', while RT claims that it also applies to the notion of 'what is said' and they label this an 'explicature'. I will discuss this in detail in the next chapter.

Consequently, both the Gricean theory and RT belong to inferential pragmatics. 'The goal of inferential pragmatics is to explain how the hearer infers the speaker's meaning on the basis of the evidence provided' (Sperber and Wilson 2006). This means that meaning is recovered on the basis of some conscious or unconscious inference. This inference is carried out on the basis of multiple factors provided by the context. Moreover, RT 'shares the Gricean intuition that utterances raise expectations of relevance' (Sperber and Wilson 2006). Grice voiced this intuition by postulating his maxim of relation, which compelled the speaker to be relevant but—at least in the classical version—it was only one of the four maxims which developed the cooperative principle. By contrast, relevance is the central claim of RT. The major drawback of the described stance is that the definition of relevance is not fully clear, and all the remaining claims of RT rely on this notion. RT claims that relevance is 'a potential property of (…) utterances' (Sperber and Wilson 2006). This property is assessed with respect to contexts which are sets of propositions. The assessment that requires least effort and provides the most effects is the answer to the question of what is relevant:

> It is usual to treat relevance as a property of utterances or a relation between an utterance and a text or discourse. However, relevant information may be derived not only from utterances and other communicative acts, but also from memory, observation, and inference. We

[1] 'So there must be a place for an unsimplified, and so more or less unsystematic, logic of the natural counterparts of these devices; this logic may be aided and guided by the simplified logic of the formal devices but cannot be supplanted by it.' (Grice 1975).

> shall treat relevance in the first instance as a property of propositions (information units, combinations of sense and reference); subsidiary definitions of relevance for utterances or discourses are relatively easy to construct. Similarly, we shall treat a proposition as relevant in the first instance, not to a text or discourse but to a context, which is a stock of information derived not only from preceding discourse, but also from memory, observation, and inference. From the formal point of view, a context is simply a set of propositions of arbitrary size and content. From the psychological point of view, both size and content are subject to considerable constraints (…). (Sperber and Wilson 2004)

The issue with applying the technical notion of relevance to the legal realm is that the pragmatic phenomenon selected on the basis of the strategic framework does not always have to carry a technical property of relevance because it is as if the interpreter ascribes this property to the interpretation he has chosen (for some strategic reasons). Consequently, relevance would be dependent on the immediate strategic goal, thus, this is incompatible with the claim that there is always an interpretation that carries the property of relevance in a somehow 'objective' manner. Moreover, the fact that lawyers have construed so many complex theories of interpretation over the years proves that interpretation often requires a considerable amount of cognitive effort that is much larger than the amount required to get default cognitive effects (as defined by RT).

Analogously to Grice, RT sees communication as just one example of a much broader set of human rational behavior. It claims that people seek relevance in every kind of action they pursue, not only speaking. Such action is labeled 'input' and is 'relevant to an individual when it connects with background information he has available to yield conclusions that matter to him; for example, by answering a question he had in mind, improving his knowledge on a certain topic, settling a doubt, confirming a suspicion or correcting a mistaken impression.' (Sperber and Wilson 2006) In a nutshell, a relevant input yields a positive cognitive effect which is a 'worthwhile difference to the individual's representation of the world – a true conclusion, for example.' (Sperber and Wilson 2006) Only inputs that yield positive effects matter—other inputs are a cognitive waste of time.

Coming back to the definition of relevance, being relevant is a matter of degree. It is often the case that an individual has several competing relevant inputs in a situation and she chooses the most relevant one. The choice is made on the basis of interplay of effort and effect. This means that the chosen input will generate the greatest effects in terms of relevance with the lowest necessary cognitive effort (Sperber and Wilson 2006). The effect is measured in terms of its contributing a 'worthwhile difference', such as a true conclusion.

RT questions the most fundamental Gricean thesis: the necessity of cooperation. In other words, RT does not need a cooperative principle and maxims to explain communication. It can explain pragmatic phenomena such as implicatures without assuming cooperation. The entire Gricean framework is replaced by a single cognitive principle of relevance which claims that 'human cognition tends to be geared to the maximization of relevance' (Sperber and Wilson 2006).

RT also claims that it has improved the explanation of silence proposed by Grice. For Grice, silence meant an opt-out—a refusal of cooperation. By contrast, Sperber and Wilson write that 'an ostensive stimulus (for instance an utterance) is the most relevant one that the communicator is WILLING AND ABLE to produce' (Sperber and Wilson 2006). Consequently, if the speaker asks a question and the hearer remains silent, there are two possibilities. First, the hearer may be unable to answer and her silence is non-ostensive (Sperber and Wilson 2006). This means that silence cannot be a basis for inferring any content; however, the hearer can also remain silent on the grounds of RT because she is unwilling to convey more information. This will clearly be an ostensive silence and thus, allegedly contrary to Grice, the interlocutor can infer some content on the basis of such silence:

> On a Gricean account, violation of the first Quantity maxim ('Make your contribution as informative as required') is invariably attributed to the communicator's INABILITY – rather than UNWILLINGNESS – to provide the required information. Unwillingness to make one's contribution 'such as is required' is a violation of the Cooperative Principle, and, in some cases, is a suspension of the Cooperative Principle that should make it impossible to convey any conversational implicatures at all. We have argued that, although much communication is cooperative in the sense that the communicator is willing to provide the required information, cooperation in this sense is not essential for communication, as it is for Grice. (Sperber and Wilson 2006)

However, I am not sure whether the notion of silence constitutes a genuine problem for the classical Gricean version of the theory. It is true that, on the sole basis of the quantity maxim, remaining silent would entail being unable to say more than one has said so far. Yet the Gricean idea is much more complex than just the maxim of quantity. It describes four main ways of failing to fulfill the maxims (see previous chapter). One of them is called 'opt-out', which occurs when the speaker indicates that he does not abide to the CP and maxims:

'He [the speaker] may opt out from the operation both of the maxim and the CP; he may say, indicate, or allow it to become plain that he is unwilling to cooperate in the way the maxim requires. He may say, for example, *I cannot say more; my lips are sealed.*' (Grice 1975) Thus, an opt-out clearly indicates that the speaker is unwilling to convey more and remains silent.[2]

Nevertheless, RT (just like most neo-Gricean theories) brings an improvement to the classical Gricean version of the theory as far as the notion of 'what is said' is concerned. RT reads Grice as claiming that, as far as 'what is said' is at stake, the only elements that may require context are reference assignment and disambiguation. Thus, we may look at context to find the referent of indexicals such as 'he' or 'she', and we may look at the context to decide whether 'bank' means a riverbank or a financial institution. However, all neo-Gricean theories (including RT) point to the fact that there are more elements of 'what is said' that need context for a proposition to be grasped. They claim that 'the explicitly communicated content of an utterance goes well beyond what is linguistically [syntactically and lexically]

[2]This section aims to analyze solely the relation between claims about silence in RT and the Gricean theory. Nevertheless, legal theory has constructed all kinds of interesting distinctions concerning silence. Since Roman times, the saying 'qui tacet consentire videtur' has been applied to, for instance, administrative law. The application of this saying is forbidden in criminal law. For a detailed account see Dobosz (2011).

encoded'. RT defines the explicitly communicated content as 'a communicated proposition recovered by a combination of decoding and inference which provides a premise for the derivation of contextual implications and other cognitive effects' (Sperber and Wilson 2006).

Again, the fundamental difference between Grice and RT appears on the horizon. Grice claimed that only implicatures are recovered through the CP and maxims. By contrast, RT 'treats the identification of explicit content as equally inferential, and equally guided by the Communicative Principle of Relevance, as the recovery of implicatures' (Sperber and Wilson 2006). Thus, we get a picture of where pragmatics plays an important role in understanding 'what is said', which is referred to as 'explicature' by RT. The job of semantics is further reduced, and solely semantic input will not be sufficient to understand what the speaker says.

Another difference pertains to the fact that Grice assumed that the decoding of content takes place in sequential order. We need first to decode the literal meaning and 'what is said' to be able to infer implicatures on the basis of the CP and maxims. The neo-Griceans, including RT, question this. The way people process language in their minds does not seem to have a sequential order and, in any case, the Gricean order is not respected: 'The hearer does not FIRST decode the logical form of the sentence uttered, THEN construct an explicature and select an appropriate context, and THEN derive a range of implicated conclusions. Comprehension is an on-line process, and hypotheses about explicatures, implicated premises and implicated conclusions are developed in parallel against a background of expectations (or anticipatory hypotheses) which may be revised or elaborated as the utterance unfolds.' (Sperber and Wilson 2006) Thus, the human mind mixes all the Gricean stages of meaning recovery, achieving the same result but without a specific order.

RT takes a specific stance on what Grice labeled Generalized Conversational Implicatures (GCI—see previous chapter). While most neo-Gricean approaches treat them as 'stereotypical narrowings analyzed as default interpretations derivable via default rules', RT sees GCI as a type of pragmatic enrichment (Sperber and Wilson 2006). This means that the kind of resort to context we need for a Gricean GCI probably contributes to the content of an explicature (and not implicature). In other words, RT restricts the Gricean list of implicatures because it removes GCIs from this list. Further, it claims that GCIs belong to the 'what is said' notion.

RT claims that an explicature conveys a basic explicature as well as some higher-level explicatures. This is similar to Kent Bach's idea that a single utterance may convey several truth-apt propositions. Consider the following conversation:

(I.) Peter: Will you pay back the money by Tuesday?
(II.) Mary: I will pay it back by then. (Sperber and Wilson 2006)

Mary's answer conveys the basic explicature that she will pay back the money by Tuesday. However, according to RT, it also conveys at least two higher-order explicatures such as 'Mary is promising to pay back the money by Tuesday' and 'Mary believes she will pay back the money by Tuesday' (Sperber and Wilson 2006). Note that Bach's theory and RT are accounts based on the Gricean tradition. This is the reason for using terms such as second-order 'implicatures'. By contrast, for Austin, such second-order explicatures would have been listed as the felicity conditions of a speech act (Austin 1962; Grabowski 1999).

3.2 Relevance Theory and the Legal Discourse

Some of the amendments to the classical Gricean picture proposed by RT are helpful to better explain the functioning of legal language. However, the overall claim presented in this chapter will be that RT is not a theory that could be helpful in fully depicting the differences between the kind of enterprises in which natural and legal languages are involved. I will first present the amendments and analyze whether they are genuinely useful. Second, I will argue that RT cannot serve as an appropriate theory of legal pragmatics.

3.2.1 The Amendments to the Classical Gricean Picture

RT does not postulate the necessity of assuming the CP and maxims in order to explain implicatures. Thus, on the basis of RT it could be possible to explain implicatures in law without claiming that legal discourse is cooperative. The entire Gricean framework is replaced by a single cognitive principle of relevance, claiming that humans have a universal tendency to maximize relevance wherever it is possible. This is supposed to make it possible 'at least to some extent, to **predict and manipulate the mental states of others**.' (Sperber and Wilson 2006)

Both the lack of cooperation as well as the possibility of predicting the mental states of others is in line with my idea outlined in the previous chapter. The strategic principle and the maxims that develop it require only a counterfactual assumption of cooperation to infer the possible implicatures [see the content of the strategic principle in the previous chapter]. However, this assumption does not require this cooperation to be genuinely present. Moreover, the maxim of anticipation ('anticipate the goal of your interlocutor and anticipate what content he may wish to deny') concentrates on the issues of predicting the mental states and consequently the behavior of others.

Since the lack of cooperation in RT and the strategic framework seems compatible, let us now verify whether the consequences they yield are also consistent. The absence of CP and maxims in RT does not preclude an effort on the part of the hearer toward finding the proposition that has the property of relevance:

> Given the universal tendency to maximize relevance, an audience will only pay attention to a stimulus that seems relevant enough. By producing an ostensive stimulus, the communicator therefore encourages her audience to presume that it is relevant enough to be worth processing. **This need not be a case of Gricean cooperation**. Even a self-interested, deceptive or incompetent communicator manifestly intends her audience to assume that her

stimulus is relevant enough to be worth processing – why else would he pay attention? [emphasis mine] (Sperber and Wilson 2006)

As I have already emphasized, this consequence cannot be accepted in the strategic framework and exchanges in the realm of law because in such exchanges the effort of the hearer is not oriented at finding the proposition that has the property of relevance as defined by RT. Take legal interpretation for instance: it is not oriented at finding a proposition whose processing requires least effort; quite the contrary, the interpretive process will often involve very high levels of cognitive effort and reflection on the interpreted sentence.

Even if legal pragmatics is not interested in the kind of psychological approach proposed by RT, a legal theorist can still learn something important from RT. Grice did not elaborate much on the notion of 'what is said', as it was not his central point of interest. Thus, this notion has been put under intensive criticism (more on this criticism in the next chapter). Consequently, Grice did not spend much time on a theory explaining how people process denotations and other single units that can form sentences when aggregated. For Grice, this was not an element that was important for the coherence of his theory but, by contrast, it is crucial in analyzing legal language. Since RT's ambition is to provide an account of how the mind works and processes language, RT has an account of how pragmatic processes can affect single extensions. This is the idea of loosening the encoded meaning and broadening the denotation (for example, prominent brand names such as *Hoover, Xerox, Kleenex* etc.). Brand names such as *Hoover* denote an entire category rather than just objects labeled with a specific brand. Other instances include approximations of well-defined terms such as *square, painless or silent* (Sperber and Wilson 2006). Sperber and Wilson also give the example of the ambiguous word 'bank', which could denote not only a natural area near a river or an institution, but also a cash dispenser. Moreover, it could be used to denote any other device with a similar function to the stereotypical financial institution we call a bank, for instance a website. This idea seems to me to be an account of polysemy in terms of a philosophy oriented at the functioning of the mind. I believe that this explanation is useful for lawyers and I will demonstrate why.

Coming back to the example from the previous chapter concerning the *Smith vs. US* case,[3] the discussion on the meaning of the phrase 'use a firearm' is a typical description of the phenomenon of polysemy. There are multiple theories that attempt to explain this phenomenon (Recanati 2017). RT explains it by use of the notion of loosening. This is a pragmatic process of the modulation of meaning which

[3] Briefly the facts of the case were the following: 'The issue was whether a man's exchanging a machine gun for narcotics constituted his 'use' of a firearm 'during and in relation to…a drug trafficking crime' within the meaning of Statute 18 U.S.C. s. 924(c)(1) (hereafter referred to as Stat-18). The statute imposes an additional five-year prison term when a gun is used, and if the weapon is a machine gun, the mandatory sentence is 30 years. The defendant, John Angus Smith, offered to trade a MAC-10 machine gun with an undercover federal agent for two ounces of cocaine. He was convicted of conspiracy to possess and distribute cocaine, and of 'using' the machine gun in relation to the conspiracy in violation of Stat-18. On appeal, Smith argued that trading a gun was not among the 'uses' of a firearm defined by the statute. He lost his appeal.' (Carston 2013).

results in broadening the scope of a notion's referents. In Smith vs US, the court ruled that 'using a firearm' means not only firing it, but also using it to pay for drugs. Thus, explaining this decision as an example of loosening fits neatly into the explanation of what is at play in the language of law.

Furthermore, RT proposes a different definition of implicature: 'An implicature is a contextual assumption or implication which a speaker, intending her utterance to be manifestly relevant, manifestly intended to make manifest to the hearer' (Sperber and Wilson 2001). Such implicatures can be of two types: implicated premises and implicated conclusions. 'Implicated premises must be supplied by the hearer, who must either retrieve them from memory or construct them by developing assumption schemas retrieved from memory.' (Sperber and Wilson 2001) They must be the most relevant in terms of effort and effect. By contrast, implicated conclusions are 'deduced from the explicatures of the utterance and the context' (Sperber and Wilson 2001). The speaker must predict in advance that the hearer will deduce such conclusions.

RT further amends the classical Gricean project by depicting that the strength of such implicatures is gradable:

> A proposition may be more or less strongly implicated by an utterance. It is STRONGLY IMPLICATED (or is a STRONG IMPLICATURE) if its recovery is essential in order to arrive at an interpretation that satisfies the expectations of relevance raised by the utterance itself. It is WEAKLY IMPLICATED if its recovery helps with the construction of an interpretation that is relevant in the expected way, but is not itself essential because the utterance suggests a range of similar possible implicatures, any one of which would do (Sperber and Wilson 2006).

Consequently, some implicatures deduced from one utterance are stronger than others which have been deduced from the very same utterance. The strongest ones are 'fully determinate' and the speaker is 'responsible for their truth' (Sperber and Wilson 2001). This is a substantial difference compared to the Gricean version of the theory, in which all implicatures were indeterminate.[4] Thus, according to RT, some implicatures are strong, while others are made only weakly manifest. Consider again the example:

(III.) Peter: Would you drive a Mercedes?
(IV.) Mary: I wouldn't drive any expensive car. (Sperber and Wilson 2001)

According to RT, the strong implicatures derived from Mary's answer are:

(V.) A Mercedes is an expensive car. (implicated premise)
(VI.) Mary wouldn't drive a Mercedes. (implicated conclusion)' (Sperber and Wilson 2001)

---

[4] 'Since, to calculate a conversational implicature is to calculate what has to be supposed in order to preserve the supposition that the Cooperative Principle has been observed, and since there may be various possible specific explanations, a list of which may be open, the conversational implicatum in such cases will be a disjunction of such specific explanations; and if the list of these is open, the implicatum will have just the kind of indeterminacy that many actual implicata do in fact seem to possess.' (Grice 1975).

By contrast, RT claims that other implicatures derivable from Mary's answer will be weak, for instance:

(VII.) A Rolls Royce is an expensive car.
(VIII.) A Cadillac is an expensive car.
(IX.) Mary wouldn't drive a Rolls Royce.
(X.) Mary wouldn't drive a Cadillac'.
(XI.) People who refuse to drive expensive cars disapprove of displays of wealth.
(XII.) Mary disapproves of displays of wealth. (Sperber and Wilson 2001)

Such weak implicatures do not have to be recovered at all by some agents, or could be recovered by others. Their relevance is lower than the relevance of the strong implicature. Consequently, the speaker will not be held responsible for his truth.

By contrast, he will be held responsible for the truth of strong implicatures. According to RT, the criteria leading to the distinction of strong implicatures are the following: 'The strongest possible implicatures are those fully determinate premises or conclusions, such as (V.) and (VI.) which must actually be supplied if the interpretation is to be consistent with the principle of relevance, and for which the speaker takes full responsibility.' (Sperber and Wilson 2001)

The above criterion is problematic in the realm of law because, according to RT, the recovering of a strong implicature is necessary to be able to ascribe the property of relevance to an utterance. Without recovering the strong implicature, the agent will not consider the utterance as relevant at all. In the realm of law, there exist cases in which an implicature is clearly strong (in terms of effort and effect interplay), yet the courts ignore it. This was the case in *Holy Trinity Church vs US.* In terms of effort and effect, the most accessible understanding of a list of exceptions is that it is exhaustive; however, the decision of the court was to ignore this pragmatic effect.

The last major modification (mentioned in this chapter) introduced by RT to the Gricean picture is a new theory of irony. However, the discussion of irony is irrelevant for the present considerations as it is absent in legal discourse. Irony can be used in some discussions in the courtroom; it will usually have limited importance yet, by contrast, you cannot say that a legal decision is ironic.

To sum up, the rejection of the assumption that communication is cooperative, and the idea of lexical narrowing and broadening are undeniably interesting for the legal theorist. Let me now argue why, despite apparent similarities to legal reasoning, RT cannot be an explanatorily sufficient theory of legal pragmatics.

3.2.2 *Why RT Cannot Be a Sufficient Theory of Legal Pragmatics*

RT shares with Grice the conviction that psychology is primordial to semantics. RT claims that the derivation of implicatures is a non-demonstrative inference. In other words, the inference can be, for instance, induction or other kinds of defeasible reasoning (Neale 2016). RT is supposed to be a 'psychologically plausible theory' that can be verified through empirical experiments. This last element differentiates it from the Gricean idea, since the British philosopher did not consider whether his theory could ever be confirmed in empirical research.

The problem with viewing RT as a theory of legal pragmatics can be stated in one sentence: legal decisions are often counterintuitive. People often look at a legal rule and claim that they would understand it as A, yet the court decides that the proper meaning is B. Thus, speaking in RT's terms, the most relevant interpretation is A. This is the interpretation of the sentence that leads to the decoding of an utterance that bears the property of relevance because it is the most accessible in terms of the effort–effect interplay. Nevertheless, the court chooses interpretation B. This proves that, for the court, relevance is by no means a decisive factor.

I have described this example many times but let me repeat the claim. I am positive that if a poll was made among the population of English speakers or Polish speakers as to how people understand the phrase 'use a firearm', the tremendous majority would have responded that they understand this as an implicit narrowing 'as a weapon'. Yet the court did not uphold this intuition in *Smith vs US*, indeed, it rejected this narrowing. Analogously, the most relevant interpretation of an enumeration or list in a legal rule is that it is exhaustive. Nevertheless, this is not the interpretation that is always accepted by those who interpret it.

The problem of counterintuitive decisions is not restricted to the exchange between the legislature and courts. It equally applies to other strategic exchanges. If parties argue in a courtroom and one of them pronounces a statement that carries a strong implicature that does not conform to her immediate argumentative goal, she might try to deny the implicature and uphold a weaker pragmatic phenomenon. Such moves may not always be very successful, but this is a different discussion. What counts is that the strategic ignoring of the implicature might be a reasonable thing to do in the circumstances.

The question arises of whether legal pragmatics need RT at all because hard cases in legal discourse seem to require from us a reason for having chosen one rather than another interpretation of what an utterance implicates. Consequently, 'automatic' or 'spontaneous' processes should not be of central interest to the study of such situations. The kind of strategic uses of language described in the previous chapter are far from being 'automatic' or 'spontaneous'. Instead, they require a careful, reflective analysis and reasoning of which pragmatic effect (ex. implicature content) will be most suitable to reach one's argumentative goal.

Robyn Carston gives a few examples of valid cognitive-psychological arguments that find support in RT and have been used in famous debates in the Supreme Court of the United States. Recall the *Smith vs. US* case discussed in the previous chapter:

> 'In the absence of other evidence, the very fact that an interpretation is the first to come to mind lends it an initial degree of plausibility'. Recall O'Connor's concession (…) that the first interpretation of 'use a firearm' to come to mind (…) is that of the use for which the firearms were designed, that is, as weapons. (Carston 2013)

This shows that the court did take the cognitive kind of argument proposed by RT under consideration as one of the arguments. Nevertheless, this argument did not prevail as the sentence of the Supreme Court claimed that 'using a firearm' could mean more than just firing it. As a result, while RT neatly explains one kind of argument made in the debate, it cannot explain the overall mechanism that leads to the decision (by contrast, the strategic principle and the maxim of selectivity do provide such an answer).

Carston's reading of RT also neatly explains the kind of argument judges make when they resort to the mysterious notion of common knowledge or common sense. On this reading, any interpretation in line with the purpose of an utterance would fall within the communicative relevance of this utterance. The reasoning goes as follows: the speaker produces an utterance and the hearers must presume its relevance. Carston claims that every rational hearer will make a similar inference as to what is relevant in the circumstances. Thus, such a relevant interpretation is treated as common sense or common knowledge because any rational agent is able to infer this same content and treats it as relevant in the circumstances. In other words, common sense is 'a case where the relevant contextual assumptions are available to all ordinary mentally able citizens and would be immediately activated by the text itself' (Carston 2013).

A good example is the Garner vs. Burr case. A relevant section of the Traffic Act of 1930 stated that 'Any vehicle traveling on a public highway must be fitted with pneumatic tires'. The question was whether a chicken coop on wheels fell within the scope of 'vehicle'. The court ruled that it did fall within the scope of a 'vehicle'. In RT's terms, this word was broadened, and this was done on the basis of the functioning of the statute. This functional reasoning was as follows: 'public roads are used by many people; keeping the roads in good order benefits all road users; it also helps save on unnecessary expenditure of public funds; running heavy structures on iron wheels may damage a road's surface; fitting such structures with pneumatic tires greatly reduces the likelihood of damage' (Carston 2013). Note that deploying such arguments does not require any meticulous analysis of legislative records. This line of reasoning is based on common sense which is well reflected in the technical relevance postulated by RT (Carston 2013).

Another example in which common-sense arguments prevailed is the interpretation of a sign hanging in a railway station proclaiming that 'It shall be a misdemeanor… to sleep in a railway station'. How to interpret the word 'sleep'? According to Carston:

> No (rational) policeman who noticed the briefly dozing passenger would feel impelled to bring the force of the law down on him. On the other hand, the policeman might well take

> the law to apply to a man who throws a blanket onto the station platform, lies down on it, and stares up at the ceiling, showing no signs of intending to move on, but who does not in fact sleep. (Carston 2013)

However, while this explains why arguments from common sense may sometimes win the debate, it tells us nothing about the strategic character of interactions in the realm of law. In other words, it does not explain why some decisions (based on inferred implicatures) seem counterintuitive to a standard observer. Moreover, courts often take decisions (especially in 'hard cases') that seem counterintuitive to the wider public. These can be interpretive decisions based on the inference of one rather than another implicature. Yet, under closer scrutiny, they are revealed to be supported by thorough reasoning, just as the decision in *Smith vs US*. In other words, the first and most intuitive understanding of an expression (or the first implicature that comes to mind) is not always the most reasonable one in terms of an immediate, strategic, argumentative goal in legal circumstances. The strategic principle and the maxim of selectivity explain the mechanism that causes common-sense interpretations (including common-sense inferences of implicatures) to be rejected: courts usually take the legislature as willing to achieve some concrete state of affairs by enactment of a statute. According to the strategic principle and the maxim of selectivity, the relevant interpretation will be ignored if it could lead to consequences that do not conform to the discussed state of affairs. Consequently, the broader public could perceive such decisions as counterintuitive if they do not conform to RT's most accessible (in terms of effort and effect) understanding.

Carston also notes that counterintuitive decisions are impossible to explain on the grounds of RT. She discusses the *Church of Holy Trinity vs US* case. The discussion was whether a provision forbidding the importing to the US of labor (or service) of any kind, followed by a list of exceptions (singers, actors, lecturers), also precluded the importing of a priest. The court decided that the American church was allowed to employ the clergyman. Carston claims that this decision is counterintuitive:

> It is difficult to see any kind of grounding for a narrowing of the phrase "labor or service of any kind" to "manual labor or service of any kind", especially given the explicit list of exceptions, which any such narrowing would render redundant (hence irrelevant). Not all speaker/author preferences are transparent to the interpreter or are intended to be. When there is a sufficiently relevant interpretation derivable without seeking them out, that is the warranted interpretation. (Carston 2013)

Thus, RT will not be helpful in explaining counterintuitive judicial decisions.

Moreover, I do not want to claim that analyzing unconscious processes and the way our mind functions in legal situations is completely uninteresting for a legal theorist. This can be useful, for instance when analyzing the psychology (which cognitive processes occur) of the speakers in a courtroom. Second, it is useful when unconscious processes are employed; for instance, a witness is being cross-examined and it is the reaction time that matters. In other words, someone is supposed to answer as quickly as possible and his answers may heavily rely on unconscious processing. Third, it is interesting to analyze the cognitive traps of the unconscious that influence directly conscious processes. In other words, we are curious what potential differences there may be between the functioning of the human mind in natural language processing and in legal language processing.

A purely psychological approach can also be used in the interpretation of wills. Carston gives the example of a testator who wrote simply 'All for mother':

> The testator's mother was, however, long dead. The court accepted evidence that the testator habitually used the word 'mother' to refer to his wife and the occurrence of 'mother' in the will was duly interpreted (in accordance with its author's naming preference) as meaning his widow. (Carston 2013)

However, this cognitive and psychological approach is insufficient to fulfil the goal of legal pragmatics, which generally aims to account for the mechanism of conscious and reflective argumentation that is supposed to convince others to choose an interpretation of a statute. Judges and all other kinds of participants in the legal enterprise (barristers, prosecutors etc.) will use all kinds of arguments (not only linguistic-psychological arguments of the kind proposed by RT) to achieve their goals. To explain the kind of strategic speaking described in the previous chapter, we will need more than a theory that explains how the human mind processes natural language.

Thus, RT does not rule out the idea laid out in the previous chapter, it is just that RT aims at something different, namely explaining the functioning of the human mind rather than the reasons for which we interpret a statute one way rather than another. While in the law there are often multiple competing interpretations of one statute, the basic task of a judge is to choose one on the basis of convincing argumentation. Consequently, legal pragmatics will need a theory of building such a convincing argumentation and constructing arguments. RT sees situations in which more than one interpretation is possible as 'unnecessary effort':

> An utterance with two apparently satisfactory competing interpretations would cause the hearer the unnecessary extra effort of choosing between them, and the resulting interpretation (if there were one) would not satisfy (…) the definition of optimal relevance. (Sperber and Wilson 2006)

This claim is fundamentally flawed as far as legal considerations are concerned. Claiming that the job of a judge is 'unnecessary effort' contravenes the very idea of legal interpretation and the application of the law. Judges are precisely interested in explaining the logical considerations that lead to the choice of one interpretation rather than another.

Robyn Carston makes an analogous claim:

> It should be that the first-pass reading of any legal document does fall quite straightforwardly within the general pragmatic story. However, one of the ways in which legal interpretation is special is in the kind of conscious effortful scrutiny a legal text may be subjected to in a bid to find an interpretation which may benefit a particular individual's case in a situation where the stakes are very high for that individual. To extrapolate validly from the one kind of interpretive process to the other and to provide cognitively grounded reasons for favoring a particular interpretation in the case of an explicit interpretive dispute is an important challenge for relevance theory. (Carston 2013)

I started this chapter with the observation that neo-Gricean theories have brought two principal amendments to the classical Gricean view. First, they denied the necessity of operating on four maxims; they then showed that the notion of 'what is said' involves more pragmatic processes than just disambiguation and reference assignment.

The first amendment as formulated by RT has already been analyzed. I have argued in this chapter why replacing the four Gricean maxims with a single principle of relevance can be useful in a cognitive approach to language. However, I have also tried to give arguments why this replacement cannot be useful in building a comprehensive theory of legal pragmatics. The second amendment will be discussed in the next chapter.[5]

Let us now continue to seek a neo-Gricean approach that would deal with the two amendments in a manner which is useful for legal pragmatics. At least two main

[5] Just to remind the reader at this point: As far as the second amendment is at stake, the neo-Griceans are surely right that there is more of pragmatics in 'what is said' than Grice initially thought. He defines this notion in the following paragraph: 'In the sense in which I am using the word say, I intend what someone has said to be closely related to the conventional meaning of the words (the sentence) he has uttered. Suppose someone to have uttered the sentence "He is in the grip of a vice". Given a knowledge of the English language, but no knowledge of the circumstances of the utterance, one would know something about what the speaker had said, on the assumption that he was speaking standard English, and speaking literally. One would know that he had said, about some particular male person or animal x, that at the time of the utterance (whatever that was), either (1) x was unable to rid himself of a bad character trait or (2) some part of x's person was caught in a certain kind of tool or instrument (approximate account, of course). But for a full identification of what the speaker has said, one would need to know (a) the identity of x, (b) the time of utterance, (c) the meaning, on the particular occasion of utterance, of the phrase in the grip of a vice, [a decision between (1) and (2)]. This brief indication of my use of say leaves it open whether a man who says (today) Harold Wilson is a great man and another who says (also today) The British Prime Minister is a great man would, if each knew that the singular terms have the same reference, have said the same thing.' (Grice 1989) As quoted, when Grice uses the term 'what is said' he encompasses in this very term only three, simple, pragmatic effects. First, under the label (a) is the assignment of a referent to an indexical (here 'he'). Note that he mentions only explicit indexicals, which are pronounced or written. There is no mention of implicit indexicals at all. Second, under the label (b) comes the time of utterance, indicated by the tense, because it is something we have to determine for practically all utterances. Grice does not mention other parameters such as the place of utterance. Finally, under the label (c) Grice mentions disambiguation. Moreover, he speaks only of classical cases where there are two distinct meanings that are only very remotely (or not at all) related to one another, i.e. homonyms. He does not include unarticulated constituents or polysemy. As a consequence of these omissions, researchers that came after Grice, RT included, noticed that 'what is said' needs far more pragmatics than just (a), (b) and (c). Consider the sentences: Have you had breakfast? He is tall. According to dual pragmatists these sentences contain unarticulated constituents that need a double pragmatic inference. First, we need to notice that there are some variables and then we need to assign a reference to them: Have you had breakfast [today]? He is tall [for a schoolboy]. Thus, the bracketed content is not a case of simple reference assignment, and RT is right in postulating more pragmatic processes in the decoding of explicatures. The texts enacted by legislatures as legal statutes will also be subject to such various pragmatic enrichments. To state what the legislator has said, one will need more pragmatic data than just standard disambiguation or reference assignment. I will return to this issue in more depth in the next chapter.

questions remain to be answered. First, whether a theory that reduces the number of maxims does not leave some issues in legal interpretation unanswered. The reduction of the number of maxims in explaining natural language is a perfect application of Ockham's razor. It is extremely valuable to construct a theory that is simpler and still explains all the phenomena at stake. The problem with legal pragmatics is that we cannot make a direct transposition. The reduction of the number of maxims may result in some legal language issues being left unexplained. Thus, I need to first verify whether a theory with a limited number of maxims (as compared to Grice's number) explains all the issues that I am interested in. Only secondly will I answer the question of whether this approach explains the mechanism of legal pragmatics better than the Gricean theory.

3.3 The Q and R Principles

Lawrence R. Horn has formulated an interesting theory that aims to give an account of pragmatic inferences based on logic and linguistics. His idea is interesting for legal theorists for two main reasons. First, it is much less reliant than RT on psychological considerations and on what biologically grounds our language processing. Additionally, the concepts are not as deeply entangled in psychology as the concepts of RT. Consequently, it is easier to separate the notions created by Horn's theory and transfer them to a different theory—a theory of legal pragmatics. Second, it depicts how (in natural language) the four Gricean maxims can be reduced to two main principles: sufficiency (Q) and least effort (R).

Horn introduces the idea by quoting Martinet, who seems to share Sperber and Wilson's intuition concerning the importance of the effort factor:

> In order to understand how and why a language changes, the linguist must keep in mind two ever-present and antinomic factors: first, the requirements of communication, the need for the speaker to convey his message, and second, the principle of least effort, which makes him restrict his output of energy, both mental and physical, to the minimum compatible with achieving his ends. (Horn 1984)

What Horn aims to prove is that these same two 'antinomic forces' and their interaction produces the pragmatic phenomena described by Grice. Thus, it is a reductionist program in relation to the number of maxims postulated by Grice. The idea is that the maxim of quality (roughly: be truthful) must always be retained as a condition *sine qua non* for the 'entire conversational and implicatural apparatus' (Horn 1984). This is a substantial difference in comparison to RT, which rejects the maxim of quality.

Apart from the maxim of quality as a basic condition, what is retained by Horn is the maxim of quantity and the maxim of relation. The Gricean maxim of quantity is constituted by two sub-maxims:

> QUANTITY
>
> 1. make your contribution as informative as is required (for the current purposes of the exchange).
> 2. Do not make your contribution more informative than is required. (Grice 1975)

The first sub-maxim of quantity (quantity$_1$) reflects 'the need for the speaker to convey his message fully'. By contrast, the second sub-maxim of quantity (quantity$_2$) reflects the principle of least effort. Horn claims that this second sub-maxim of quantity boils down to the Gricean maxim of relation/relevance (be relevant) because:

> what would make a contribution more informative than required, except the inclusion of material not strictly relevant to and needed for the matter at hand? (Horn 1984)

Roughly, the claim is this: the principle of quality is so obvious that it need not be inscribed as a maxim precisifying the principle of cooperation. Moreover, all the pragmatic processes described by Grice can be explained by the maxim of quantity. In fact, the maxim of relevance also contains the maxim of quantity (more precisely, its second sub-maxim) as well as the remaining maxim of manner (which is mostly stylistic). Thus, the Gricean quantity$_1$ maxim is called the Q principle (from the word 'quantity') and the quantity$_2$ maxim, which equates with the relation/relevance maxim, is called the R principle (from the word 'relevance'):

> (1a) The Q principle (hearer-based):
>
> MAKE YOUR CONTRIBUTION SUFFICIENT (cf. Quantity$_1$)
>
> SAY AS MUCH AS YOU CAN (given the R principle)
>
> [It is a] lower-bounding principle, inducing [generating] upper-bounding implicata
>
> (1b) The R principle (Speaker-based):
>
> MAKE YOUR CONTRIBUTION NECESSARY (c.f. Relation, Quantity$_2$, Manner)
>
> SAY NO MORE THAN YOU MUST (given the Q principle)
>
> [It is an] upper-bounding principle, including [generating] lower-bounding implicata (Horn 1984)

In the citation above, Horn uses 'implicata' as implicatures. One may perhaps wonder what the above bounding is supposed to mean. Horn's Q and R principles are supposed to generate complementary bounding effects, and Carston describes the Q bounding effects particularly lucidly:

> The Q- and R-principles are claimed to have complementary bounding properties. [...] in the Q cases: what is encoded or said sets a lower bound, e.g. "at least three/some/possible" and the Q-based implicature provides an upper bound, e.g. "at most three/not all/not certain":
>
> (1) a. Utterance: Max ate some of the cakes.
>
> b. Implicature: Max didn't eat all of the cakes. (Carston 2005)

As far as the R principle is concerned, the idea is less clear. Roughly, in the R cases what is encoded or said sets an upper bound (for instance: my finger or someone else's finger) and the R-based implicature sets a lower bound or restricts the possibilities (here: my finger):

(2) a. I broke a finger yesterday.

b. Implicature: The finger is mine. (Carston 2005)

Carston criticizes the above idea because it remains unclear what 'R places an upper bound on – is it speaker effort, or information given, or (somehow) both?' (Carston 2005). Moreover, as Carston further stresses, there is no mirroring, but, on the contrary, both Q and R act similarly in that they narrow the interpretation in the implicature (from at least some to just some, or from 'a finger' to 'my finger'). Thus, we will have to proceed cautiously with the mysterious notion of bounding.[6]

This framework can account for a range of interesting pragmatic phenomena. However, before discussing some particular examples I would like to clarify how the two principles interact to produce implicatures.

Let us come back to the non-controversial bounding of the Q principle. This is a mechanism that generates so called 'scalar implicatures'. Recall the contrast between the said at least *three/some/possible* and the implicated *at most three/not all/not certain*. Scalar implicatures are special because they are based on conventional meanings attributed to words with the use of lexical scales (Horn 2006). If you hear 'some of the students have passed the exam', you will infer that not all of them have passed. Placing a word in a definite position on a scale enables the speakers to attribute a definite meaning to it that does not have to be consistent with the lexical meaning of the word. The most discussed example is the quantifier "some", which can mean either 'at least some' or 'some but not all'. Yet, in ordinary conversation 'some' is understood as 'some but not all'.

Consider the following example:

II. Some of the guests have gone.

When uttering (II) the speaker is normally taken as implicating that not all of the guests have gone. This is because, had the speaker wanted to be understood as implicating 'at least some of the guests have gone, in fact all of them' she would

[6]It is considerably less clear how the alleged reverse pattern of bounds pans out in the R cases. What does the R Principle place an upper bound on—is it speaker effort, or information given, or (somehow) both? Consider some examples standardly cited as giving rise to R-based implicatures: (2)a. Utterance: Hannah insulted Joe and he resigned. b. Implicature: Hannah's insulting Joe caused him to resign. (3)a. Utterance: I broke a finger yesterday. b. Implicature: The finger is mine. (4)a. Utterance: Can you reach the salt? b. Implicature: I request you pass the salt to me. In what sense are the implicatures here lower-bounding? The idea seems to be that, on the basis of the speaker having said that p, there is an R-inference to 'more than p' and the hearer has to go on to figure out what this more is. In the case of 'and'- conjunctions such as (2), it is a stronger relation between the conjuncts; in (3), it is a narrowing to a specific domain of fingers; in cases of indirect speech acts such as (4), it is simply a different speech act from the (irrelevant) one directly expressed. But one could say much the same of the Q cases: something is explicitly said and what is communicated is stronger (more informative/relevant). In both kinds of case, there is a strengthening of communicated content: from 'at least some' to 'just some', from 'a finger' to 'my finger', etc. I find little support for the claim (Horn 1984) that the effects of the two principles are mirror images of each other. (For fuller discussion of this point, see Carston 1998: section 3). (Carston 2005).

have used the word 'all' rather than 'some'. The above considerations are valid in situations in which the speaker and hearer have full contextual knowledge. This means that the speaker knows how many of the guests have gone. She knows whether all of them have gone or only a number of them have gone. Moreover, the hearer knows that the speaker has this knowledge. Thus, the scale is the following:

- <some, all>

The above reasoning has been confirmed in experiments carried out not only on adults, but also children (Noveck 2001).

Let us consider another example: A says to B that 'some philosophers are boring'. This warrants the implicature that not all of them are boring, because if they were all boring A would have instead said 'all philosophers are boring'. Once again, this mechanism works because of the existence of a conventional lexical scale, <some, all>, on which using a weaker term means that one is not warranted to use the stronger term. Such an implicature is dependent on context. As a result, it can be cancelled either explicitly ('Some, if not all/and perhaps all, of philosophers are boring') or implicitly ('by establishing an appropriate context, in which all that is relevant, or can be known, is the lower bound.') (Horn 1984).

The same reasoning applies to numerals such as 'two'. Thus, the idea is this: Semantically, an assertion of 'two' means something like 'at least two' (two if not more), so it formulates a lower bound. Pragmatically, 'two' implicates 'at most two' (two but not more) and formulates an upper-bound. 'The conjunction of assertion and implicature results in conveying the corresponding "two-sided" understanding ("exactly…")' (Horn 1984).

By contrast, the R-principle works in just the opposite way: 'a speaker who says "…p…" may license the Q-inference that he meant "…at most p…"; a speaker who says "…p…" may license the R-inference that he meant "…more than p…"' (Horn 1984).

Horn illustrates this reversed pattern with the following example:

> If I ask you whether you can pass me the salt, in a context where your abilities to do so are not in doubt, I license you to infer that I am doing something more than asking you whether you can pass me the salt – I am in fact asking you to do it. (If I know for a fact that you can pass me the salt, the yes–no question is pointless; the assumption that I am obeying the Relation maxim allows you to infer that I mean something more than what I say). (Horn 1984)

Additionally, Horn discusses a different taxonomy of the Gricean versions of not observing the maxim. Just to briefly remind the reader, Grice identified four ways to not observe maxims: violation, opt-out, clash and flout (see previous chapter). The first (violation) was specific because the hearer did not know that the speaker was not simply obeying the standard maxim, and this resulted in lies.

Horn modifies the taxonomy by claiming that intentional (and covert) violation of the quality maxim results in lies, while unintentional violation is just misleading. Violating other maxims has different consequences:

> Intentional violations of the Q-based sufficiency principle result in a speaker's misleading the addressee, and intentional violations of the R-based least effort principle are often simply unhelpful or perverse. A courtroom witness must swear to tell the whole truth and nothing but the truth, i.e. to obey quantity and quality, while violations of relevance lead only to a possible lawyer's objection or judge's scolding. (Horn 1984)

Having outlined Horn's idea, let us now proceed to assessing whether this framework can help shed further light on legal linguistic issues.

3.4 The Q and R Principles in Legal Discourse

The reformulation of the four Gricean ways of not observing the maxims (violation, opt out, flout and clash) is interesting from the point of view of a legal language theorist. Horn's taxonomy permits us to exclude the possibility of lying in a courtroom (as intentionally and covertly violating the maxim of quality will result in penal consequences). Moreover, it will exclude opt-outs (except from the refusal to testify, or the need to comply with a secrecy regulation). However, flouting and clashing the Q and R principles will—just as in natural speech—be possible and in fact will carry some special characteristics. Let us now take a closer look at them.

According to Horn, violating the Q principle, which means saying less than you can actually say, would be misleading. This is true for the natural language context, but the legal context could be more complex, perhaps because a speaker in the realm of law will often say less than they can for various reasons. For instance, the legislature could say less than it can in a statute to leave discretion to the courts. A barrister may also often say less than he knows to properly defend his client. Thus, situations in which the Q principle is violated are much more common in the legal realm and may, of course, result in the hearer being misled, but they do not have to be.

I believe that this is just another form of indirect evidence for the functioning of a strategic framework of the kind described in the previous chapter. This is because there seems to again be a strategic principle of the form: 'assume that the speech is cooperative, infer all the implicatures and then apply the second-order strategic maxims to the inferred implicatures (anticipate which implicatures your hearer/speaker will choose/ignore)'. It is just that here the implicatures counterfactually derived from cooperative maxims will be derived not on the basis of the four Gricean ones, but on the basis of the Q and R principles. Moreover, there will be another possible strategic behavior: the speaker can predict that if he says more, then his hearer will be licensed to infer more implicatures that may contradict the strategic goal of the speaker. If the speaker's goal is to prove the innocence of his client, he may wish to avoid utterances that will license the hearer to infer implicata that could lead to the incrimination of the client.

By contrast, violations of the R principle—saying more than one must say—also occur sometimes in the legal realm. For instance, a barrister could also be interested in providing a torrent of information so as to make his opponent lose track and fail to choose the possible pragmatic implicatures that suit his strategic goal (he will intend to be 'unhelpful or perverse').

As a result, the general picture that looms out of the above observations is that the strategic meta-framework causes the boundaries of the Q and R principles to be way more stretched than in ordinary conversation. In other words, on the basis of the strategic framework, a speaker in the legal realm will sometimes say less than he can or more than he must.

To depict more clearly how this strategic framework works, consider the following citation:

> A speaker obeying only Q would tend to say everything she knows on the off-chance that it might prove informative, while a speaker obeying only R would probably, to be on the safe side, not open her mouth. (Horn 1984)

Thus, the idea seems to be that in natural language the competing principle makes speakers strike a balance to find a natural equilibrium between Q and R. By contrast, in strategic speech this equilibrium need not be achieved and one of the principles can simply prevail over the other. It is striking how strategic speech in a courtroom resembles politeness as described by Horn: 'avoid saying too much when you can get it across by hints' (Horn 1984). Using the R principle allows one to deny having implicated content that does not fulfill one's strategic goal. It is easier to deny an implicature than a pronounced assertion, which is already 'out there'.

The sociological studies invoked by Horn are another factor that could be interesting for legal language theorists and which could confirm the intuitions about the possibility and ubiquity of strategic speech. In 1976, Keenan analyzed the language of the Malagasy-speaking culture of Madagascar. This 'is a speech community in which the Cooperative Principle, and in particular the maxim of Quantity, is not observed.' (Horn 1984) In this culture there is no informativeness principle and Q-based inferences do not occur (people say less than they could say):

> Interlocutors regularly provide less information than is required by their conversational partner, even though they have access to the necessary information. If A asks B, "Where is your mother?" and B responds, "she is either in the house or at the market", B's utterance is not usually taken to imply that B is unable to provide more specific information needed by the hearer. The implicature is not made because the expectation that speakers will satisfy informational needs is not a basic norm. (Keenan 1976)

It seems very hard to believe that no cooperative principle is in force and yet the language exists, persists, and communication occurs. However, upon closer scrutiny, both Keenan and Horn conclude that it is not the case that the CP and maxim of quantity are completely not in force, but rather that the CP is often in force. In fact, cases in which the maxim of quantity does not seem to be in force are just cases in which 'Quantity is overridden by a countervailing R-based principle, in particular the imperative of avoiding *tsiny* (the responsibility, guilt, or other unpleasant consequences incurred by uttering claims which turn out to be false and/or offensive to other members of the society, living or dead)' (Horn 1984).

Thus, it is not a culture in which there is no CP or quantity maxim. It is just that the R-principle may more often override the Q-principle than in other cultures. In other words, the usual equilibrium between the Q and R principles is different. I believe a similar mechanism is in place in a courtroom when a barrister says less just because he believes it will be easier to deny having implicated some content rather than deny content that has been pronounced. Thus, lawyers in our culture deploy similar pragmatic abilities as the ones possessed by speakers in the Malagasy culture; therefore, the Keenan–Horn framework is useful for the theorist of legal language.

Now let me return to the aforementioned notion of scalar implicatures. Scalars are based on lexical scales and they are the source of implicated upper bounding (for instance, 'some' is restricted to 'some but not all'; the higher word on the scale is excluded; there is an upper bound on the scale which is placed between some and all). They warrant an inference from quantity: 'what is communicated is more informative, more definite than what is said' (Horn 1984). Here are some examples:

some $\longleftrightarrow$ not all

may $\longleftrightarrow$may not[7]

3 $\longrightarrow$ not more than three

p or q $\longrightarrow$ not both p and q

a believes that p $\longrightarrow$ a does not know that p (Horn 1984)

Let us now analyze whether the interpretation of statutes always gives rise to standard scalar implicatures. Imagine a statute containing the following provision: 'Applicants that fulfill some of the criteria for enhanced additional tax relief are entitled to standard tax relief.'

No reasonable interpreter would claim that the provision above would preclude an applicant that fulfills all criteria for enhanced additional tax relief from receiving standard tax relief. Thus, the reading of 'some' in the statute is 'some if not all' or 'at least some'. The implicated upper bound does not occur. Why?

The reasoning is based on a well-known interpretive rule called the *a fortiori* argument. In this particular case, it is the *a minori ad maius* version that is being employed. The reasoning goes as follows: If someone that fulfills only some and not all of the criteria of enhanced, additional tax relief is entitled to standard tax relief, then someone that fulfills all of these criteria is even more strongly entitled to standard tax relief.

Consequently, the *a fortiori* argument allows us to ignore the implicature that some but not all the criteria can be fulfilled. How does this fit the idea from the previous chapter? The strategic nature of speech is a matter of degree. While the linguistic exchange within a legislative body is in fact pure political speech and happens to be an almost unconstrained strategic enterprise, statutory interpretation is very different. Statutory interpretation cannot be an unconstrained strategic enter-

[7] Horn's idea is that if you tell someone that he may do something, you are not warranted to tell him that he may not do something, and this is because of pragmatic reasons. This also works the other way around, so if you tell someone that he may not do something, then you are not warranted to tell him that he may do something.

prise because this would amount to giving up the rule of law. Consequently, interpretation needs to be at least partly constrained by the rules that govern it. As a result, 'ignoring' a scalar implicature is possible only when ignoring is warranted by an interpretive rule. In the example above, it is the *a fortiori* argument.

The Q principles can create another interesting mechanism: the 'restriction of a more general predicate to a stereotypical instance (...):

The secretary smiled ⟶the female secretary smiled

John had a drink ⟶ John had an alcoholic drink.' (Horn 1984)

For instance, if you apply this mechanism to the interpreting of the expression 'to use a firearm', what you will receive will be 'to fire a gun/firearm'. Unless some interpretive rule licenses you to ignore the stereotypical narrowing, the understanding of the statute boils down to the stereotypical case. This is a point for which the necessity of introducing a second-order maxim of selectivity is clear. As already emphasized, without this maxim it is impossible to account for the ruling in *Smith.*

Another phenomenon mentioned by Horn which is interesting from the point of view of a theorist of legal language is indirect speech acts (ISA), which are derived on the basis of the maxim of Relation. Some ISAs are so often used in natural language that they become somehow 'conventionalized', although it is a very peculiar kind of 'convention'. Horn explains these weird 'conventions' by quoting Searle: 'there can be conventions of usage that are not meaning conventions by which certain forms will tend to become conventionally established as the standard idiomatic forms for indirect speech acts' (Searle 1975). Thus, they are not meaning conventions, so they are not semantic but they still have a pragmatic character (Gizbert-Studnicki 1983). It is just that they are frequently employed. Consider the examples:

Can you please close the window?

Could you please close the window?

Are you able to (please) close the window?

It's ((...)please) cold in here.

(please) close the window. (Horn 1984)

The first two examples are the 'conventionalized' ones in the sense that they are often employed to convey the relevant ISAs that are, for instance, orders to close the window. The remaining ones are more unusual. Within the realm of law, legal statutes often convey normative orders through ISAs. Consider the following example from the Polish penal code:

'art 148. Whoever kills a man, is subject to a punishment of...'

The statute above pragmatically implicates the ISA (order) that: 'You should not kill men'. Every legal system contains a large quantity of this kind of pragmatic implicata (Gizbert-Studnicki 1983).

The linguistic analysis proposed by Horn also provides interesting conclusions for legal language as far as double negation is concerned. He claims that double negation will have a weakening effect in comparison to a simple affirmative assertion: 'two negatives of the form not – (not p) do not cancel out functionally even when they do semantically; they convey a positive [p – clarification mine] which is characteristically weaker than the corresponding simple affirmative.' (Horn 1984)

In everyday Polish, double negation functions in a slightly different way and it does not always have the weaker effect described. However, Polish legal language seems to exhibit some similarities because some of the sentences formulated by the Polish Constitutional Court (PCC) in the Polish legal system take the form of a double negation, and this also seems to have a weakening effect.

The PCC can issue a few types of decisions. If an applicant asks the Tribunal to compare the statutory provision with the wrong article of the constitution (i.e. an article that concerns a different matter than the one at stake), the sentence takes the form 'the statute is not inconsistent with the Polish constitution' rather than 'is consistent with the constitution'.

The third type of PCC decisions clearly contain an implicature that weakens the message because of the use of a double negation rather than an affirmative sentence. Horn explains this situation with the use of his two principles:

> With double negation, as with indirect speech acts, we see an especially clear correlation between the stylistic naturalness of a given form, its relative brevity and simplicity, and its use in stereotypic situations (via R-implicature). The corresponding periphrastic forms, stylistically less natural, longer and more complex, are restricted (via Q-implicature) to those situations outside the stereotype, for which the unmarked expression would have been inappropriate. (Horn 1984)

Finally, Horn discusses the idea of lexical broadening and narrowing that RT will later employ and modify. However, while RT explains it through some psychological apparatus, Horn explains it with the Q and R principles that are independent of psychological assumptions and for this reason his account seems to fit legal language better. As a quick reminder, the mechanism consists of lexical shifts: either a reduction (narrowing) or an expansion (broadening) of meaning (Horn 1984). Moreover, narrowing may be the consequence of both the Q and R principles, while broadening is solely a consequence of the R principle.

> Narrowing generally involves an R-based shift from a set denotation to a subset (or member) of that set, representing the salient or stereotypical exemplar of the general category. (…) In these instances, the shift has become virtually complete (although the original, broader extension may persist in marginal uses). (Horn 1984)

Consequently, the word 'color' usually excludes black and white, for instance when we speak about color TV or state that something is 'in color'. If someone states, 'I have a temperature', she will be understood as having a 'fever'. If you are ordered to pick a number from 1 to 10, you will pick an integer. If someone asks you if you would like a drink, you will be warranted in taking this as an alcoholic drink. If a German man speaks about his 'Frau' or a French man speaks about his 'femme', you will also be warranted in understanding that he is speaking about his wife (Horn 1984).

Narrowing can also be based on the Q principle if it concerns the specialization of a hyponym. It is based on an inference such as the following: 'the author of the utterance could not be more specific, so he used a more general term (otherwise he would have used a more precise one).' The 'more general term' is very special because the term employed by the author used to be a hyponym—it used to encompass an additional category or subset that has been excluded from its scope. For example, the words 'cow' (excluding bulls), 'rectangle' (excluding squares), 'finger' (excluding thumbs) etc. (Horn 1984).

By contrast, broadening is based exclusively on the R principle and Horn defines it as 'the generalization of a term for a species to cover the encompassing genus, from genus to phylum, from subset to superset' (Horn 1984). The examples provided are analogous to the one given by Sperber and Wilson: brand names such as Xerox or Kleenex.

To sum up, the theory advanced by Horn seems to provide the legal realm with many interesting solutions and Robyn Carston has created an interesting interpretation of Horn's theory which she has applied to explain the issues faced by courts when interpreting statutes. Let us now have a look at her theory and analyze whether her intuitions could fit into the strategic framework.

3.5 Q and I Heuristics

Carston claims that the two complementary principles—as defined by Horn—that speakers are supposed to follow are mirrored by interpretive heuristics deployed by hearers. The heuristics are based on both the Gricean maxim of quantity and Horn's Q and R principles. Moreover, these heuristics are defeasible, just as any other pragmatic inference. Thus, we get three types of theories that describe similar phenomena: the Gricean version, Horn's version, and heuristics. As far as the first complimentary principle is concerned, the rules are as follows:

> [A] Grice's first maxim of quantity: Make your contribution as informative as is required (for the current purposes of the exchange).
>
> Q-principle: Say as much as you (truthfully and relevantly) can. (…)
>
> Interpretive heuristic (Q): What isn't said, isn't the case (Carston 2013)

The reasoning is the following: the speaker is abiding by the principles/maxims. Consequently, if she knew something relevant she would have said so. If she remains silent, then it must be because she does not have information to confirm the more relevant statement.

Scalar terms are a classical example of employment of such heuristic. Consider the following lexical scales:

- <some, most, all>
- <good, excellent, outstanding> (Carston 2013)
- <one, two, three, …>

If you hear 'some of the guests have gone [from the party]', you will probably infer that 'not all of them are gone'. This is because if all of them had gone, then the speaker would have said 'all of the guests have gone'. If someone says 'take a coffee or a tea' you will most probably infer that he intends you to take one or the other but not both. Otherwise she would have said 'take a coffee and a tea'. However, it is a defeasible inference and will not hold in all contexts (Carston 2013).

In contracts governed by common law, if one wants to convey the meaning one or the other or both, one has to write 'or/and'. The default interpretation of 'or' is treated as exclusive.

Having discussed the heuristic related to the Q principle, let us now sum up the ideas related with the second complementary rule:

> [B] Grice's second maxim of quantity: Do not make your contribution more informative than is required.
>
> Grice's maxim of relation: Be relevant.
>
> I-principle: Say no more than you must.[8]
>
> Interpretive heuristic (I): What is simply/briefly described is the stereotypical or normal (default) instance. (Carston 2013)

Thus, the idea is that what is obvious in the circumstances does not need to be pronounced. Moreover, the hearer should understand a sentence in accordance with what comes first to his mind. Consider the following example:

> a. John will give you £10 if you mow his lawn. Implicates: He'll give you £10 only if you mow his lawn. [If you don't, he won't.]
>
> b. Mary turned the key and the motor started.
>
> Implicates: Mary's turning of the key caused the motor to start. (Carston 2013)

On the basis of the I-principle, the 'if then' formula in sentence (a) will be interpreted as 'if and only if'. Analogously, the 'P and Q' formula in sentence (b) will be enriched to the form 'P and this caused Q'. (Carston 2013)

However, the problem is that the two heuristics may come into conflict in some situations and yield opposite, contradictory results. The above considerations seem clear on the basis of the I-principle. By contrast, if the Q-principle was to be applied, the results would be different. If the speaker had said 'if then' rather than 'if and only if', then she must have meant only 'if then'. Otherwise, she would have used the phrase 'if and only if'. Analogously, if she had uttered 'P and Q', then she did not mean 'P and this caused Q' (Carston 2013). Carston gives further examples:

> I've lost an earring/a contact lens.

---

[8] Horn calls this the R-principle. I think Carston's label is more intuitive because it comes from the word 'informativeness'. This was the second Gricean sub-maxim of quantity.

Implicates: It's one of my own earrings/contact lenses. (…)

I've found an earring/a wallet.

Implicates: It's not one of my own earrings/wallets. (Carston 2013)[9]

The first sentence usually relies on the I-principle. The standard, stereotypical case is when we lose one of our own earrings. However, the second sentence relies on the Q-principle. If the speaker had meant something different, she would have said so and thus the decision as to which heuristic should be applied is highly context dependent.

The heuristics can be held responsible for the previously described cases of lexical broadening and narrowing. If you see the sentence:

There's a vehicle blocking the driveway. (Carston 2013)

You can interpret it according to the I-principle and conclude that the most stereotypical case of a vehicle is a motor car. However, you are equally warranted to interpret this in accordance with the Q-principle and claim that 'given the salient semantic entailment scale <vehicle, car> and the fact that the speaker has chosen to use the semantically weaker [broader] word, we can infer that (as far as the speaker knows) it is not a car' (Carston 2013).

The natural question to then ask is what is the point of having a theory that could explain each interpretation both ways? What is the decisive factor that makes us understand utterances we hear in accordance to only one of the heuristics? Carston claims that the decisive factor is an underlying principle of relevance:

> these context-sensitive maxims/heuristics, while they both reflect certain recurrent patterns of pragmatic inference, can be seen as somewhat superficial manifestations of some other deeper or more general principle underlying all pragmatic inferences. I would maintain that a properly developed concept of communicative "relevance" is required. (Carston 2013)

While I do agree that in natural language there is an underlying, probably psychologically bound principle of relevance that makes us decide which heuristic to employ when interpreting a sentence, I do not think legal interpretation can be explained in this way. There are various types of discourses that take place in the social enterprise that we call law and they all share a strategic character. This character is a matter of degree, with some of discourses being more strategic and others less so. Consequently, this special feature makes the principle of relevance insufficient to explain the legal case and a more elaborate strategic principle of selectivity is required. Nevertheless, before proceeding to a more detailed discussion on the point, let me present another interesting idea for theorists of legal language. Robyn Carston suggests that the heuristics laid out above are mirrored in the traditional canons of construction.

---

[9] This will not work in languages in which there are no articles. For instance, if you say in Polish 'I have found wallet' (no article!), you can mean either your own wallet or the wallet lost by a stranger. The disambiguation will be purely contextual.

3.6 The Canons of Construction

Canons of construction or interpretation are traditional rules employed by lawyers, especially judges, to justify their decisions. Carston showed that they mirror the reformulations of the Gricean principles by Horn. The Q-principle is mirrored by the canon *'Expressio unius est exclusio alterius'* (expression of the one is exclusion of the other). By contrast, the I-principle is expressed by the canon *'Eiusdem generis'* (of the same kind) (Carston 2013; Macagno et al. 2017).[10]

There are cases in which the canons yield converging results:

> Children under ten get in free
>
> Inference: Children ten or over do not get in free. (Carston 2013)

Imagine the above in a notice at a swimming pool. The notice does not mention older children, so they are excluded from getting in for free (Q heuristic). Simultaneously, this is 'equivalent to an utterance of "If a child is under ten, then he/she gets in free" and so should fall under the I-principle and accompanying heuristic ("Say no more than you must," "Enrich to the stereotypical/normal case").' (Carston 2013)

Nevertheless, it is often the case that the two principles lead to contradictory conclusions. In the already mentioned *Church of the Holy Trinity vs United States* the *expressio unius...* should lead to the exclusion of clergymen from the exception. By contrast, the *eiusdem generis* should allow the exemption to encompass the activities at stake.[11]

In the continental legal tradition, a similar issue would arise if the *a contrario* and the *per analogiam/a simile* reasoning methods clashed. The *a contrario* method means not applying a legal rule when it does not explicitly state itself that it is applicable to the case at stake. By contrast, the *per analogiam* method means applying a rule to cases which do not fall within the scope of a rule, yet are similar enough (Ziembiński 2000).

Herbert Hart also notices that sole canons of construction are never sufficient because they can yield contradictory results and must themselves be interpreted:

> Canons of "interpretation" cannot eliminate, though they can diminish, these uncertainties; for these canons are themselves general rules for the use of language, and make use of general terms which themselves require interpretation. (Hart 2012)

Carston concludes that there is need for an 'antecedent decision' on the application of one of the canons/methods of reasoning. Sometimes the legislator makes the

---

[10] In the Polish legal tradition, the *expressio unius* canon is often labeled the 'a contrario' reasoning or argument. The canon *eiusdem generis* is often labelled the 'a simile' or 'a simili' reasoning or argument (Zieliński 2012).

[11] Nevertheless, sometimes the eiusdem generis canon actually narrows down the scope of interpretation. Brian Slocum provides an example: 'a law concerning the regulation of (1) gin, bourbon, vodka, rum, and other beverages would not likely (absent some unusual context) be interpreted as including Coke (the soda), even though it is a "beverage".' (Slocum 2016).

decision for the interpreters. This is the case when he adds to a list of exceptions the words ‘and others’ or ‘in particular’. Similarly, in contracts one can add the clause ‘without limiting the generality of the foregoing’. These are cancellations of the implicature by the speaker that is based on the rule ‘what is not said is not the case’ (Carston 2013). Brian Slocum argues that such cases should be dealt with by a theory that combines the idea of scalar implicatures and the eiusdem generis canon. He claims that the ‘scale’ in such cases is the following: <specific list, list 1 ‘other’ clause, general term> (Slocum 2016). Slocum provides an example by considering three legal rules:

1. No dogs, cats, or birds allowed.
2. No dogs, cats, birds, or other animals allowed.
3. No animals allowed.

According to Slocum, the first rule above should be treated as exhaustive. The second, rule should be interpreted as narrower than the third. In other words, the word ‘other’ in the second rule is narrower than in the third rule (Slocum 2016). For instance, the second rule could be narrowed to animals kept in households or something similar depending on the context. While this seems an interesting normative theory, this does not explain why courts sometimes follow such patterns and sometimes ignore them, even in the exact same context.

However, the cases that are the most problematic (and for which interpretation is most needed) are those which contain no such explicit indication. Consequently, there remains the need of an overarching principle.

As far as everyday exchanges in natural language are concerned, the principle of psychological and contextual relevance could be sufficient. However, in the realm of law, interpretive decisions happen to be opposite to the first interpretation that comes to mind according to some relevant heuristic. To account for this counterintuitive character of enterprise, Relevance Theory is insufficient. Thus, I suggest, instead of a relevance principle, it is the strategic super-maxim of selectivity that gives a more adequate account of what is going on in the legal language. As I emphasized in the previous chapter, hearers in legal discourse (including interpreters) choose implicatures in accordance with their strategic, interpretive goal. Thus, they choose the principle/maxim that generates the implicature that fits their goal. However, contrary to political discourse, the strategic nature of legal discourse is very much constrained through all kinds of rules that are supposed to guarantee the sane functioning of the legal system. Any legal interpreter is bound not only by textual canons of the kind already mentioned, but also by substantive canons. Carston gives the example of the Rule of Lenity, ‘according to which an ambiguous criminal statute is to be resolved in favor of the defendant.’ (Carston 2013)[12] Another example could be the separation of powers principle or the *lex retro non agit* rule. Thus, within the constraints posed by the system, strategic agents choose the impli-

[12] In the Polish legal tradition, the rule of lenity is labelled as the rule forbidding a reasoning based on analogy to the detriment of the accused (Spyra 2006).

catures that fit their goals. Moreover, it is possible to predict which implicatures they will choose. The Q and I maxims are just ways of justifying the choice.

I will elaborate more on this subject in further parts of this study. However, I would like to formulate just a few comments on how the jurisprudential theory of legal interpretation could fit into the strategic picture. The basis of justificatory interpretation in common and (in some theories) in civil law systems is the *Plain Meaning* rule (‘*dyrektywa języka potocznego*’ (Wronkowska 2005)):

> The meaning of a statute is to be understood as the ordinary (plain) meaning of the language of the statute (**except when it makes explicit that a word is a technical term or provides a special legal definition**). [emphasis mine] (Carston 2013)

Polish legal theory has developed an interesting debate on an issue related to the Plain Meaning Rule in which two main claims are distinguished.

First, there is Wróblewski’s school, which favors the canon *clara non sunt interpretanda*. Thus, if we understand the text of the law, we do not need to interpret it. If we do not understand the law—that is, we are not sure if the rule applies to the case at hand—interpretation becomes necessary. Interpretation stops when it results in understanding, which is expressed by the canon *interpretation cessat in claris*. (Wróblewski 1990)

Secondly, there are Zieliński’s followers, who claim that we always need to interpret and there is no such notion as direct understanding which does not require any interpretation. It is expressed by the canon *omnia sunt interpretanda*. Moreover, the interpretation process only ends when we have verified that the three types of directives (linguistic, systemic and ‘functional’) do not yield any issues (Grabowski 2015). The functional directive is a directive to interpret the text in accordance with its purpose.

However, there are exceptions when we cannot resort to systemic or ‘functional’ arguments:

> For instance, we have to accept a linguistically univocal meaning of legal definitions, the norms of legislative competence (as far as they directly and unambiguously indicate the law-making authorities) and legal provisions that confer legal rights to the citizens etc. (Zieliński and Radwański 2006; Zieliński 2012)

Interestingly, the two canons *clara non sunt interpretanda* and *interpretatio cessat in claris* seem to have the same antinomic structure as Horn’s Q and R principles. Moreover, judges sometimes use one of them and sometimes the other, just as we in conversation sometimes employ the Q principle and sometimes the R principle. Thus, the *clara non sunt interpretanda* could be a correlate to the Q principle ‘say as much as you can’. This is because the more content the legislator explicitly says, the more content is treated by interpreting judges as something clear that has to be understood and not interpreted. In this way, the legislator guarantees himself that his will is more respected and judicial activism is limited. By contrast, the *Omnia sunt interpretanda* principle seems to mirror the R principle ‘say no more than you must’. This is because everything the legislator says is put under ‘scrutiny’ (interpretation) and the outcomes may be influenced by factors that could be beyond the legislator’s full control.

The employment of the plain meaning rule in Polish legal theory is slightly more nuanced yet still similar to the common law approach in an important way. Consequently, according to the *clara non sunt intrepretanda* canon, in clear, unambiguous cases, the statutes should be understood according to the 'ordinary, literal sense' (Wronkowska 2005). Because in hard cases there is no clear, unambiguous meaning and the 'ordinary, literal sense' could be either the syntactic-semantic-encoded meaning or the most frequently used interpretation, the plain meaning rule is not explanatorily sufficient. Consequently, 'folk' jurisprudential theories create all sorts of additional, justificatory levels. In civil law systems, the next level is the so-called systemic interpretation. It incites the interpreter to search for disambiguation hints in other rules or statutes of the legal system, such as searching for a definition of a term in another rule of the same statute or in another statute. Continental systems tend to have a strict hierarchy and structure of legal texts and the rules governing this structure and hierarchy can also constitute a systemic argument (Chauvin et al. 2014). In common law systems, such an idea is mirrored by the possibility of searching for cases with similar contextual factors. Finally, if this kind of systemic justification is not available, there remains the purposive interpretation, which claims that the aim of the statute is to be decoded on the basis of its context. To sum up, the *clara non sunt interpretanda* canon claims that interpretation is necessary only in hard cases, Moreover, it resorts to systemic arguments only when the plain meaning approach fails. Additionally, if the systemic interpretation still does not help, functional or teleological arguments ensue (there can be exceptions; for a detailed picture see Gizbert-Studnicki 2010).

By contrast, according to the *Omnia sunt interpretanda* canon, even understanding the ordinary literal sense means interpreting. Moreover, systemic and functional arguments need always to be considered so as to verify whether there is no 'hidden' interpretive issue (Grabowski 2015).

The common-law tradition has developed a plethora of doctrines based on the kind of intention a legislative speaker can have. Thus, we have the intentionalist, textualist and purposivist doctrines of interpretation (Gizbert-Studnicki 2012).

The approach that gives priority to statutory meaning (understood as dictionary definitions) is one of the tenets of formalism. Formalism aims to—among others—reduce the number of premises in an interpretive reasoning. It proclaims itself as a doctrine that protects the rule of law, yet this is a mistaken deception: in reality, it leads to dangerous simplifications of the interpretive process (Matczak 2018).

For this reason, a non-formalist[13] approach to legal interpretation is needed.[14] As Marcin Matczak convincingly argues: 'legislative history, other judicial rulings, and

[13] 'An example of a critique of the formalistic reductionism from a utilitarian point of view is Eskridge's and Frickey's opinion that fully fledged legal reasoning should be based on the idea of practical reasoning, which incites disposing of the maximum amount of data and premises used in the process of taking a decision, rather than limiting it. Due to the maximum of premises, the final decision is optimal.' [translated by IS] (Matczak 2007).

[14] 'As critics emphasize, the "standard meaning" approach, for which there are no criteria of being "standard", enables a huge amount of discretion for judges which has a negative influence on the

views expressed in legal literature, as well as the functional and purposive aspects of legal language can all be treated as elements that help in analyzing the meaning of legal terms. An interpretation guided by historical, comparative, or legal literature perspectives goes hand in glove with the rule of law, especially with the claim that provisions and rules are essentially of a linguistic nature. This, in turn, unseats formalism, along with its textual perspective, as the exclusive method of interpretation compatible with the rule of law. Critics of non-formalism who fear excessive discretionary powers being handed to lawyers or judges have nothing to fear. Paradoxically, the non-formalist approach to legal interpretation can ensure the better predictability of judicial decisions and the stricter curtailment of judicial discretion by broadening the scope of the interpretive premises on which judges base their decisions.' (Matczak 2018) I will return to this issue in the third chapter.[15]

I believe that the strategic selectivity of pragmatic effects comes into play on the third level, namely the functional. The plain meaning and systemic levels are just constraints on the kind of strategic behavior described in the previous chapter. Thus, at the functional level the plethora of possible utterance interpretations is chosen on a strategic basis. This strategic basis remains constrained through syntactic-semantic meaning, systemic considerations and substantive principles. Nevertheless, within these constraints strategic behavior of the kind described in the previous chapter is allowed. For instance, a functional decision can be taken in terms of which parts of the system of rules should be taken into account in the interpretive decisions and which should be ignored. Or a functional decision can be taken as to which dictionary definition of a word should be employed. Finally, different functions of the same rule can be promoted through an interpretive decision. However, the strategic framework differs from the psychological and cognitive relevance we use in our everyday linguistic exchanges.

---

principle of the predictability of the outcome of applying the law, although this aspect is seen as an asset of the formalistic approach (…) the notion of the standard understanding of a text is dependent on many factors, in particular on the context in which this meaning is to be reconstructed. This means that searching for an objective criterion for the standard meaning of a text is not a good solution since it suffices to change the context (for example the interpreter) for the standard meaning of the text to change.' [translated by IS] (Matczak 2007).

[15] '(…) it is far from obvious that legal formalism should be supplemented by formalistic application of the law. Quite the contrary: modern legal systems have developed numerous mechanisms to avoid the flaws of a formalistic approach to the application of the law. These conceptions usually order the setting aside of formalism in the application of legal rules; instead, one should focus on the formulation of rules about the usage of other prescriptive rules as well as rules about the construction of legal declarations of intent. These rules order taking into account their aim and function, which renders the process of their application non-formalistic. If a formally applied rule leads to a state that contravenes its aim, then the metanorms, which are found in constitutions or legal codes, order a direct realization of the goal, thus leading to a modification of the initial rule. This modification negates the idea of the formal stability of rules, which is a basic precondition of formalism in the law.' [translated by IS] (Matczak 2007).

3.7 Conclusion

The behavior of communicators in the legal realm is often counter-intuitive because they choose interpretations that are not the first, most 'obvious' interpretations that come to mind (for instance 'use a firearm' as 'use a firearm as a weapon'). Thus, a theory of cognitive relevance that is supposed to explain the psychology of speaking or explain why an interpretation comes first to mind is insufficient for a theorist of legal language. Consequently, I am skeptical of interpretive heuristics ('What isn't said, isn't the case', 'What is simply/briefly described is the stereotypical or normal (default) instance' etc.). Heuristics are processes that remain to a large extent unconscious or subconscious. By contrast, legal interpretation should be a conscious, rational enterprise of justifying the decisions taken. Moreover, the kind of strategic behavior deployed by legal communicators in all sorts of contexts related to the legal realm often seems counter-intuitive. No heuristic can account for the counter-intuitiveness and the need to extensively justify (give reasons for) legal decisions.

Nevertheless, I believe that the Q and R principles as defined by Horn are a very neat simplification of the Gricean framework. They shed light on linguistic issues, especially scalar terms. These issues are also present in legal language. Thus, I am sympathetic to the claim that the Gricean basis for strategic behavior could be replaced by Horn's idea. Moreover, reformulating the Q and R principles with canons of construction such as *expression unius est exclusio alterius* and *eiusdem generis* seems to be an appropriate move because it shows that the 'folk', jurisprudential theory of interpretation is based on at least partially correct intuitions about the nature of legal language and its pragmatics.

References

Austin JL (1962) How to do things with words: [the William James lectures delivered at Harvard University in 1955], 2nd edn, [repr.]. Harvard University Press, Cambridge

Carston R (1998) Informativeness, relevance and scalar implicatures. In: Carston R, Uchida S (eds) Relevance theory: applications and implications. John Benjamins, Amsterdam, pp 179–236

Carston R (2005) Relevance theory, Grice and the neo-Griceans: a response to Laurence Horn's "Current issues in neo-Gricean pragmatics". Intercult Pragmat 2. https://doi.org/10.1515/iprg.2005.2.3.303

Carston R (2013) Legal texts and canons of construction: a view from current pragmatic theory. In: Freeman MDA, Smith F (eds) Law and language, 1st edn. Oxford University Press, Oxford

Chauvin T, Stawecki T, Winczorek P (2014) Wstęp do prawoznawstwa [Introduction to Jurisprudence]. Wydawnictwo C.H. Beck, Warszawa

Dobosz P (2011) Milczenie i bezczynność w prawie administracyjnym [Silence and omission in administrative law]. Wydawnictwo Uniwersytetu Jagiellońskiego, Kraków

Gizbert-Studnicki T (1983) O sposobach formułowania dyrektyw [A few remarks on the ways of formulating norms]. Studia Semiotyczne XIII:91–109

Gizbert-Studnicki T (2010) Dyrektywy wykładni drugiego stopnia [Second order directives of interpretation]. In: Choduń A, Czepita S (eds) W poszukiwaniu dobra wspólnego - księga jubileuszowa Profesora Macieja Zielińskiego. Uniwersytet Szczeciński Rozprawy i Studia T., Szczecin

Gizbert-Studnicki T (2012) Oryginalizm i living constitutionalism a koncepcja państwa prawnego [Originalism, living-constitutionalism and the concept of the rule of law]. In: Kardas P, Wróbel W, Sroka T (eds) Państwo prawa i prawo karne: Księga jubileuszowa Profesora Andrzeja Zolla. Wolters Kluwer, Warszawa

Grabowski A (1999) Judicial argumentation and pragmatics: a study on the extension of the theory of legal argumentation. Ksiegarnia Akademicka, Krakow

Grabowski A (2015) Clara non sunt interpretanda vs. omnia sunt interpretanda: a never-ending controversy in Polish legal theory? Revus:6797. https://doi.org/10.4000/revus.3326

Grice P (1975) Logic and conversation. In: Cole P, Morgan J (eds) Syntax and semantics. Academic Press, New York

Grice HP (1989) Studies in the way of words. Harvard University Press, Cambridge

Hart HLA (2012) The concept of law, 3rd edn. Oxford University Press, Oxford

Horn LR (1984) Toward a new taxonomy for pragmatic inference: Q-based and R-based implicature. In: Schiffrin D (cd) Roundtable on languages and linguistics, meaning, form, and use in context: linguistic applications. Georgetown University Press, Washington, DC

Horn LR (2006) Implicature. In: The handbook of pragmatics. Blackwell, Malden

Keenan EO (1976) The universality of conversational postulates. Lang Soc 5:67. https://doi.org/10.1017/S0047404500006850

Macagno F, Walton D, Sartor G (2017) Pragmatic maxims and presumptions in legal interpretation. Law Philos. https://doi.org/10.1007/s10982-017-9306-4

Matczak M (2007) Summa iniuria: o błędzie formalizmu w stosowaniu prawa [On the mistake of formalism in applying the law]. Wyd. 1. Wydawn.Nauk. "Scholar," Warszawa

Matczak M (2018) Why judicial formalism is incompatible with the rule of law. Can J Law Jurisprudence 31(1):61–85. https://doi.org/10.1017/cjlj.2018.3

Neale S (2016) Silent reference. In: Ostertag G (ed) Meanings and other things. Themes from the work of Stephen Schiffer. Oxford University Press

Noveck IA (2001) When children are more logical than adults: experimental investigations of scalar implicature. Cognition 78:165–188. https://doi.org/10.1016/S0010-0277(00)00114-1

Perry J, Korta K (2015) Pragmatics. Stanford Encyclopedia of Philosophy

Recanati F (2017) Contextualism and polysemy. Dialectica 71:379–397. https://doi.org/10.1111/1746-8361.12179

Searle J (1975) Indirect speech acts. Syntax Semantics 3:59–82

Slocum BG (2016) Conversational implicatures and legal texts: conversational implicatures and legal texts. Ratio Juris 29:23–43. https://doi.org/10.1111/raju.12114

Sperber D, Wilson D (2001) Relevance: communication and cognition, 2nd edn. Blackwell Publishers, Oxford

Sperber D, Wilson D (2004) On defining relevance. In: Grandy RE, Warner R (eds) Philosophical grounds of rationality: intentions, categories, ends, Reprinted. Clarendon, Oxford

Sperber D, Wilson D (2006) Relevance theory. In: Horn LR, Ward GL (eds) The handbook of pragmatics. Blackwell, Malden

Spyra T (2006) Granice wykładni prawa: znaczenie językowe tekstu prawnego jako granica wykładni [The limits of legal interpretation: the linguistic meaning of a legal text as a limit of interpretation]. Zakamycze, Kraków

Wróblewski J (1990) Rozumienie prawa i jego wykładania [Understanding the law and interpreting]. Zakład Narodowy im. Ossolińskich. Wydawnictwo Polskiej Akademii Nauk, Wrocław

Wronkowska S (2005) Podstawowe pojęcia prawa i prawoznawstwa. Ars boni et aequi, Poznań

Zieliński M (2012) Wykładnia prawa. Zasady, reguły, wskazówki [Legal interpretation. Principles, rules, hints], 6th edn. Lexis Nexis, Warszawa

Zieliński M, Radwański Z (2006) Wykładnia Prawa Cywilnego [The interpretation of civil law]. Stud Prawa Prywatnego 1–40

Ziembiński Z (2000) Logika praktyczna [Practical logic]. Wydaw. Naukowe PWN, Warszawa

Chapter 4
Propositionalism and the Law

4.1 The Completeness of Legal Propositions

In the previous chapters I argued that the classical Gricean project offers the basis for an explanatorily valuable framework in constructing a theory of legal discourse. I claimed that this discourse consists of generating content according to a classic Gricean-like procedure. The second-order framework later modifies this first-order framework and consists of the strategic principle and the maxim of selectivity. I have also emphasized that the neo-Griceans are warranted in formulating two reproaches of the classical picture. First, the four maxims that were supposed to precisify the cooperative principle can be reduced to two: the Q and R principles. Moreover, in the legal framework they can be replaced by canons of construction such as 'expressio unius est exclusio alterius' and 'eiusdem generis'. Second, the Gricean notion of 'what is said' (in contrast to 'what is meant') is much more open to pragmatic enrichments than just the resort to context for disambiguation and reference assignment of the terms contained in a sentence. The first reproach has been discussed in detail in the previous chapter; in this chapter I would like to focus on the second reproach.

To grasp the stakes of the debate on propositionalism, the notion of a propositional radical needs to be introduced. What distinguishes a 'propositional radical' from a 'proposition' is its truth-evaluability. Only a proposition is truth-apt; a propositional radical is not truth-apt. Thus, the benchmark point between a propositional radical and a proposition is the point where the entity can be evaluated as true or false. This is the point where the entity is complete. For instance, take the example:

(I.) He is ready.

Most theorists in the debate—except, for instance, Emma Borg—claim that the above sentence does not express a proposition, since we do not know for what John is ready. Moreover, if the truth conditions only require something for which he is ready, then the truth conditions are trivial. By contrast, the sentence:

I. Skoczeń, *Implicatures within Legal Language*, Law and Philosophy Library 127, https://doi.org/10.1007/978-3-030-12532-5_4

(II.) John is ready to start the exam.

is obviously more complete than the previous example. This expresses a proposition, since it can be ascribed non-trivial truth conditions. In other words, only propositions are truth-apt. It makes sense to speak of a proposition only when the content evaluated is complete and truth-apt. The debate on propositionalism is in fact a debate about when linguistic content is complete enough to be assessed in terms of truth or falsity.

Before proceeding, let me briefly clarify some terminological issues. In this chapter I will use the distinction between complete and incomplete content: incomplete content is not truth-apt; complete content is truth-apt. Thus, complete content and propositional content are used interchangeably. An expression is roughly understood as a sub-part of a sentence (this does not preclude that a special expression could be by itself a sentence). For the purposes of the present chapter, let a sentence type be a syntactic string built in accordance with grammatical rules and equipped with the lexical (dictionary) meaning of the words that constitute it. Each such sentence type can be uttered as a sentence token—an utterance of a sentence by a speaker at a place and time and in a context. Two distinct utterances need not involve two distinct tokens of a sentence. A token of a sentence can be reused. For instance, if I leave the same piece of paper with the inscription 'Back in 5 minutes' pinned to the door each time I leave the office during office hours, I am reusing the same token of a sentence to produce a different utterance each time (Perry 2012).

4.1.1 Why Is 'What Is Said' Not Said?

Just to remind the reader at this point, Paul Grice defined his notion of 'what is said' as the basis for the inference of implicatures made by the hearer. The 'what is said' notion was supposed to be strictly semantic and the only elements that involved pragmatics in the reconstruction of 'what was said' were, according to Grice, disambiguation and reference assignment of contextually sensitive terms. Researchers that reflect on the Gricean legacy have challenged this thinking about the borders between semantics and pragmatics. This debate is sometimes labeled 'the border wars' because it focuses on trying to define a border between the semantic and pragmatic enterprise (Horn 2006).

There are three principal points of interest in this debate: first, it aims to answer the question of whether it is possible to recover a proposition from solely syntactic and semantic input; second, the debate questions whether what we call 'literal meaning' can be traced to some entity at a cognitive level; finally, researchers who claim we need pragmatics to decode a proposition from 'what is said' disagree over what sorts of pragmatic processes are involved. I will now provide a brief overview of the stances in the debate, then I will try to show that this debate can be a source of interesting conclusions for the role of jurisprudence in general.

Let me start with the debate on whether pragmatic processes are necessary to decode a proposition. This is in fact a debate about the role of semantics as a topic of research. If it is possible to get a proposition from strictly semantic input, then semantics is a field that is able to account for the truth-aptness of propositions. In other words, semantic data will be all that is needed to evaluate a proposition in terms of truth or falsity.

The stance claiming that only semantics can lead to a proposition is labeled minimalism and Emma Borg is its chief proponent (Borg 2006, 2012). She defines semantics roughly as 'features of the literal meaning of linguistic terms' (Borg 2012). By contrast, she defines pragmatics as 'roughly, features emerging from the context within which such items are being used' (Borg 2012). She claims that there is only an extremely limited set of (lexically or syntactically marked) context-sensitive expressions whose literal content can be affected by pragmatics: indexicals, demonstratives and tense markers (Borg 2012). This view assumes a strict compositionalism: the meaning of a sentence is fully determined by the meaning of the words that constitute it.[1] All of these claims make the Borgian notion of 'what is said' very close to Grice's idea, since he also postulated a limited set of context-sensitive expressions that contains only those subject to reference assignment and disambiguation. To sum up, Borgian minimalism is defined by four key claims:

i. Semantic content for well-formed declarative sentences is truth-evaluable content.
ii. Semantic content for a sentence is fully determined by its syntactic structure and lexical content: the meaning of a sentence is exhausted by the meaning of its parts and their mode of composition.
iii. There are only a limited number of context-sensitive expressions in natural language.
iv. Recovery of semantic content is possible without access to current speaker intentions (crudely, grasp of semantic content involves 'word reading' not 'mindreading'). (Borg 2012)

Borg's minimalism claims that we need to separate two questions: first, the question of which processes are involved in generating intuitive truth conditions; second, the question of which truth conditions are yielded by strictly semantic (lexical) and syntactic input. To illustrate this division, consider the examples provided by Borg:

(I) Jane is ready.
(II) Jane can make it.
(III) Jane can continue (Borg 2006).

If you hear the sentence 'Jane is ready' completely out of context, you would probably ask 'ready for what?' Theorists take this reaction as an indication that to evaluate a proposition conveyed by a sentence, we need more than just semantic and syntactic information. If this is correct, then there is no escape from pragmatic inferences in the process of reconstructing a proposition by the hearer. What we receive

[1] 'It is possible to recover the proposition literally expressed by a well-formed declarative sentence (its semantic content) simply on the basis of knowledge of the lexical entries for the expressions involved and an understanding of the syntactic construction of that sentence, plus, for sentences which contain genuinely context-sensitive elements, a merely minimal conception of the context within which the sentence was produced.' (Borg 2012).

from mere semantic and syntactic input is merely a 'propositional radical'. This is an incomplete entity that demands pragmatic completion until it becomes truth-apt. Kent Bach is a proponent of this view, which he labels *radical semantic minimalism* (Bach 2006).

The problem that this reasoning faces is that it significantly reduces the importance of semantics as a field of inquiry because it deprives semantics of the ability to define the truth-aptness of propositions. To save semantics as a fully fledged research field on propositions, Borg claims that we do need pragmatics, yet only to receive the intuitive truth conditions of a proposition. By contrast, semantic and syntactic input can provide us with so-called 'liberal truth conditions' (LTC). Here are some examples:

(a) If u is an utterance of 'Jane can't continue' in a context c, then u is true iff Jane can't continue something in c.
(b) If u is an utterance of 'Steel isn't strong enough' in a context c, then u is true iff steel isn't strong enough for something in c.
(c) If u is an utterance of 'Fido is bigger than John's dog' in a context c, then u is true iff Fido is bigger than the dog bearing some relation to John in c.
(d) If u is an utterance of 'The apple is red' in a context c, then u is true iff the apple is red in c. (Borg 2006)

Thus, the LTC program should rescue semantics as a field of inquiry that analyzes truth conditions. However, another question arises: can such a rescue plan be at all successful? Many theorists have presented counter-arguments, a detailed account of which can be found in (Skoczeń 2015). Here, I will only briefly recall the three major counterarguments to LTC: their triviality, artificiality and inability to explain possessive constructions.

First, there is always something in every context that Jane cannot continue, which means that LTCs are trivial. They always generate the value of truth. Consequently, LTCs seem to have little explanatory value because they do not allow discrimination between the truth and falsity of propositions. Second, LTCs are an artificial theoretical construct because they do not find any support in cognitive research. E. Borg claims that we have a linguistic module[2] in the brain that takes semantic and syntactic input, applies to it some deductive, computational processes and generates minimal propositions as output (Borg 2012). This is not confirmed by cognitive research. Speaking in terms of the type–token distinction, Borg claims that sentence types generate LTCs, while concrete tokens of sentences generate intuitive truth conditions. However, the human brain does not process information in terms of sentence types, it uses tokens (Gibbs 2002). If this is correct, then the reason for postulating LTCs remains a mystery. Third, minimal semantics has a problem with explaining a crucial constituent of every natural language, namely possessives. Consider the phrase:

(IV) John's dog

[2] E. Borg was inspired by J. Fodor and his claims on the modularity of the human mind, see (Fodor 1983).

On the basis of Borgian minimal semantics, this could be 'a dog bearing some relation to John'. The possessive relation is by no means the default one for (IV) according to the minimal semantics theory. Yet a theory of semantics that does not explain something as basic for any natural language as the possessive relation seems simply inadequate (Skoczeń 2015).

However, if Borgian minimalism is not helpful in explaining standard mechanisms of natural language functioning, does this mean it is completely useless? I believe not. Borg claims that:

> Children, **legislators**, and philosophers often seem to operate precisely with the kind of strict, syntax-based model of meaning which minimalism suggests, so to claim that the readings the account predicts fail to match any of our intuitions about utterance content would be far too strong. [emphasis mine] (Borg 2012)

Moreover, there is a limited class of phenomena in natural language that employ the described kind of minimal meaning. Borg claims that 'We are all used to sarcastic or uncooperative responses to something we have said which pick up not on obvious features of the conveyed content, but instead insist on a minimal, literal interpretation of our words.' (Borg 2012) This is best illustrated by jokes, irony or sarcastic behavior that are supposed to 'trade on' literal meaning. Consider the following example:

> A, B and C are standing in front of a lake. A points toward the water and says:
>
> A. Look! A hippo's head!
> B. Oh! It is.
> C. It's probably a whole hippo; it's just that the rest of him is under the water.
>
> The mechanism that C adopts to produce the joke is to refuse to enrich A's utterance with contextual features. Thus he treats A's literal utterance as a truth-evaluable proposition and reacts to it.' (Skoczeń 2015)

Nevertheless, as experimental research proves (Gibbs 2002), there is no 'refusal' to enrich. Rather, agents first decode the enriched proposition and only next turn to the literal one. 'The mechanism is comparable to taking a step backwards from a full proposition to one in which an element is not disambiguated or pragmatically enriched.' (Skoczeń 2015) Crucially, the step backwards is very often local. This means that it can only involve one term in the sentence, leaving other context-sensitive expressions enriched. Take the example:

A: Everyone loves this teacher.
B: Even the queen of England? (Jaszczołt 2016)

In the above example, B treats the word 'everyone' as literal. By contrast, he does not seem to deny the contextual determination of the referent of 'this teacher'.

Moreover, this is far from being the only issue minimal semantics faces. LTCs provide a problematic analysis for any sentence that contains an indexical or context-sensitive expression (from the limited set of context-sensitive expressions she assumes at the outset). This is because the minimal, computational, devoid-of-context meaning of such an expression is just its Kaplanian character. A character is a rule, a function from contexts to contents. For the expression 'I', the 'character' would be something like 'the person who is currently speaking'. Yet, as Kaplan argued, the sole 'character' will never yield truth conditions. To get truth-aptness we need content, which is the value of the character-function in context. For instance, for the expression 'I', the content will be the person who is the speaker (Kaplan 1978). Borg needs an additional element to the 'character', but it remains unclear what this element is according to her theory.

Consequently, there remains the question: what exactly is literal meaning? Is it possible to formulate a definition of this notion? The answer to the above question constitutes the second part of the 'border wars' dispute. I hope that the above considerations have shown that there is no truth-apt literal meaning without context. Thus, the definition of literal meaning we are left with is roughly provided by Recanati: 'Literalism in its modern form holds that the truth conditions of a sentence are fixed by the rules of the language (with respect to context) quite independently of the speaker's meaning.' (Recanati 2004)

This entails that from the point where 'minimalism' or 'literal meaning' are used in the present chapter, they are not used any more in the Borgian sense because, from that point, it is a notion that involves some contextual elements.

Metaphor theorists and experimental pragmatists have questioned the above definition of literal meaning. Roughly, if you hear a metaphor, you will need more than just the rules of language (such as, for instance, compositionality rules) to recover the meaning. By contrast, the meaning recovered on the basis of the sole rules of language (even with context) will not generate truth conditions (Carston 2012). Usually, the first truth-apt entity that comes to mind when processing metaphors involves a substantial deviation, especially from the compositionality rules (Sternau et al. 2015; Jaszczolt 2005).

The present considerations will concentrate on the ways in which syntactic and semantic rules need to be supplemented with pragmatic, contextual factors in order to yield a proposition (a truth-apt entity). In other words, we need to answer the question: what exactly are the 'necessary contextual elements' from the above definition of literal meaning? This question is important for legal theory because every judge, when interpreting a legal rule, must enrich the incomplete content of a legal text with at least the necessary contextual elements. Otherwise, he will get not complete content, but incomplete content. Moreover, he may enrich more than just the necessary amount and get 'richer' propositional content. Thus, the second question pertinent to jurisprudence is how much can a judge legitimately enrich? By legitimately I mean in a way that does not infringe the separation of powers principle or the principle of equality of the subjects in the eyes of the law. The latter could be infringed if when deciding on case A, a judge enriches the rule recovered from the legal text in a different manner than when deciding some similar case B on the basis of the same rule.

Recanati has clarified the relation between literal meaning and 'what is said': 'The meaning of an expression may be insufficient to determine its referential content; this is so whenever the expression is indexical or otherwise context-dependent. In such cases, the meaning of the expression provides a rule which, given a context, enables the interpreter to determine the content of the expression in that context.

The content thus determined in context by the conventional meanings of words is their literal content. The literal content of a complete declarative utterance is 'what is said', or the proposition expressed by that utterance.' (Recanati 2004).

Theorists have formulated arguments backing the claim that the notion of 'what is said' involves more than just disambiguation and reference assignment. However, what is this mysterious 'more'? First, it could be contextual factors that are exclusively 'bottom-up'. This stance is labeled indexicalism or minimalism. Indexicalism claims that we can supplement 'what is said' with contextual elements only when the syntax or semantics of this sentence require this. For instance, when there is a hidden variable or argument position in the logical form of the sentence that needs to be filled, this process is referred to as 'saturation'. Jason Stanley is a proponent of this view, claiming that 'much syntactic structure is unpronounced, but no less real for being unpronounced' (Stanley 2002).

Second, one can claim that saturation is not enough; this stance is referred to as contextualism. According to contextualists, we can only analyze sentences in use which are concrete utterances. There are two main versions of this view: moderate and radical contextualism. The debate between the two stances is another focal point of the 'border wars'.

Moderate contextualists claim that contextual effects can be not only bottom-up, but also 'top-down'. The latter are not required by anything in the syntax or semantics of the sentence. They are possible only in virtue of the context of use. Such processes are labeled 'free enrichment'. Yet since moderate contextualists are moderate, they claim that free enrichment is needed only sometimes rather than always. They still attribute an important role to syntax (Jaszczołt 2016). Francois Recanati is a proponent of this stance:

> I think the objection [to this stance – added IS] is confused. Even though free pragmatic processes, i.e. pragmatic processes that are not mandated by the standing meaning of any expression in the sentence, are allowed to enter into the determination of truth-conditional content, in the framework I have sketched they still come into the picture as part of the compositional machinery. Semantic interpretation remains grammar-driven even if, in the course of semantic interpretation, pragmatics is appealed to not only to assign contextual values to indexicals and free variables, but also to freely modulate the senses of the constituents in a top-down manner. Semantic interpretation is still a matter of determining the sense of the whole as a function of the (possibly modulated) senses of the parts and the way they are put together. (Recanati 2012)

Top-down processes are not triggered by anything in the syntax or semantics of the sentence. They are utterly pragmatic developments of the logical form of 'what is said'. In other words, no hidden variables in the syntactic structure or semantic meaning point to the necessity of enriching the proposition decoded on the basis of 'what is said'.

Radical contextualism, which is advocated by Charles Travis, is a stance which is also referred to as occasionalism or meaning-eliminativism. This stance claims that only 'top-down' processes count because there is no meaning outside context (Travis 2008).

Let me now respectively turn to the tenets of indexicalism as well as moderate and radical contextualism. As a reminder, minimalism and indexicalism allow the saturation of content. Saturation is defined as 'the contextual provision of a value for a syntactically marked context-sensitive item' (Carston 2012) For instance, in the sentence 'it is raining here', the indexical expression 'here' requires saturation to recover the place where it is raining. By contrast, if you hear the sentence 'it is raining'[3] *tout court*, then the place where it is raining is an unarticulated constituent of the sentence. To recover the place, a top-down process that is referred to as free enrichment is required.

Minimalists do not allow free enrichment to affect 'what is said'. As a result, they 'say that the aspects of utterance meaning which result from free enrichment do not belong to what is strictly and literally said, but either are "conversational implicatures" or (if one wants to restrict the term "conversational implicatures" to things that are intuitively 'implied by' the utterance) belong to an area of meaning that is intermediate between what is said and the conversational implicatures. Bach calls the things in that area the "impliciatures' of the utterance".' (Recanati 2002) For moderate contextualists such as Recanati, free enrichment is a third contextual process which is different than saturation. Moderate contextualists claim that truth conditions that do not take top-down processes into account are too minimal. For this reason, moderate contextualists claim that free enrichment is sometimes necessary to arrive at the intuitive truth conditions of a sentence. Moreover, it is the intuitive truth conditions that we are genuinely interested in. To illustrate the dispute, consider the following example:

(V) 'I've had a very large breakfast' (Recanati 2002)

For minimalists, 'what is strictly and literally said by (1) would be true if the speaker had had a large breakfast only once, twenty years ago. But what the speaker of (1) actually states is quite different: it is true iff the speaker has had a large breakfast on the day of utterance.' (Recanati 2002) Here, the disagreement between minimalism/indexicalism and moderate contextualism is merely terminological. The two stances are simply interested in different definitions of truth conditions. Minimalists are interested in some abstract truth-aptness of the sentence, while moderate contextualists are interested in the intuitive truth conditions which are genuinely and consciously considered by interlocutors when interpreting sentences.

Jason Stanley made an attempt to rescue indexicalism from the reproach that it generates unintuitive truth conditions. His strategy was to show that top-down processes such as free enrichment do in fact reduce to bottom-up processes such as saturation. He stated that 'for each alleged example of an unarticulated constituent [mentioned in the literature], there is an unpronounced pronominal element in the

[3] This example works on the assumption that this sentence does not have a hidden, syntactical argument for the place. Recanati assumes this on the basis of the following example: imagine a crazy scientist that wants to control the amount of rain across the entire planet (or universe etc.) and places rain detectors all over its surface. Whenever it rains somewhere on Earth, a bell rings. If the scientists says 'It is raining!', he does not have in mind a concrete location on Earth (Recanati 2004).

logical form of the sentence uttered, whose value is the alleged unarticulated constituent' (Stanley 2000). In other words, he claimed that free enrichment is articulated at a deeper level of syntax (Recanati 2002). Stanley's claim transformed the debate between indexicalists and contextualists into a genuine empirical dispute because he wished to conflate the definitions of truth conditions of sentences provided by both indexicalists and contextualists. For him, intuitive truth conditions contained only 'bottom-up' processes because all 'top-down' processes are reduced to 'bottom-up' ones. According to Recanati:

> Stanley (…) uses data of the sort originally collected by Barbara Partee (Partee 1989) to show that whenever an alleged unarticulated constituent has been postulated to account for the intuitive meaning of an utterance, one can intuitively "bind" the alleged unarticulated constituent, i.e. make it vary according to the values introduced by some operator. For instance, the temporal location of the breakfast event, which was said to be an unarticulated constituent of the speaker's response in example (1) can be bound by a quantifier. We can say:
>
> (4) No luck. Each time you offer me lunch, I've had a very large breakfast.
>
> The temporal location of the breakfast event now systematically varies with the temporal values introduced by "each time you offer me lunch". It follows (according to the argument) that the alleged unarticulated constituent in the original example was not really unarticulated: it had to be the (contextual) value of a variable in the logical form of the sentence, since without a variable there could not be the sort of binding that occurs in (4). (Recanati 2002)

Before summarizing Recanati's counterargument to Stanley's claims, we need to introduce the distinction between communicational and metaphysical unarticulated constituents (UCs). A communicational UC is 'part of the interpretation of an utterance and, as such, is 'available' to whoever fully understands the utterance.' (Recanati 2002) By contrast, metaphysical UCs are not subject to such a constraint. Take the example:

> It is a metaphysical fact that every action takes places somewhere. The action of dancing is no exception. It follows that, if we say that Mary danced, we describe a state of affairs (Mary's dancing), which is bound to involve a place. (…) in virtue of the fact that the sentence describes an action, a truth-maker for that sentence is bound to involve a place. (Recanati 2002)

Some UCs can be both communicational and metaphysical. For instance, the sentence 'It is raining' requires the place to be properly interpreted both communicatively and metaphysically. By contrast, the sentence 'Mary danced' is understandable even if we do not know where she danced (Recanati 2002). The present considerations are restricted to communicational UCs.

Crucially, the discussion between Recanati and Stanley is different from the discussion between contextualists and the Borgian minimalist. This is best illustrated by the different consequences that Borgian minimalists and indexicalists together with contextualists (like Stanley or Recanati) draw from the same situation: imagine that there is a sentence with a variable in its hidden syntactic or semantic structure and the hearer is unable to fill the argument place. For Borg, the hearer is recovering a minimal proposition with LTCs. By contrast, the indexicalists and contextualists claim that such an entity is 'vacuous'. This means that what the hearer has received is merely a 'propositional radical', an entity that is not truth-apt. In this case, saturation is absolutely necessary to receive a proposition, while free enrichment is only optional. Consider the examples:

(argumental underdetermination):

- Mary finished. (what?)
- The cow jumped over. (what?)
- Gentlemen prefer blondes. (to what?)
- Mutual knowledge is not relevant. (to what?)
- John is ready. (for what?)
- (parametric underdetermination):
- That lamp is short/cheap/old. (relative to what?)
- That employee is good/talented/valuable. (in what respect?)
- Even cowgirls sing the blues. (in addition to whom?) (Recanati 2002)

In these cases, what is required is saturation because it is the structure of the sentence itself that requires contextual completion (or so Recanati claims).[4]

However, if a failure to recover a UC does not result in the incompleteness of the proposition but in a 'mismatch' between the proposition asserted by the speaker and the proposition recovered, then free enrichment is genuinely required (Recanati 2002). Thus, the discussion between Stanley and Recanati is in fact a discussion concerning 'mismatch' cases (recall the breakfast example) rather than vacuity cases.

If we follow Recanati in claiming that free enrichment is not triggered by anything in the (even deepest) syntax, we must conclude that free enrichment is not an argument place filler in some sub-syntactic structure. Consequently, we need to answer the question about the mechanism that guarantees the unity of a freely enriched proposition. Recanati suggests that this 'glue' that holds the proposition together is a 'variadic function'. This is 'a function from relations to relations, where the output relation differs from the input relation only by its decreased or increased adicity. Adding a predicate modifier (adverb or prepositional phrase) to a predicate expressing an n-ary relation R^n thus results in a complex predicate expressing an n+1-ary relation in which the nth+1 argument is a *circumstance*: a time, a location, a manner or what not.' (Recanati 2002).

The 'decreased or increased adicity' means that there are two sorts of variadic functions, recessive and expansive, and the latter is supposed to pragmatically expand a semantic property:

[4] 'When the relevant parameter – the comparison class in the case of 'small' – is contextually provided rather than made explicit in the sentence, there is an obvious sense in which the parameter in question is not articulated: no word or morpheme in the sentence stands for it. But there is also a sense in which it is "articulated". As we have seen, there is an expression in the sentence, namely the adjective "small" itself, that triggers the search for a relevant comparison class, just as an indexical triggers the search for an appropriate contextual value. A truly unarticulated constituent resulting from free enrichment must not even be articulated in that second, weaker sense. It must not result from an obligatory process of saturation or "completion".' (Recanati 2002).

> The effect of an "expansive" variadic function of the sort contributed by adverbial modifiers is that it adds an argument role. The output relation therefore contains the same argument roles as the input relation, plus the extra argument role provided by the variadic function. For example, in the statement "John eats in Paris" the prepositional phrase "in Paris" contributes a variadic function which maps the property of eating, which is ascribed to John in the simpler statement "John eats", onto the dyadic relation Eat_in (x, l) between an individual and a location. That relation is predicated of the pair ⟨John, Paris⟩ in the more complex statement. Note that the prepositional phrase "in Paris" contributes not only the variadic function, but also the argument (Paris) which fills the extra argument-role. (Recanati 2002)

By contrast, 'there are also "recessive" variadic functions that decrease the valence of the input relation by suppressing an argument role. In English, various alternations such as the passive alternation and the intransitive alternation (Levin 1993) can be described in such terms. The operation of passivation ("John kisses Mary" → "Mary is kissed") suppresses the argument role that corresponds to the subject of the active sentence, whereas intransitivation ("John eats the apple" → "John eats") has the effect of suppressing the argument role that corresponds to the direct object of the verb.' (Recanati 2002).

Let us take stock. The discussion between Recanati and Stanley is about the existence of truly unarticulated constituents. These are constituents that are pragmatic and are not triggered by anything in the syntax or semantics. Stanley claims that such constituents do not exist because there must always be something in the syntax or semantics that can, at least hypothetically, bind a variable. In other words, we must always be able to put an operator before the sentence that will bind it. Recanati disagrees with this claim. For him, there exist genuine unarticulated constituents which are the result of free enrichment. He labels this claim the 'optionality criterion' and defines it in the following words: 'Whenever a contextually provided constituent is (truly) unarticulated, we can imagine another possible context of utterance in which the contextual provision of such a constituent would not be necessary for the utterance to express a complete proposition.' (Recanati 2002).

For Stanley, nothing can fulfill the optionality criterion, since for him unarticulated constituents are either required by the syntax or are bound by a quantifier. This entails that there are no genuine unarticulated constituents. Recanati labels Stanley's argument 'the binding criterion' and defines it in the following way: 'A contextually provided constituent in the interpretation of a sentence S is articulated whenever the argument role it fills can be intuitively "bound", that is, whenever what fills that role can be made to vary with the values introduced by some operator prefixed to S.' (Recanati 2002).

Recanati further argues that the binding criterion does not stand. Take the example of the verb 'eat'. There is nothing in the semantics of the verb 'eat' that would require the specification of the thing eaten. We can perfectly say that someone is eating *something or other.* Now consider the sentence:

(VI) John is anorexic, but whenever his father cooks mushrooms, he eats. (Recanati 2002)

Intuitively, one wants to claim that John eats precisely what his father cooks. In other words, intuitive binding occurs. Yet it is perfectly possible to imagine a context in which John eats something else (other than the mushrooms his father cooks)! What John eats does not have to be specified. Completion of the variable is not necessary, so there is no free variable in the logical form. The variable is optional. Thus, intuitive binding does not entail articulatedness. Stanley's 'binding criterion' fails (Recanati 2002).

To sum up, the border wars have not yet ended, and new arguments are constantly appearing. Nevertheless, some rough formulations of the answers to the three questions stated at the outset are starting to appear more clearly on the horizon. The first question was about the possibility of Borgian minimal content being truth-apt. Minimal content, in E. Borg's theory, means content yielded solely by syntax and semantics. The number and seriousness of the counterarguments to Borg's theory tilts the balance toward a negative answer to the first question or an extremely limited set of sentences in natural language that can be ascribed the Borgian literal truth conditions. The second question was about the nature of literal meaning. There is an increasing amount of (experimental among others) data and arguments that suggest that we do not think in terms of literal meaning. This is an abstract construct rather than a cognitive concept. Finally, as for the third issue, there is some intermediate level of pragmatic meaning that is neither an implicature nor a bottom-up process triggered by something in the syntactic or semantic structure of the sentence. This level differs from implicatures because it does not express a distinct proposition from the proposition recovered on the basis of what was said. On the contrary, the content added by 'top-down' processes such as free enrichment is part of the proposition recovered on the basis of 'what was said'.

4.2 What Can a Theorist of Legal Language Learn from the 'Border Wars'?

The aim of this section is to show that adopting a particular stance in the debate on propositionalism has a great influence on the theory of interpretation that one adopts. What is more, the theory of interpretation one chooses usually depends on one's preferred stance in political philosophy—values such as the division of powers principle etc. Before depicting this interrelation, let me add a few comments about modern approaches to the separation of powers principle and the rule of law.

4.2.1 The Separation of Powers Principle

Every language theorist that undertakes the challenge of providing a theory which accounts for what is going on in the law considers the exchange between legislatures and courts as a real pain in the neck. The principal hurdle—the inconspicuous monster that deprives the poor scholar of sleep and peace of mind—has a name. This is political morality.

To identify the roots of the theorist's nightmare we have to jump back in time to the year 1748 and the publishing of 'The Spirit of the Laws' by Charles Montesquieu; specifically, to the passage tackling the separation of powers principle. This groundbreaking idea which underlies every modern democratic system contains the assumption that causes the unbearable suffering of the theorist: legislative and judicial powers have different, separate tasks. Legislative power (collective body or single person) cannot infringe on the competence of judicial power, and vice versa. The result is two elements in the structure with different competences—philosophical torture. In the Obamacare ruling, Justice Scalia puts the point neatly:

> The Court's decision reflects the philosophy that judges should endure whatever interpretive distortions it takes in order to correct a supposed flaw in the statutory machinery. That philosophy ignores the American people's decision to give Congress "[a]ll legislative Powers" enumerated in the Constitution. Art. I, §1. They made Congress, not this Court, responsible for both making laws and amending them. This Court holds only the judicial power – the power to pronounce the law as Congress has enacted it. We lack the prerogative to repair laws that do not work out in practice, just as the people lack the ability to throw us out of office if they dislike the solutions we concoct. (…)

One of a democratic system's most crucial elements that guarantees the respect of the separation of powers is the rule of law principle. Roughly, this principle forces both institutions and their subjects to act in accordance with the law. In other words, everyone must respect the rules of the game accepted at the outset. Rule of law is a rather complex concept that encompasses many more specific requirements. Namely, theorists claim that there are three main subsets of principles that precisify it: the formal aspects of governance by law, the procedural aspects, and certain substantive values (Waldron 2016). The procedural aspect is inherently related to the separation of powers idea:

> Some procedural requirements are also institutional in character: there must be courts and there must be judges whose independence from the other branches of government is guaranteed. This side of the Rule of Law is related to the constitutional principle of the separation of powers. That principle is sometimes justified simply on the grounds that it is unhealthy for power to be institutionally concentrated in society. But it also has a Rule of Law justification inasmuch as it assigns distinct significance to distinct stages in the making and application of laws (Waldron 2013).

One of the most recent and systematic accounts of the components of the rule of law is the 'Rule of Law checklist' adopted on the 11th of March 2016 by the Venice Commission of the Council of Europe. It develops the following values: 'legality; legal certainty; prevention of abuse of powers; equality before the law and non-discrimination; as well as access to justice'.[5]

Since it is not the purpose of this study to analyze all of the sub-principles of the rule of law, I will confine myself to requirements which are interesting from the

---

[5] See http://www.venice.coe.int/images/SITE%20IMAGES/Publications/Rule_of_Law_Check_List.pdf.

point of view of a theorist of language. Firstly, according to the rule of law principle, laws must be epistemically accessible: 'the laws should be a body of norms promulgated as public knowledge so that people can study it, internalize it, figure out what it requires of them, and use it as a framework for their plans and expectations and for settling their disputes with others.' (Waldron 2016) This means that any theory of legal language must duly consider any epistemic limitations that could arise.

The reason for the above is the legal certainty requirement identified in the Venice Commission's checklist. If epistemic access is not guaranteed, then legal certainty fails. There is however an interesting discussion between the formalist and anti-formalist camp. The formalists claim that to guarantee legal certainty, the number of interpretative premises must be limited. (…) Classic formalists believed that law should fulfill three requirements: first, it must be determinate, its judgments following from the application of norms to facts; second, it must be systematic, creating a coherent structure of relatively abstract concepts and principles; and thirdly, it must be autonomous, deriving its norms only from legal sources rather than from the contestable claims of religion, philosophy, or political economy (Matczak 2007, 2018).

In a nutshell, the more limited the number of premises, the more predictable the decision. The Venice Commission identifies the principal questions that must be answered in the affirmative if a state wants to have foreseeable, or predictable laws:

Are court decisions accessible?

i. Are court decisions easily accessible to the public?
ii. Are exemptions sufficiently justified?

Are the effects of laws foreseeable?

i. Are the laws written in an intelligible manner?
ii. Does new legislation clearly state whether (and which) previous legislation is repealed or amended? Are amendments incorporated in a consolidated, publicly accessible, version of the law?[6]

The Commission further argues that 'foreseeability means not only that the law must, where possible, be proclaimed in advance of implementation and be foreseeable as to its effects: it must also be formulated with sufficient precision and clarity to enable legal subjects to regulate their conduct in conformity with it'.[7]

By contrast, the anti-formalist camp warns against this approach. Only an 'all things considered' decision can be a fair and just decision. This line of thought has a long tradition. A critique of formalism and a support of judicial discretion is given by Plato (c. 370 BC): 'insistence upon the use of law in government was like a stub-

[6] See http://www.venice.coe.int/images/SITE%20IMAGES/Publications/Rule_of_Law_Check_List.pdf.

[7] See http://www.venice.coe.int/images/SITE%20IMAGES/Publications/Rule_of_Law_Check_List.pdf.

born, stupid person who refuses to allow the slightest deviation from or questioning of his own rules, even if the situation has in fact changed and it turns out to be better for someone to contravene these rules.' (Plato 294AD; Waldron 2016).

Another early criticism comes from the Roman jurist Cicero, who in 1 BC coined the maxim 'summum ius, summa iniuria' ('The highest law, the highest injustice') (Cicero 2008, I, 10, 33). This can be paraphrased as 'rulings rigidly that stick to the letter of the law often have little to do with justice.' (Matczak 2018)

The Venice Commission also warns against a formalistic approach. In the commentary to the checklist, we read that 'The Commission warned against the risks of a purely formalistic concept of the Rule of Law that merely requires that any action of a public official be authorized by law. "Rule by Law", or "Rule by the Law", or even "Law by Rules" are distorted interpretations of the Rule of Law.'[8]

A warning against formalism was also formulated by Herbert Hart:

> we cannot ab initio foresee what combinations of circumstances will arise nor foresee what interests will have to be sacrificed or to what extent if precaution against harm is to be taken. Hence it is that we are unable to consider, **before particular cases arise**, precisely what sacrifice or compromise of interests or values we wish to make in order to reduce the risk of harm. [emphasis mine] (Hart 2012)

To sum up, respecting the Rule of Law means carefully striking a balance between formalist and anti-formalist arguments so as to render just decisions. As I intend to depict below, choosing a stance in the debate on propositionalism can either strengthen the rule of law in a state or undermine it. Thus, in coining a theory of legal language, we need to pay constant attention to this issue.

4.2.2 *The Consequences of Choosing a Stance in the Debate on Propositionalism for the Separation of Powers Principle*

As far as legal interpretation is concerned, the stance in the debate on propositionalism and the stance on the separation of powers principle are deeply interrelated. The preferred answer to the first question entails a choice of the preferred answer to the second question. I will consecutively discuss these relations with the following three stances: the Borgian minimalist idea, the necessity of saturation to receive a proposition, and the possibility of free enrichment in legal interpretation.

Just to remind the reader, minimalists claim that we can get a complete proposition from strictly syntactic and semantic input plus the rules of compositionality. This means that the reconstruction of the proposition by the hearer is supposed to have a computational character. In the continental legal tradition, since 1748, when Montesquieu published 'The Spirit of the Laws', the division of powers idea is con-

[8] See http://www.venice.coe.int/images/SITE%20IMAGES/Publications/Rule_of_Law_Check_List.pdf.

sidered the very heart of the state. Roughly, the idea behind the traditional formulation of this principle is that the legislature enacts a statute and the judge only applies the law. Judges are often called the 'mouth of the law'. Thus, the strictest possible definition of the word 'application' is precisely the minimalists' idea because the computational character of decoding a proposition renders it as predictable as possible. Since the legislative context may sometimes prove barely accessible to judges (Marmor 2014), they are able to completely ignore the pragmatic processes and still get the complete content of the statute at stake. If the judge does not have to perform pragmatic reasoning, then—since pragmatic reasoning is defeasible—she does not have to perform defeasible reasoning either. Moreover, the legislator is able to predict the outcome of judicial reasoning in detail. Unfortunately, this perfect (almost naïve) picture of the division of powers is simply not feasible.[9] The minimal propositions and liberal truth conditions described by Emma Borg are too minimal to constitute the basis of a decision because they are mostly trivial; for instance, they are always true in every context. Recall the *Smith v. US* case and the debate on the expression 'to use a firearm'. Taken minimally, any 'use' counts and Scalia's argument that even scratching your head with a firearm falls within the scope of this provision becomes valid. Thus, minimal propositions and literal meaning can be a good basis for interpretation, but they do not suffice *per se* to take decisions.

This means that to make decisions in court, pragmatics are simply a necessary tool. However, the naïve version of the separation of powers principle cannot be fully realized if pragmatic processes interfere with the judge's interpretive activity. Quite the contrary, if reconstructing 'what is said' (or actually 'what is ordered') requires pragmatics, then the division of powers principle needs reformulation. This is simply due to the nature of language. If—through interpretation—the linguistic content of the order reconstructed from the statute by the judge does not involve at least bottom-up processes (saturation), very often no decision can be taken. This is because saturation of the legal rule is sometimes required to get a fully fledged proposition. Consider an example of a legal rule: All men are equal. The question that immediately arises is: equal in respect to what? The syntax and semantics require a variable to be contextually filled. Since saturation is a process required by the syntax or semantics of the proposition, it is still possible to claim that the legislature can foresee where a variable will occur and how could it be filled by judges. This gives the judge some discretion as to the variable filling. However, this still seems like a predictable process. Thus, the division of powers principle could

[9] 'The critique of the claim on the binding of the interpreting person proves that due to the semantics of language, legal language included, a textualist approach to language is impossible, as is the limitation of lawyers' discretion proposed by textualists. Language is contextual by its very nature, which means that we cannot talk about the stability of meaning and the clarity of legal text because understanding a text is directly dependent on the context constituted by the features of the reader as well as the circumstances of reading. (…) The pragmatic nature of language is against the claim on the possibility of restricting lawyers' discretion through the text, especially the influence of pragmatics on semantics – the influence of varying circumstances, in which we employ the same text, on the changes in the meaning.' [translated by IS] (Matczak 2007).

embrace the possibility of judicial saturation. A good example is the case *United States v. Gonzales*. As Asgeirsson notices, all the parties found it clear that the expression 'term of imprisonment' needed saturation. Namely, one party claimed that this should be saturated as 'term of imprisonment {that has already been imposed}'. By contrast, the other party wanted it to be enriched as '{federal} term of imprisonment' (Asgeirsson 2017). The court had to decide on which value of the variable to choose.

A much more problematic idea is free enrichment. If we accept Recanati's argument that a variadic function allows a variable to be added first and only second can the variable be saturated, then a series of questions arises for legal interpretation. This is because free enrichment is unpredictable in the sense that there is nothing in the syntax or semantics of the sentence that require this as a variable to be filled in the future. This is because even if we have a case of quantifier bounding, the variable does not have to be a pre-existing fact of the matter—it can be added only later by the variadic function. An example of a quantifier bounding legal rule is the following: 'Every time a citizen files a motion with the Ombudsman, the Ombudsman must undertake an action'. You can imagine a context in which the Ombudsman reacts in a different way than that requested in the citizen's motion.

Since cases in which a legal rule is applied may have very varied and unpredictable contexts, free enrichment gives considerable discretion to judges. As a result, the question remains of how much a judge can freely enrich a provision so as to apply it to the case. How to strike a balance between a rational, practical interpretation and some unwanted activism by which the judicial powers take up the legislative voice? These questions arise because of the nature of the tool that we use: language. The task of jurisprudence is to design mechanisms that constrain the discretion that language grants to judges. For instance, take again the example from *Smith v. Us*. The court could repeatedly employ free enrichment to develop the expression 'use a firearm'. One can imagine something such as:

I. Use a firearm{as a weapon}{without control}{in an unrestricted area}{for self-defense purposes} etc.

Note that one could explain the linguistic mechanisms lurking behind the example above with variadic functions. This is because expressions such as 'as', 'without', 'in', 'for' etc. are functions that take arguments 'as *x*', 'without *x*', 'in *x*', 'for *x*' etc. The mechanism is the following: first, there is a free enrichment procedure that consists in adding a variadic function. Since this is a function from relation to relation, the output can generate a variable that has to be filled. Second, through saturation, the variable is supplied, and the result is, for instance, the expression 'as a weapon' or 'without control'.

A mechanism determining when to stop free enrichment in such a case is necessary. In analysis of an everyday conversation it is possible to claim that a hearer enriches only so as to get what he thinks the speaker intended to communicate. However, the matter is more complicated when we come to what a legislature communicates. Since a parliament is a collective body composed of multiple agents, the laws enacted are the effect of an interplay of multiple individual intentions. I will elaborate on this problem in detail in the next chapter. For the purposes of the current considerations, I will only make use of Andrei Marmor's idea of an 'exhortative'. Before proceeding though, just one remark: I often employ the words imperative or order. The idea that law is constituted of orders was proposed by John Austin in his 'The province of jurisprudence determined' (Austin 1832). Nevertheless, this view has been criticized at length by many legal philosophers (including Herbert Hart) who claimed that laws are rules rather than orders (Hart 2012). Consequently, the present considerations will involve a slight simplification, as the debate on the nature of laws is independent of considerations concerning the debate on propositionalism.

John Langshaw Austin is the author of the speech act theory, which explains how it is possible that we do things with words. On his account, imperatives are acts which enable us to issue orders. In Austin's version of the theory, the intention of the speaker to issue an order is a necessary and constitutive element of the felicity of an imperative (Austin 1962). As already stated, the implementation of this idea in the pragmatics of legal language can be problematic because—as I will argue in the next chapter—intention is a problematic feature of the theory of meaning in the law. Even if everyday communication is heavily reliant on people's intentions, the meaning in law is more external and independent of intention. Thus, there remains the question of how to modify Austin's theory so as to make it more independent of intention. Marmor proposes such a solution: he labels such imperatives without intention 'exhortatives' and thus coins a new term 'exhortatives' so as not to confuse it with the Austinian one. The genuine intention of the speaker is not a constitutive element of an exhortative:

> If the propositional content of an exhortative is, as I suggest, self-referential, describing the speaker's state of mind, then one might have to conclude that the relevant state of mind is what determines the propositional content asserted. And this would be a problematic result. For example, it would mean that in the example of collective speech, in which different participants have somewhat different intentions, wishes, etc., the propositional content would vary with the participants involved; that seems like a mess. (Marmor 2014)

Consequently, for an exhortative to occur, it is sufficient that an objective hearer understands this as an imperative. Moreover, this, on Marmor's account, applies equally to exhortative and assertive content:

> The truth-evaluable, asserted content consists in what is said or asserted by a speaker in a given context, not by what the speaker intended to say. I am not suggesting that communication intentions are irrelevant, far from it. Under normal circumstances, in an ordinary, conversational context, it is precisely the communication intentions of the speaker that we try to grasp by figuring out what is said (and perhaps implicated etc.). But again (…) the assertive content of an utterance is determined by what a reasonable hearer – knowing the relevant conversational background and context – would infer about the speaker's communication intentions from the words or sentences uttered in that context. (Marmor 2014)

The problem with the objective hearer is that it generates a question concerning the determinants of the standard of an objective hearer (which criteria define an objective hearer). Moreover, it must be verifiable that the relevant institution empowered by the legal system has provided the exhortative. However, since most often it is the judge that is supposed to decide on the 'objective hearer's' interpretation, this is an issue concerning legal interpretation.

Judicial interpretation is the descriptive reconstruction of the exhortative (through available contextual cues). It is reasoning of what a reasonable hearer would infer from the utterance. The judge must reconstruct the rule so as to be able to apply it to a concrete case; however, it is not clear when the reconstruction is complete and should be stopped. Marmor's account does not solve this issue because it is relative to the standard of a reasonable hearer. It is not clear to what extent the proposition can be pragmatically enriched; especially, it is not clear to what extent (and if at all) free enrichment can occur. The safest idea (in terms of the rule of law) is probably to allow free enrichment only when the contextual elements of the concrete case make it impossible to apply the exhortative and make a decision. The idea is that in such cases the judge 'discovers' a part of the abstract order that was never acknowledged before. This freely enriched exhortative also needs to be applied in further cases so as to guarantee equality in the eyes of the law.

J. Goldsworthy provides another idea. He introduces two tests for determining when it is necessary to allow judges to undertake 'creative' actions. Note that this is not a necessity in the logical sense. The first test is 'practical efficacy':

> It asks whether or not the alleged implication is necessary to make particular provisions, or the document as a whole, operate effectively. (Goldsworthy 1994)

A similar test was developed by Scott Soames in relation to constitutional interpretation. Soames argues that the courts are allowed to make a 'minimum, necessary precisification' of the text (Soames 2013).

The second test provided by Goldsworthy is labeled the 'obviousness test' or 'the test concerning psychological necessity':

> It asks whether or not interpreters are compelled to acknowledge the alleged implication because it is so obvious as to be inescapable. In contract law, the question has been said to be whether the Court is "necessarily driven" to the conclusion that some term is implied. The term "necessity" is used loosely here; what is really required is not that the implication cannot possibly be denied, but that it cannot reasonably be denied. In a case involving statutory interpretation, Isaacs, Barton and Rich [judge's names – clarification mine] said that "necessary intendment only means that the force of the language in its surrounding carries such strength of impression in one direction, that to hold the opposite view appears wholly unreasonable".[10] Obviousness is a more accurate term than "necessity" for what is required'. (Goldsworthy 1994)

Goldsworthy emphasizes that in such cases the courts should not pretend to be discovering some hidden 'intention' of the legislature, but rather they should openly and frankly admit that they are supplementing the law. There is nothing wrong in such conduct (Goldsworthy 1994). As we have seen, such behavior does not have to contradict the rule of law or the division of powers principle; quite the contrary, it can strengthen them (Matczak 2018).

---

[10] Worrall v. Commercial Banking Co of Sydney Ltd (1917) 24 CLR 28 at 32.

All these considerations may seem somewhat abstract. For this reason, let me now discuss some examples of pragmatic enrichment found in the literature. Next, I will try to apply the strategic framework to these cases.

4.3 Some Famous Examples of Pragmatic Enrichment in the Law

Richard Ekins claims that pragmatic enrichment in interpretation is frequent and provides four examples:

A. Witnesses who attest 'any will or codicil {*of real estate*}' under which they are beneficiaries shall be treated as good witnesses, but the gifts made to them shall be void.
B. All drug shops "shall be closed at 10 pm on each and every day of the week {*and shall stay closed until morning*}".
C. It is an offence to "stab, cut or wound" any person {*with a weapon or instrument*}.
D. Every person who fraudulently harbors uncustomed goods shall forfeit a specified sum, "and the offender {*or apparent offender*} may either be detained or proceeded against by summons". (Ekins 2012) (Bennion 1990) (Asgeirsson 2017)

The text in italics and brackets is the content added through pragmatic enrichment. Ekins argues that enrichment is very frequent in the law. In other words, he claims that the legislator often makes use of non-literal enactment. The examples above are supposed to prove his thesis. By contrast, Andrei Marmor argues that non-literal legislative speech is very rare. This is because—given that the stakes are so high—the enrichment must be obvious and this almost never happens since the legislative context is usually too thin (Marmor 2014). As Asgeirsson convincingly argues, neither of the extremes is correct. Non-literal legislative enactment is neither ubiquitous nor very rare. Marmor's requirement that the context needs to be obvious is too strict. It is sufficient that it is 'significantly more probable than not that the speaker is not intending to assert what she literally says' (Asgeirsson 2017).

The idea is that in ordinary conversation there are many situations in which we are not sure if the speaker meant the literal content of the proposition or some enriched version. However, this, does not matter—the communication succeeds anyway. In other words, it does not really matter whether the hearer decodes the enrichment or not. Asgeirsson gives many examples, let me just recall one of them:

> imagine that someone asks an artist how her show went and that in response she utters the following: "Nobody came to my show!" In most situations, a rational hearer would infer that the artist intended to communicate that almost nobody came to her show. But it's not outright impossible that the artist is intending to assert that zero people showed up. However, given that it is rare that absolutely nobody shows up for a show, the artist has given her interlocutor good reason to believe that she is intending to communicate that almost nobody came to the show – it is significantly more likely than not that she is so intending. Moreover, it does not matter – vis-à-vis this particular context – which proposition the artist in fact intended to communicate; either way, the artist has conveyed that the show didn't go well, which suffices for the purposes of the conversation. As before, it may not be outright silly to ask the artist whether she meant that absolutely nobody or almost nobody showed up, but in the stipulated scenario there is – given what is "required by the accepted purpose of the

> conversation" – no reason to ask for clarification that is independent of the interlocutor's desire to know for certain. (Asgeirsson 2017)

You could object that the above is possible only because in ordinary conversation the 'stakes are not so high'. By contrast, this kind of incertitude seems hard to accept in the legal realm, in which precision is called for. Asgeirsson has an answer to this:

> Typically, a legal system will contain a considerable amount of relatively insignificant run-of-the-mill legislation, such as littering laws and pet identification regulations, to name some examples. While there is of course generally good reason to have laws of this sort, the stakes associated with their interpretation are in most cases not very high – certainly not high enough to provide sufficient support for the claim that, in law generally, successful non-literal assertion requires obviousness. (It is important to keep in mind that the need for legal interpretation is not confined to court cases; officials often have to interpret the law in situations with little or no danger of evolving into full-fledged legal disputes. In many cases, the absence of such danger is exactly due to the relatively low stakes) (Asgeirsson 2017)

Even though there can be good reason to claim that the stakes are even higher in criminal law than in other legal areas, Asgeirsson claims that 'legal systems typically also have a number of relatively insignificant criminal laws – laws with low fine-only options provide a good case in point'. (Asgeirsson 2017)

If the above is correct, then pragmatic enrichment is an important part of legal interpretation that is brought about by the very nature of the tool we call language. Moreover, since the inference does not have to be obvious—just significantly more probable than not—then the requirement to share the contextual background (or information) also becomes weaker. In other words, less shared background is necessary (Asgeirsson 2017).

However, the smaller amount of common ground is not without influence on the enrichment:

> Although a rich conversational background is not – as a general matter – required for successful non-literal assertion, the conversational background will still limit the possibility of such assertion by limiting the ways in which the conversational maxims can be violated and by **limiting the range of plausible candidates** for intended assertive content. [emphasis mine] (Asgeirsson 2017)

If the range of plausible candidates for intended assertive content gets limited, this only facilitates the task of the judge. Such cases are labeled 'easy cases'.

Asgeirsson notices that shared information plays two analytically distinct roles in non-literal assertion: 'the role it plays in determining *that* the speaker intends to assert something other than what she says and the role it plays in determining *what* the speaker intends to assert (instead)' (Asgeirsson 2017). Thus, the difficulty is twofold: even if it is clear that there is need for enrichment, it often remains unclear what sort of enrichment is needed. Consequently, we need a jurisprudential mechanism that mitigates the difficulty.

Let us now come back to Ekins' examples cited at the outset. Asgeirsson claims that only case B can be genuinely explained through a straightforward enrichment of the kind we find in natural language (with the classical Gricean kind of framework). In the other cases, he claims, something else is going on and a different explanation is necessary (Asgeirsson 2017). In case B, 'the Canadian case of Rex v. Liggetts-Findlay Drug Stores Ltd. (…) the issue was whether closing a drug store at 10pm and opening it a little later constituted a violation of a law requiring drug stores to close at 10pm (without further explicit specification).' (Asgeirsson 2017) The enrichment 'and shall stay closed until morning' was quite uncontroversial.[11] By contrast, the other three cases were controversial.

In case A, the court reached a decision that was a clear contradiction of a decision taken 15 years ago on an analogical interpretive issue (Asgeirsson 2017). This is worrying because, as already mentioned, the pragmatic enrichment of a provision by a judge should ideally constitute a 'discovery' of a previously undiscovered content conveyed by the legislature. Yet since the content is developed, then it needs to be consistently applied in future similar cases. Otherwise, we get a peculiar differentiation, which unless justified by a special feature of the context of the case, creates an inequality of subjects in the eyes of the law.[12] The facts of case A, namely Brett v. Brett, were the following:

> the issue was whether the phrase "any will or codicil" – occurring in the Wills Act 1752 – was being used literally by the legislature or to mean 'any will or codicil {of real estate}'; if the former, the phrase included reference to personal property. The judgment in the case was provided by Sir John Nicholl, who held that the phrase, viewed in "connection with its whole context in the statute, is not even difficult to interpret, and was clearly being used to convey the more limited meaning. The judgment was affirmed on appeal by a court of nine judges after hearing Counsel for the Appellant only. (Asgeirsson 2017)

However, 15 years earlier, in *Lees v. Summersgill,* Sir William Grant argued that the context indicates the general interpretation of the expression. As Asgeirsson concludes, 'there is plenty room for disagreement among competent, well-informed interpreters about what the legislature's communicative intention was in enacting the statute.' (Asgeirsson 2017).

Analogously, in case C, the verdict was reached in a ratio of seven to six. Thus, only a single vote decided that an interpretation should prevail. Case D is also problematic: it relies on a mistake of fact made by the legislature (the drafter), rather than an interpretive dispute. 'In Barnard v. Gorman, the issue was whether officials had the authority to detain merely suspected offenders in virtue of the Customs Consolidation Act 1875, which provides that an "offender may either be detained or proceeded against by summons". If not, then persons who are detained but turn out to be innocent are able to recover damages for false imprisonment. It was unanimously held that the only way to make sense of the Act was to read it to include reference to apparent offenders.' (Asgeirsson 2017) Any other interpretation would 'require a conclusive determination of guilt before action could be taken' and this seems absurd (Asgeirsson 2017).

---

[11] Asgeirsson notes that Marmor has a similar example: 'Suppose that a municipal regulation requires cafés and restaurants to have "clean and well-kept indoor restrooms". Given the context of such a requirement, surely it would be implicated by this regulation that the restrooms must be actually open for the patrons to use.' (Marmor 2014).

[12] This is a worry that also appears when one analyses Larry Solum's definition of construction.

While I agree with Asgeirsson that case D is a drafter's mistake, I do not accept the fact that cases A and C cannot be treated as non-literal legislative speech. I believe that if a different framework is applied to them, the mechanisms at stake become clearer and the outcomes less random. Before proceeding to a discussion of this mechanism, let me discuss two more examples provided by Asgeirsson.

The first example has already been mentioned in the previous chapters. It is the case *Church of the Holy Trinity v. US*. Just as a reminder, the purpose of the Alien Contract Labor Act was 'to prohibit the importation and migration of foreigners and aliens under contract or agreement to perform labor in the United States, its Territories, and the District of Columbia'. There was a list of exceptions, including actors, singers etc., but the list did not contain clergyman. The question was whether or not a priest could work in the US. As Asgeirsson notices, even though the ruling claimed that it was commonly understood between Congress and the courts that the aim of the statute was to prevent the importation of 'cheap, unskilled labor', the exception that mentioned 'professional artists' contradicted this claim. Asgeirsson concludes that:

> In this case, it seems to me reasonable to say that the common ground between Congress and the courts was neither rich enough to make it significantly more likely than not that Congress did not intend to prohibit the importation of all types of labor or service, including those of rectors and clergymen, nor rich enough to make it significantly more likely than not that they positively did intend to do so. Taking everything into account, the evidence seems to favor neither claim over the other. If that is correct, the content of the Alien Contract Labor Act was to some extent indeterminate. There is simply no answer to the question "Does the Act apply to people intended to serve as pastors?" (Asgeirsson 2017)

However, does the fact that there is no answer to question mean that the decision was absolutely random?

The second example is *Ali v. Federal Bureau of Prison*. The facts were the following: the Federal Torts Claim Act guaranteed the government immunity from '[a] ny claim arising in respect of [...] the detention of any goods, merchandize, or other property by any officer of customs or excise or any other law enforcement officer'. Taken literally, this should apply to officers of any kind. Yet the court decided to limit this to officers 'working in customs or related domains'. Asgeirsson notes that no element of the context of enactment was such that it could decide whether the narrowing was meant (Asgeirsson 2017). However, again, does this mean that the court made an arbitrary decision?

The above two cases have contexts for which it is not clear *that* the legislature wanted to convey non-literal content. However, Asgeirsson notices similar issues of indeterminacy in cases in which it is indeterminate *what* the enriched content was. An example is *United States v. Gonzales*. The question was whether 'the court could order that a federal prison sentence could run concurrently with a state-imposed sentence, despite the fact that a section of 18 U. S. C. §924 states that a sentence imposed under it "shall [not]... run concurrently with any other term of imprisonment"'. The literal meaning of the provision was excluded since it would be odd, as justice Stevens argued, if a federal statute could command state judges. Moreover, it would be absurd if federal sentences were suspended because of the passing of a state sentence. Thus, on this argumentation, it was highly probable that a non-literal reading was needed. The question remained of *what* the enrichment should be: 'Either Congress intended to use the phrase "any other term of imprisonment" to mean any other term of imprisonment {that has already been imposed} or to mean any other {federal} term of imprisonment' (Asgeirsson 2017).

As stated above, the decision was not whether to enrich but rather, how to enrich. Yet does this mean that the choice between the options was random? Asgeirsson comments that in these cases: 'The general principle here is that even if it may be indeterminate what the content of a particular statute is, the statute still determinately applies to those cases to which it applies on any ***reasonable*** enrichment.' [emphasis mine] (Asgeirsson 2017) The problem with such a formulation is that, as Andrei Marmor argues, there are cases for which there are many 'reasonable' options and some different criterion is needed (Marmor 2016).

Marmor identifies a narrow class of inferences that exhibit a specific kind of defeasibility. He labels this kind of defeasibility 'the conflicting defeat'. This is supposed to generate a genuine indeterminacy of the kind Asgeirsson mentions in his paper. This occurs when 'it becomes indeterminate whether the putative conclusion follows or not; namely, it is a conclusion that **one would not be unreasonable to deny, nor unreasonable to affirm**.' [emphasis mine] (Marmor 2016).

This is supposed to occur in contexts in which 'an inference to implicated content comes into conflict with a salient contextual fact presumed to be common knowledge between speaker and hearer' (Marmor 2016). This happens because a 'superseding premise demonstrates that the usual or the typical fails to obtain in the particular case' (Marmor 2016).

Recall the examples provided by Marmor that I described in chapter one, such as the *FDA vs Brown and Williamson Tobacco Corp* case or the *West Virginia Hospitals vs Casey*. The FDA example especially concerned strong pragmatic effects like conversational implicatures rather than pragmatic enrichments. Nevertheless, the indeterminacy issue was analogous to the one described by Asgeirsson.

As a judge, you cannot ask the legislature for clarifications, thus indeterminacy is inquiry resistant. Does this mean that in the case of an indeterminate hard case it is impossible to predict the judgment? Is the choice of contradictory implicatures or enrichments completely arbitrary? Isn't there a mechanism that descriptively explains what will happen? I attempt to answer this question through the second-order strategic framework that I outline in the present study.

4.4 Baum-Levenbook's Set of Ordered Norms

In her paper 'Beyond legislative intent', Barbara Baum-Levenbook argues that the enrichments are generated by a set of ordered norms. She discusses the following examples:

The already mentioned *Smith v United States* case, the *Regina v. Liggets-Finlay Drug Stores Ltd,* the *Smith v. Hiatt* case and a case discussed by Pufendorf. As a reminder, in *Smith v. US* the statute 'stated that stiffer penalties must be visited upon a defendant who "during and in relation to … a drug trafficking crime, uses …a firearm"'. The added enrichment was 'as a weapon'. (Baum-Levenbook forthcoming) *Regina v. Liggets-Finlay* concerns the Canadian statute, which specifies that all drug shops shall be 'closed at 10 p.m. on each and every day of the week'. The added enrichment is 'and shall not reopen until morning'. In *Smith v. Hiatt* the issue concerned 'the Massachusetts Public Ways and Works Statute', section 21 of the chapter on the 'Repair of Ways and Bridges' notice of claims for injuries from [outdoor] ice and snow suffered on private property must be given in writing to the owners within a certain period of time. The enrichment is in brackets. Finally, Baum-Levenbook cites a statute from Pufendorf, a German jurist from the seventeenth century, that prohibits 'drawing blood in the streets'. The added enrichment is 'by antagonists' (Baum-Levenbook forthcoming).

Her thesis is that all these examples are governed by a set of norms. Moreover, like Marmor, she also deploys the concept of an enrichment based on what an objective hearer would understand in the circumstances. In other words, she claims that sometimes there can be enrichment without intention (more on the issue of challenging Grice's theory of meaning in the next chapter). This is supported by examples of signs or newspaper headings:

1. Don't let worries kill you. Let the church help.
2. Panda mating fails; veterinarian takes over. (Baum-Levenbook forthcoming)

She labels these, after Kent Bach, contextual implicatures. They do not require intention to occur. It is sufficient that the average hearer is able to recover them in the circumstances. She concludes that there must be some epistemic standards or norms for generating such context-independent enrichments. These norms should select some of the most salient features of the context. With this move, Baum-Levenbook wants to avoid a consequence stemming from J. Goldsworthy's moderate intentionalism, namely, epistemic relativism (Goldsworthy 2005). If Baum-Levenbook is correct, then the epistemic norms are stable and they do not vary depending on the epistemic possibilities of the audience. Let us now have a look at the norms. There are four main standards:

1. Normality
2. Unity of subject
3. Relevance
4. Limitation to Jurisdiction (Baum-Levenbook forthcoming)

The normality rule is applied when 'the type of act, situation, circumstance or agent referred to in the statute is the normal or expected type or the difference is made explicit in the statute (As a maxim to legislative drafters: If you want people to do or refrain from doing something normally done one way or under one circumstance in a different way or unusual circumstance, you must make the latter explicit).' (Baum-Levenbook forthcoming) This rule is strikingly similar to a heuristic described by Robin Carston, which can be incorporated into a judicial canon of construction. Remember, the heuristic comes from Grice's second maxim of quantity, 'Do not make your contribution more informative than is required', combined with the maxim of relation, 'be relevant'. This leads to Horn's I principle, 'Say no more than you must'. The I-principle leads Carston to identify a heuristic, 'What is simply/briefly described is the stereotypical or normal (default) instance' (Carston 2013). This seems analogous to the normality rule. As a canon of construction, it has the form '*Eiusdem generis*'. Nevertheless, as already stated in previous chapters, this heuristic has in every context a competing heuristic which leads to contradictory results. This competing heuristic is based on Grice's first maxim of quantity, 'make your contribution as informative as is required (for the current purposes of the exchange)'. This leads to Horn's Q-principle, 'say as much as you (truthfully and relevantly) can'. This in turn leads Carston to the heuristic, 'What isn't said, isn't the case'. This is expressed by the canon, '*Expressio unius est exclusio alterius*'. As Carston has shown, the two often compete with each other and other criteria for making an interpretive decision are employed. This is because, if we apply the two canons to the *Smith v. US* case, we get exactly contradictory results. The *eiusdem generis* canon leads to the interpretation of using a firearm as a weapon. By contrast, the *expressio unius…* leads to the interpretation that any use of a weapon falls within the scope of the provision (Carston 2013).

The second norm identified by Baum-Levenbook is the unity of subject: 'In a written text, a change of subject is explicitly indicated in ways appropriate to the conventions of the genre. (…) As a maxim to writers: make the change of subject explicit in ways appropriate to the genre. The absence of a change of subject marker defeasibly implies a unity of subject.' (Baum-Levenbook forthcoming) Again the expressio unius canon respects the unity of subject. This is because, if the change of subject is explicitly indicated in ways appropriate to the genre, then the subject must be interpreted as the same, following the *expressio unius est exclusion alterius* canon. Unfortunately, the eiusdem generis does not lead to the same result. Quite the contrary, it allows any kind of analogy or broadening of the scope of subjects concerned.

The third norm is relevance. Baum-Levenbook claims that: 'All parts of a single statute are relevant contributions, and so are the statutory title and subtitles of sections. (As a maxim to legislative drafters, a special adaptation of one of Grice's maxims for conversational speakers is required: Make each contribution to the statute relevant)' (Baum-Levenbook forthcoming). This corresponds to a broadly accepted interpretive rule in the Polish tradition (Wronkowska 2005; Zieliński 2012). As claimed in the previous chapters, if we understand relevance in a technical sense, such as for instance Sperber and Wilson, we can genuinely escape relativism and try to find the most relevant result in each case (Carston 2013). The issue is however, that this works only as a normative theory. It does not descriptively explain what judges actually do because, in terms of relevance, the court decisions in hard cases are often counterintuitive, as in *Smith vs US* (see previous chapter).

Finally, Baum-Levenbook's fourth norm is limitation to jurisdiction. 'Absent explicit words to the contrary, the laws, persons, actions, circumstances, and locations referred to in a statute are limited to the jurisdiction of the enacting legislature.' (Baum-Levenbook forthcoming) Again this inference can be defeated with the two contradictory heuristics. Moreover, the recent development of private international law, especially European regulations, seems to contradict this norm.

To sum up, the four norms provided by Baum-Levenbook provide a valuable normative theory of how an idealized interpretive process should be carried out. However, the theory described above is not sufficient to explain why cases involving indeterminacy that could be cured by enrichment or implicature are decided the way they are. A different explanatory framework is necessary.

4.5 Conclusion: Strategic Speech and Pragmatic Enrichment

Let us have a look again at the problematic examples in Table 4.1:

As I hope to have shown, neither Asgeirsson's criterion of reasonableness nor Baum-Levenbook's norms explain the mechanisms that lead to decisions on enrichments or implicatures in such cases. A different framework is needed. As have already stated, I believe that Marmor's strategic framework, with modifications, can give a satisfying explanatory answer. Asgeirsson also seems to have a similar intuition when he writes that 'in the context of directives, the so-called maxim of Quality—which is normally the operative maxim in non-literal assertion—is perhaps best taken to be something like the following: **Do not direct a person to do that which you do not desire/intend/etc.**[13]' [emphasis mine] (Asgeirsson 2017).

This is in line with the strategic principle that I have proposed; let me recall its definition:

I. **Strategic principle (SP): assume that the speech is cooperative, infer all the implicatures/enrichments and then apply the second-order strategic maxims to the inferred implicatures/enrichments (anticipate which implicatures/enrichments your hearer/speaker will choose/ignore)**

The above second-order framework can be equally well applied to implicatures as to enrichments. It fits all the pragmatic processes at stake because it depicts how judges choose from the pragmatic options in indeterminate contexts that follow their goals or purposes, which are often extra-linguistic, namely, political or moral. As you may recall, the content of second-order maxims is the following:

1. The strategic maxim—pursue your goal (independently of your interlocutor's ultimate goal).

[13] You might wonder whether such a reformulation works with an externalist account of meaning. However, to be an externalist does not mean than one is precluded from speaking about legislative intentions. It does not mean claiming that judges cannot reconstruct legislative intentions. It means only to claim that legislative intentions are not reducible to a sum of the psychological mental states of the legislator. Thus, it is always possible to reconstruct the intention on the basis of context and conventions (for instance documents issued by legislative committees about the grounds of legislation, purposes of a statute, social campaigns etc.).

Table 4.1 Famous cases containing discussion of possible pragmatic enrichments

Name of the case	Option 1	Option 2
Pragmatic enrichments		
Brett v. Brett	Any will or codicil	Any will or codicil {of real estate}
Rex v. Harris	Stab, cut or wound any person	Stab, cut or wound any person {with a weapon or instrument}
Barnard v. Gorman	The offender may either be detained or proceeded against by summons	The offender {or apparent offender} may either be detained or proceeded against by summons
Church of the Holy Trinity v. US	Prohibit the importation and migration of foreigners and aliens under contract or agreement to perform labor	Prohibit the importation and migration of foreigners and aliens under contract or agreement to perform {manual} labor
Ali v. Federal Bureau of Prison	[A]ny claim arising in respect of [...] the detention of any goods, merchandize, or other property by any officer	[A]ny claim arising in respect of [...] the detention of any goods merchandize, or other property by any officer {working in customs or related domains}
United States v. Gonzales	Term of imprisonment {that has already been imposed}	{Federal} term of imprisonment
West Virginia University Hospitals v. Casey	A reasonable attorney's fee	A reasonable attorney's fee {as well as expert fees}
Smith v. Hiatt	Notice of claims for injuries from ice and snow suffered on private property must be given in writing to the owners within a certain period of time	Notice of claims for injuries from {outdoor} ice and snow suffered on private property must be given in writing to the owners within a certain period of time
Smith v. US	Use a firearm	Use a firearm {as a weapon}
Pufendorf	Drawing blood in the streets	Drawing blood in the streets {by antagonists}
Implicatures		
FDA vs Brown and Williamson Tobacco Corp.	FDA cannot prohibit the sale of tobacco because it is legal	FDA has the authority to prohibit the sale of tobacco entirely

2. The selectivity maxim—Deny implicated/enriched content that does not conform to your goal.
    a. Maxim of selectivity for the speaker: deny implicated/enriched content formed on the basis of standard maxims if it does not conform to your goal (admit only the implicatures/enrichments you want to admit)
    b. Maxim of selectivity for the hearer: take into account only the content that does conform with your goal (hear only what you want to hear)
3. The anticipation maxim—anticipate the goal of your interlocutor and anticipate what content he may wish to deny

4. The persuasion maxim—model your strategic contribution so as to convince the hearer to join your goal.

These formulations can be boiled down to one super-maxim:

- **The strategic maxim—pursue your goal by selecting conforming implicatures/enrichments**

This is a point at which we come back to the issue stated at the outset of this chapter. The reason for this second-order framework is that the pragmatics of law need a different explanatory theory than the pragmatics of natural language. This intuition is shared by Asgeirsson:

> In the context of non-literal directives, then, the common ground has to contain information about the speaker's relevant attitudes, i.e. about her desires/ends/values/preferences. However, the common ground has to not only contain information about particular attitudes but also – crucially – information about their interrelationship. In this sense, then, the pragmatics of directives is different from – and more complex than – the pragmatics of constatives. And in many types of speech contexts, it is rarely the case that information about the interrelation between the speaker's desires/ends/values/preferences can be taken for granted. This includes law, or so I argue. (Asgeirsson 2017)

Since the legislative goals and ends are often indeterminate, the goals and purposes must be supplied by judges.[14] This is a consequence of the very nature of the language we use:

> the context of legislation rarely determinately contains facts about the appropriate weight to be given to law's various ends, vis-à-vis the relevant legislative utterance. As a result, the common ground relevant for generating non-literal directives is not sufficiently rich, even if the total information knowingly shared is often substantial. (Asgeirsson 2017)

Now, this is not done deliberately by legislatures to render the judicial job more challenging. This is just a consequence of the complexity of democratic procedures of legislation:

> The reason that the relevant information is scarce in the legislative context (…) is that law's ends compete with each other in extremely complex ways – generally, so complex that the structure of "law's preferences", i.e. the relationship that holds between law's various ends, is too complex to be part of what is genuinely taken for granted in legislative speech contexts. (Asgeirsson 2017)

Yet this scarce information cannot be an obstacle to the functioning of the system. Thus, judges are forced to use the strategic framework, due to the 'lack of unequivocal information about legislative intent.' (Asgeirsson 2017)

Asgeirsson provides a definition of the concept of RICHNESS IN LAW*:

[14] In reconstructing the legislative intention, the judge uses some facts that are independent of him; for instance, the text of the statute, committee reports, social campaigns etc. In other words, there are serious constraints on the reconstruction of intentions. Imagine a situation in which 101 members of parliament vote on a statute. 50 endorse version A and 51 endorse version B (vote against version A). An internalist would have to say that it is not possible to state clearly what the legislative intention was. By contrast, an externalist would claim that the intention is the outcome of the rules of voting, namely version B.

> Non-literal legislative speech is successful only if the legislature and its audience share a great deal of (relatively) specific background assumptions regarding the interrelationship between the legislature's desires/ends/values/preferences. (Asgeirsson 2017)

This shows that cases are rather scarce in which it is clear that the legislature intended to communicate something non-literal and it is clear what it has communicated. Yet this does not mean that pragmatic effects in interpretation are scarce. This is because judges need to take concrete decisions; they need to mitigate this epistemic indeterminacy of meaning caused by the legislative process. As Asgeirsson emphasizes: 'it is rarely the case that interpreters have information unequivocal enough to warrant the conclusion that the legislature intended to communicate something non-literal, or – if it does – then to warrant a **unique conclusion** about what non-literal content the legislature intended to communicate.' (Asgeirsson 2017) I treat the strategic framework as a mechanism that explains the often counterintuitive outcomes of judicial debates on concrete decisions in concrete cases. The task of jurisprudence is to design normative mechanisms that constrain the strategic nature of the legal enterprise.

References

Asgeirsson H (2017) On the possibility of non-literal legislative speech. In: Poggi F, Capone A (eds) Pragmatics and law. Perspectives in pragmatics, philosophy & psychology, vol 10. Springer, Cham

Austin J (1832) The province of jurisprudence determined. J. Murray

Austin JL (1962) How to do things with words: [the William James lectures delivered at Harvard University in 1955], 2nd edn, [repr.]. Harvard University Press, Cambridge

Bach K (2006) The excluded middle: semantic minimalism without minimal propositions. Philos Phenomenol Res 73:435–442. https://doi.org/10.1111/j.1933-1592.2006.tb00626.x

Baum-Levenbook B (forthcoming) Beyond legislative intent

Bennion FAR (1990) Bennion on statute law, 3rd edn. Longman, Harlow

Borg E (2006) Minimal semantics. Clarendon, Oxford

Borg E (2012) Pursuing meaning. Oxford University Press, Oxford

Carston R (2012) Metaphor and the literal/non-literal distinction. In: Allan K, Jaszczolt K (eds) The Cambridge handbook of pragmatics. Cambridge University Press, Cambridge

Carston R (2013) Legal texts and canons of construction: a view from current pragmatic theory. In: Freeman MDA, Smith F (eds) Law and language, 1st edn. Oxford University Press, Oxford

Ekins R (2012) The nature of legislative intent, 1st edn. Oxford University Press, Oxford

Fodor JA (1983) The modularity of mind: an essay on faculty psychology. MIT Press, Cambridge

Gibbs RW Jr (2002) A new look at literal meaning in understanding what is said and implicated. J Pragmat 34:457–486. https://doi.org/10.1016/S0378-2166(01)00046-7

Goldsworthy J (1994) Implications in language, law and the constitution. In: Lindell G, Zines L (eds) Future directions in Australian constitutional law: essays in honour of Professor Leslie Zines. Federation Press in association with the Centre for International and Public Law and the Law Faculty. Australian National University, Sydney

Goldsworthy J (2005) Moderate versus strong intentionalism: Knapp and Michaels revisited. San Diego Law Rev 42:669

Hart HLA (2012) The concept of law, 3rd edn. Oxford University Press, Oxford

Horn LR (2006) The border wars: a neo-Gricean perspective. In: von Heusinger K, Turner K (eds) Where semantics meets pragmatics. Elsevier, Amsterdam
Jaszczolt K (2005) Default semantics: foundations of a compositional theory of acts of communication. Oxford University Press, Oxford
Jaszczołt K (2016) Minimalizm a kontekstualizm semantyczny [minimalism versus contextualism about semantics]. In: Odrowąż-Sypniewska J (ed) Przewodnik po filozofii języka [Companion to the philosophy of language]. WAM, Kraków
Kaplan D (1978) Dthat. In: Cole P (ed) Syntax and semantics. Academic Press, pp 221–243
Marmor A (2014) The language of law, 1st edn. Oxford University Press, Oxford
Marmor A (2016) Defeasibility and pragmatic indeterminacy in law. In: Capone A, Poggi F (eds) Pragmatics and law. Perspectives in pragmatics, philosophy & psychology, vol 7. Springer, Cham
Matczak M (2007) Summa iniuria: o błędzie formalizmu w stosowaniu prawa [On the mistake of formalism in applying the law]. Wyd. 1. Wydawn.Nauk. "Scholar", Warszawa
Matczak M (2018) Why judicial formalism is incompatible with the rule of law. Can J Law Jurisprudence 31(1):61–85. https://doi.org/10.1017/cjlj.2018.3
Partee BH (ed) (1989) Binding implicit variables in quantified contexts. In: Compositionality in formal semantics. Blackwell Publishing Ltd, Malden, pp 259–281
Perry J (2012) Reference and reflexivity, 2nd edn. rev. and expanded. Center for the Study of Language and Information, Stanford
Plato (294AD) (1952) Plato's statesman, 2nd edn. Bristol Classical Press, Bristol
Recanati F (2002) Unarticulated constituents. Linguis Philos 25:299–345
Recanati F (2004) Literal meaning. Cambridge University Press, Cambridge
Recanati F (2012) Contextualism: some varieties. In: Allan K, Jaszczolt K (eds) The Cambridge handbook of pragmatics. Cambridge University Press, Cambridge
Skoczeń I (2015) Minimal semantics and legal interpretation. Int J Semiotics Law - Revue Internationale de Sémiotique Juridique. https://doi.org/10.1007/s11196-015-9448-3
Soames S (2013) Deferentialism: a post-originalist theory of legal interpretation. Fordham Law Rev 82:597–617
Stanley J (2000) Context and logical form. Linguist Philos:391–434. https://doi.org/10.1023/A:1005599312747
Stanley J (2002) Making it articulated. Mind Lang 17:149–168. https://doi.org/10.1111/1468-0017.00193
Sternau M, Ariel M, Giora R, Fein O (2015) Levels of interpretation: new tools for characterizing intended meanings. J Pragmat 84:86–101. https://doi.org/10.1016/j.pragma.2015.05.002
Travis C (2008) Occasion-sensitivity: selected essays. Oxford University Press, Oxford
Waldron J (2013) Separation of powers in thought and practice. Boston Coll Law Rev 54:433–468
Waldron J (2016) The rule of law. In: Zalta EN (ed) The Stanford Encyclopedia of Philosophy (Fall 2016 Edition). https://plato.stanford.edu/archives/fall2016/entries/rule-of-law/
Wronkowska S (2005) Podstawowe pojęcia prawa i prawoznawstwa [Basic concepts in the law and jurisprudence]. Ars boni et aequi, Poznań
Zieliński M (2012) Wykładnia prawa. Zasady, reguły, wskazówki [Legal Interpretation. Principles, Rules, Hints], 6th edn. Lexis Nexis, Warszawa

Chapter 5
The Meaning of Law

In the previous chapters I argued for a strategic framework that required a counterfactual assumption of the Gricean theory and an application of second-order strategic rules. I also discussed the necessity of preserving Gricean maxims as well as the Gricean notion of 'what is said'. This chapter will be devoted to the Gricean notion of meaning and reference.

Paul Grice is mostly recognized for his pragmatic theory concerning the mechanisms leading to implicature formation and grasping; however, he also created an internalist theory of meaning. This chapter will explore the relation between the Gricean theory of implicature and the Gricean theory of meaning.

The nature of meaning has puzzled philosophers of language for centuries. There are two principal stances in the debate on what constitutes meaning: internalism and externalism. Internalism claims that a speaker's communicative intentions constitute meaning; by contrast, externalists claim that certain sorts of factors external to the speaker's mind constitute meaning. For instance, these can be conventions, fixed expression meanings, lexical meanings, compositional rules etc.

Paul Grice took an internalist stance in the debate, yet this does not straightforwardly imply that if one wants to endorse the implicature theory, one has to be an internalist about meaning. There are two possible ways of perceiving the relation between the theory of implicatures and the theory of meaning. The first way perceives the implicature theory as a metaphysical theory. This reading treats the speaker's intention as a necessary requirement of the implicature's existence and can be paraphrased with the slogan 'No intention – no implicature'. The metaphysical theory aims to answer the following question: 'In virtue of what facts does someone, S, mean whatever he or she means by performing something, x, on a given occasion?' (Neale 2016)

However, there is another interpretation, which, as I shall argue, is better for the legal realm. It claims that the implicature theory is merely an epistemological theory that aims to answer the following question: 'What sorts of information, what principles, and what types of cognitive states and processes are involved in the (typically spontaneous) arrival in the mind of an interpreter of a (typically resilient)

I. Skoczeń, *Implicatures within Legal Language*, Law and Philosophy Library 127, https://doi.org/10.1007/978-3-030-12532-5_5

conclusion about what S means by performing x on that occasion?' (Neale 2016) This, as I shall argue, entails that the Gricean theory of pragmatics stands independently of whether one is an internalist or an externalist about meaning in the metaphysical sense.

Since the strategic framework (precisely the strategic principle) requires only a counterfactual assumption of the Gricean framework, the theory of meaning in the law does not need to be internalistic. Consequently, I will depict the inadequacy of the Gricean theory of meaning in the legal framework and endorse an externalist account of meaning in the realm of law.

To sum up, in this chapter I will first discuss the range of possible views on meaning and reference in natural language, starting from a strong, reductive internalism up to a strong externalism. Second, my claim will be twofold. I will argue for a moderate internalist account of meaning in natural language and an externalist account of meaning in linguistic exchanges within the realm of law. I intend to depict that the strategic framework requires an externalist view of meaning and reference.

5.1 Intention in Natural Language

Let us first proceed with an overview of the possible stances on meaning and reference in natural language. Before proceeding let me clarify one trivial yet important claim. Both the internalist and externalist must agree that people and their communicative intentions (whatever they are) were developed prior to language. If there were no human beings, language would not exist.[1] However, the discussion between the internalist and externalist is about a different matter: it is about which factor should be decisive when deciding the meaning of an utterance. In this discussion we need to acknowledge that the chronological order of events is a bit more complex. At the very beginning of language development there were probably only intentions. However, as time passed, these intentions led to the creation of certain conventions (whatever their definition). Next, those conventions had a strong (at least causal and etiological) influence on the communicative intentions formed. Thus, the discussion between internalists and externalists is about how to strike a balance between meaning being constituted solely by a speaker's intention and meaning constituted solely by convention. The answer probably lies somewhere between the two options.

---

[1] Even the strong externalist, when faced with a sentence accidentally formed by the sea waves on the beach, has to claim that there is no meaning because there was no primary intention. 'Meaninglessness is something objective, independent of the evidence we may have for ascertaining it. If marks were not produced by a purposeful intelligence intending them to mean something, then they are meaningless whatever we may justifiably believe given the evidence available to us.' (Goldsworthy 2005).

5.1.1 The Reductive Program of the Internalist

In a paper entitled 'Dthat' from 1979, David Kaplan describes an example that has become philosophically famous:

> Suppose that without turning and looking I point to the place on my wall which has long been occupied by a picture of Rudolf Carnap and say:
>
> (I.) Dthat[2] [I point as above] is a picture of one of the greatest philosophers of the twentieth century.
>
> But unbeknownst to me, someone has replaced my picture of Carnap with Spiro Agnew. (…)[3] (Kaplan 1979)

The example is well suited for our purposes because it depicts the inherent link between meaning and reference in demonstratives. Roughly, the possible stances in the above situation are the following:

(II.) With (I) Kaplan has referred to Rudolf Carnap.
(III.) With (I) Kaplan did not refer to anyone.
(IV.) With (I) Kaplan referred to both Rudolf Carnap and Spiro Agnew.
(V.) With (I) Kaplan referred to Spiro Agnew.

The order of the possibilities is not random. (II) depicts the stance of the strongest and most reductive internalist. The next possibilities are a route toward externalism.

Since we do not dispose of any instrument that would allow us to literally read other people's minds, what could be the possible motivation of such a strong, reductive internalist as in (II)? Let me try to formulate the main argument that backs up stance (II). I will call it the argument from erasing (AE). Imagine the above situation really happened and imagine that later the speaker clarifies to the hearer what he meant. In other words, Kaplan tells his hearer explicitly that through (I) he did not mean Spiro Agnew, but Rudolf Carnap. Surely, the speaker can be criticized for being not clear enough, careless, misleading and so forth. Yet, it seems that once one is aware of what the speaker REALLY meant, one no longer feels fully warranted to claim that what Kaplan meant was Spiro Agnew rather than Rudolf Carnap. In other words, there is a tendency to either erase or put less emphasis on what the hearer previously and mistakenly thought the speaker meant. Thus, natural language communication naturally strives toward absolute transparency of intentions and the

[2] This is a special demonstrative that Kaplan introduces in his paper 'Dthat': 'It is just according to the demonstrative analysis that the sense does not appear in the proposition. Instead the sense is used only to fix the demonstratum, which itself appears directly in the proposition. I propose now to do the same for descriptions. Instead of taking the sense of the description as the subject of the proposition, we use the sense only to fix the denotation which we then take directly as the subject component of the proposition.' (Kaplan 1979).

[3] Kaplan continues and takes an externalist stance: 'I think it would be simply wrong to argue an ambiguity in the demonstration that is so great that it can be bent toward my intended demonstratum. I have said of a picture of Spiro Agnew that it pictures one of the greatest philosophers of the twentieth century. And my speech and demonstration suggest no other natural interpretation to the linguistically competent public observer.' (Kaplan 1979).

decoding of these intentions. We, as hearers, really want to understand what the speaker means. The high value we attribute to a speaker's clarifications is an argument for the strong, reductive internalist. What counts are just intentions. Mistakes and misunderstandings can be (and need to be) erased in order to favor what was really meant to be communicated.[4]

Now, while the argument from erasing seems to work fairly well in Kaplan's example, things get much less clear when we come to more controversial situations. Consider another example: a speaker wishing to refer to a cat calls it a dog. In absence of special context, it seems impossible for the average hearer to know what the speaker really meant. The hearer has no device and no cue to know the speaker's intention if the speaker does not clarify explicitly what he meant. Thus, there is the need to introduce the notion of expectations. The speaker can have many wild intentions but only some of them will be proper communicative intentions. Communicative intentions are intentions for which a speaker considers expectations of how hearers will understand his utterance. Otherwise, 'anything goes' and you could mean anything by any symbol or act (and you could never be wrong 'in saying').

[4]Montminy has a similar reflection to Gauker's example. Let me first quote Gauker's example and then Montminy's response. I owe the selection of quotes to Palle Leth: 'Suppose that Harry and Sally are at a department store and Harry is trying on ties. Harry has wrapped a garish pink-and-green tie around his neck and is looking at himself in a mirror. Sally is standing next to the mirror gazing toward the tie around Harry's neck and says, "That matches your new jacket". As a matter of fact, Sally has been contemplating in thought the tie that Harry tried on two ties back. At first, she thought she did not like it, but then it occurred to her that it would look good with Harry's new jacket. We can even suppose that in saying "that" what she intended to refer to was the tie two ties back. But under the circumstances, Harry is in no position to realize that the tie she intended to refer to was the tie two ties back and therefore is in no position to take Sally's intention into account in identifying the reference of her demonstrative "that". The only thing one could reasonably expect Sally's demonstrative "that" to refer to is the pink-and-green tie around Harry's neck. So, if we said that the referent of Sally's demonstrative was the tie she intended to refer to, we could not maintain that the proposition her utterance expressed was a proposition that Harry could assign to it using a method of interpretation that he could reliably employ on the basis of features of the situation of which he could normally be aware. Instead, we should say that the reference of her demonstrative was the pink-and-green tie around Harry's neck.' (Gauker 2008) Montminy replied: 'The intuition invoked by Gauker thus concerns the interpretation Harry may legitimately take to be the correct one rather than the correct interpretation (Åkerman, 2009 makes the same point). One may think that this debate amounts to a mere clash of intuitions. But the intentionalist position is better supported by the following scenario. Suppose that later on in the day, Sally and Harry are having this conversation: Harry: I decided to buy the pink-and-green tie because you said it matches my new jacket. Sally: I never said that. I was talking about the yellow tie, which you tried on two ties before the pink-and-green one. It would be odd for Harry to reply, "Well, I now understand that you were trying to say that the yellow tie matches my new jacket; but what you actually said was that the pink-and-green tie matches my new jacket". In other words, it would seem unreasonable for Harry to insist that when Sally said, "That matches your new jacket", 'that' actually referred to the pink-and-green tie, despite Sally's intention to refer to the yellow one. The right thing for Harry to do is to concede that he misunderstood Sally's assertion, even though, he may add, he was quite justified in believing that her utterance concerned the pink-and-green tie. (…) However, instead of saying that Sally's utterance of "that" failed to refer to what she intended to refer to, we should say, more plausibly, that Sally failed to make clear what her utterance actually referred to.' (Montminy 2010).

The introduction of even minimal expectations or communicative intention is the first step toward externalism because we need to fix the threshold for how strict the expectations must be. In other words, we need a standard for the reasonableness of the hearer. We need more than just expectations, we need reasonable expectations. Standards vary between hearers. The more we know our interlocutor and the more common knowledge and experience we have, the less strict our threshold needs to be. Blatant cases are idiolects. If, we, as hearers, are aware that the speaker is using an idiolect, and he always calls cats dogs and dogs cats, the speaker will be licensed to form a communicative intention by using his idiolect.[5] Yet if the speaker knows that the hearer has no chance of recognizing the intention whatsoever, the communicative intention cannot be formed. It will be some other non-communicative intention. You simply cannot rationally intend the impossible. Neale puts it neatly:

> The formation of genuine intentions is severely constrained by beliefs. I cannot intend to become a prime number, intend to digest my food through my lungs on alternate Tuesdays, or swim from New York to Sydney because (roughly) I cannot intend what I believe to be impossible (Neale 2005)

Thus, the overall mechanism is the following:

> What this all means is that my modal constraint on intentions has considerable bite when it comes to communicative intentions. For S to form a genuine communicative intention, S must, in effect, quickly pair a proposition and a sentence X in a special way: S must think that by uttering X, S will likely get his audience, A, to recognize that S intends A to think that p (for example), at least partly on the basis of recognizing that S uttered X intending A to think that p. The formation of such an intention is constrained by S's beliefs. If S believes A will not recognize that S intends A to think that p, for example, then S doesn't communicatively intend A to believe that p, so S does not mean that p by uttering X. (Neale 2016)

The constraints on the intention called 'expectations' seem to be the source of the concept of 'expression meaning'. Words have stable meanings because this is such an excellent device for speakers when forming their communicative intentions. Thus, speakers can use linguistic conventions, linguistic regularities, features of the context etc. to form communicative intentions. Moreover, speakers can exploit semantics and context so as to form extra-semantic meaning on the basis of inferential frameworks such as the maxims of conversation etc.

To conclude, not every intention is a communicative intention. A communicative intention is an intention at least potentially recognizable by a reasonable, objective[6] listener in the circumstances.

Coming back to Kaplan's example, if one allows that it is the speaker's intention that constitutes meaning but it has to be a communicative intention, then one should claim that the speaker has not referred to Carnap because the hearer had no way of figuring out who he genuinely wanted to refer to. Consequently, the speaker would have failed to refer to anyone and it would be a case of (III).

---

[5] Or his malapropisms.

[6] Objective in the sense used by practitioners. A hearer that has a personal interest in adopting one rather than another interpretation is not objective. A judge whose wife is counsel for a claimant is not objective.

If, however, the audience knew that previously, instead of a photo of Spiro Agnew, a photo of Rudolf Carnap had been hanging on the wall for the last 10 years, things would change. Then, the speaker would be perfectly licensed in forming a communicative intention to refer to Rudolf Carnap and the reference would be successful, as in case (II). This would be a consequence of special circumstances that would change the standard of expectations of reasonable hearers.

To sum up, the advantage of such internalist approaches is twofold. First, they favor the transparency of genuine communication. This is a communication in which no manipulative behavior occurs. What counts is to understand the speaker. This seems to capture the intuition that when the speaker tells us what he REALLY meant, we tend not to feel fully warranted to claim that he meant what we understood he meant. Second, an undeniable advantage of every reductive program is that it does not postulate any ontologically dubious entities beyond absolute necessity. There must be some intentions, but the existence of independent and objective conventions, expressions, literal meaning etc. may not be necessary. All these elements reduce to the intention of the speaker. If there is no communicative intention, then there is no speaker's meaning.

5.1.2 The Program of the Externalist

To be an externalist is to postulate the existence of literal meaning and conventions as public artefacts formed by a community. Words, expressions, sentences and utterances have a public meaning that is always constitutive of the meaning of a sentence uttered. Individual speaker intentions are not to be taken under consideration. The first step in recognizing literal and external meaning is:

1. (IV) With (I) Kaplan referred to both Rudolf Carnap and Spiro Agnew.

This is an intermittent position in which one still wants to honor the speaker's communicative intention but simultaneously wants to recognize the literal meaning of what has been said as an important factor in the meaning definition—a clear farewell to reductionism.

Finally, a fully externalist stance is:

2. (V) With (I) Kaplan referred to Spiro Agnew.

Here, speaker intentions need not even be present. They are not a determinant or constituent of meaning: only external factors count. Externalism overturns the idea of communicating as having a source in what a human wants to convey: it is not the will to convey which is of central interest; rather, it is what has been conveyed that is at issue.

The drawback is that a strong externalist must accept linguistic indeterminacy; imagine someone utters the following sentence: 'Mary has a nice green hat.'

If in the room where the speaker uttered the sentence above there are two Marys, both wearing green hats, then the externalist must conclude that the statement is indeterminate. By contrast, the internalist will claim that it was the speaker's intention that determined which Mary was indicated.

In the externalism versus internalism debate on meaning, we are not interested in how it is that speakers form utterances (what Neale refers to as formatics, see below). We are not interested in how it is possible that hearers decode the utterances (what Neale labels pragmatics, see below). We are not interested in any epistemological issue. All we are interested in is what constitutes or determines meaning, and this is an utterly non-empirical debate.

For internalists, conventions or literal meaning are just tools. For externalists they are a determinant and constituent of meaning. Even if it is never possible to state ultimately who is right and who is wrong, there seems to be one very noticeable regularity. While in natural language we have this intuitive tendency to seek to discover the real speaker's intention, in the legal realm any disputes about intention are externalist in the sense that we are arguing over what external elements of the context can count as constituents of a constructed intention (and the idea of an intention as a mental state is misguided). This is probably a consequence of a substantial difference between everyday conversation and legal discourse. In ordinary conversation we can leave some indeterminacy as to what the conveyed meaning is. By contrast, in the legal realm we have to make a clear decision within a relatively limited period of time.

Let me proceed in the following order. First, I will show the difference between the discussion on meaning and the discussion on pragmatics. Second, I will present more stances on the metaphysical nature of meaning. Third, I will reject the Gricean definition of meaning for the strategic framework and adopt an externalist definition of meaning that will suit it.

5.2 Meaning Versus Pragmatics: Some Terminological Clarifications

The discussion between internalism and externalism about meaning and reference is a discussion in metaphysics. The Gricean theory of meaning is also *par excellence* ontological:

> The definitions of speaker meaning that Griceans have articulated, examined, refuted, and refined are meant to specify what is constitutive of speaker meaning, of the facts in virtue of which someone who does such-and-such on a given occasion thereby means that so-and-so. (Neale 2016)

The discussion about what constitutes or determines meaning needs to be separated from what Neale calls pragmatics; that is, from the epistemology of language. We need to separate '(i) accounts of what S said and what S meant by uttering X and (ii) accounts of how hearers recover what S said and what S meant by uttering X' (Neale 1992).

There is a difference between what influences the formation of an intention, what makes the hearer understand what he has understood, and what constitutes the meaning itself. Moreover, this difference occurs irrespectively of whether one holds internalist or externalist views.

Usually, the speaker's expectations that influence the formation of his communicative intention are mirrored by the inferences of the hearer. For instance, if the speaker wants to use an idiolect, he needs to make some calculation—he needs to assess whether his hearer knows his idiolect. Analogously, the hearer has to reason in the following way: since I know that the speaker is using an idiolect, he intends me to understand his words according to his idiolect rather than the standard conventional meaning. Thus, if everything goes well, the calculations of the speaker are mirrored by the calculations of the hearer. Yet these calculations are separate from the question of what really constitutes or determines meaning. The latter is a purely metaphysical question that does not have much to do with the epistemology of language. The epistemological question has to be answered by a theory of interpretation, and the metaphysical question has to be answered by a theory of meaning (Neale 2005).

Stephen Neale goes one step further in the division of matters at stake and identifies three different questions. In his jargon they are respectively called metaphysics, pragmatics and formatics and are defined as below:

> (CQ – constitutive determination) In virtue of what facts someone, S, means, whatever he or she means by performing something, x, on a given occasion?
>
> (EQ – epistemic determination) What sorts of information, what principles, and what types of cognitive states and processes are involved in the (typically spontaneous) arrival in the mind of an interpreter of a (typically resilient) conclusion about what S means by performing x on that occasion?
>
> (AQ – aetiological determination) What sorts of information, what principles, and what types of cognitive states and processes are involved in the formation of the communicative intentions S has in performing x on that occasion? (Neale 2016)

The first question is metaphysical; the second is pragmatic in Neale's sense (it is about the epistemology of language); the third is formatic. They all require separate answers. Consequently, all the previous chapters of this study have been focused on answering the second question. I have argued that the Gricean answer to the second question, if modified, can be applied to the legal framework in its strategic form.

In his article 'Meaning revised', Grice formulated his final answer to the first question, and this is an internalist answer. Grice's answer to the second question is his theory of implicatures. I stated earlier that a modification of Grice's views is needed. If we are to modify the Gricean approach, then what could be perceived as unclear is the relation between the first and the second question in our modified account. There are two possibilities. First, the implicature theory could be viewed as an answer to both the first and the second questions (a conflation of both questions). This would entail that anyone who accepted the Gricean framework for recovering implicatures would have to accept the internal stance on meaning. However, there is also a second possibility, which I will endorse: Grice's implicature theory could be modified to be read as only an epistemological theory, constituting only an answer to the second question—EQ. This would entail that one could coherently accept the Gricean epistemological framework and simultaneously hold either internal or external views about the answer to the first question—CD.

The modified version of Grice's work enables me to coherently build a theory by which everyday linguistic exchanges are explained in a way closer to internalist views, while the legal language issues will find an explanation with a more externalist flavor. Simultaneously, this version does not preclude me from upholding the implicature theory and the strategic framework as epistemological devices.

The answer to the epistemological question in natural language is an answer pertaining to 'cognitive psychology' because it involves 'reaching conclusions about speaker meaning by the hearer' (Neale 2016). In natural language, these processes may be unconscious, while in the law the entire strategic enterprise and the legal interpretation processes seem to be conscious to a much greater extent. Legal interpretation aims to justify and give reasons for a decision, rather than justify an unconscious hunch.

Still, the distinction between Neale's formatics and pragmatics is useful to legal theory. Jurisprudential considerations of judicial interpretation of laws also seem to be devoted to two different issues. First, there is the question of which processes influence the formation of a legal text within the legislature. As I mentioned in chapter one, the Polish system has codified rules of drafting legal text in the form of a 'rozporządzenie' (sub-statutory document issued by a minister). Second, there are the issues of interpretation and the question of what can be taken as a cue or an indicator of the meaning of the law. Normatively speaking, the maxims of interpretation should mirror (as much as possible) the drafting rules. Analogously, when a perfect communicative success occurs in natural language, the formatic considerations of the speaker mirror the pragmatic inferences of the hearer. Together, pragmatics and formatics form a theory of communication. In the legal case, if it is communication at all, then it is communication in a broader, somewhat attenuated sense because it is often not transparent, and strategic or manipulative behavior gives it a very specific flavor.

Stephen Neale emphasizes the fact that, as a consequence of the above considerations, there are two conceptually different elements:

> (i) What S meant by uttering X (on a given occasion)
>
> (ii) What S's addressee, A, took S to mean by uttering X (on that occasion).
>
> When things go well, (i) and (ii) coincide. When they do not, it is too bad. But no philosophical puzzle results when (i) $\neq$ (ii), when, for example, S meant that p, but A took S to mean p′. (Neale 2016)

In everyday conversational context, the above claim, although controversial, could be acceptable because it is possible to leave some indeterminacy as to what has been ultimately communicated. By contrast, in the legal realm this kind of approach is not acceptable because most of the time a clear decision must be taken.

Neale concedes that even in standard conversation, a third option can be introduced:

> There is some third thing theorists can talk about, but it is **not** something for which (i) and (ii) are candidates:
>
> (iii) What a reasonable, attentive, informed interpreter would take S to mean by uttering X (on that occasion).
>
> When we construct pragmatic [in Neale's sense – IS's comment] theories of utterance interpretation, we cannot help thinking in terms of (iii), but that is because a pragmatic theory is an idealized theory of the epistemic determination of what speakers mean, not a theory of its constitutive determination. Similarly, when we construct formatic theories of utterance planning, we cannot help thinking in terms of (iv):
>
> (iv) What a reasonable, attentive, informed speaker would mean by uttering X (on a given occasion).
>
> And that's because a formatic theory is an idealized theory of the aetiological determination of the communicative intentions with which speakers produce their utterances. (Neale 2016)

This third idealizing option is precisely what should be taken under consideration by a model speaker or hearer. Thus, when legal theorists construe normative, pragmatic theories of legal interpretation, they should defer to (iii) and (iv). By contrast, (i) and (ii) are claims of descriptive theories of pragmatics. Crucially, (iii) in a particular situation can be identical to either (i) or to (ii), or it is completely different in content. Theories of interpretation of declarations of intent in contract law tend to favor (ii) or (iii). They are interesting for the present considerations because they depict how the law views questions of meaning of utterances performed by agents such as parties during negotiations.

This can be illustrated with provisions from various legal systems. I will discuss article 8 of the Vienna Convention on the International Sale of Goods, articles 60 and 65 of the Polish civil code (PCC), article 133 of the German Bürgerliches Gesetzbuch (BGB) and articles 104 and 105 of the French Code Civil (FCC).

All the above rules claim that if there is disagreement in a courtroom concerning what a party meant, the understanding of the hearer in the circumstances or the understanding of an objective hearer will be favored. They clearly favor an externalist view of meaning in natural language. Consider article 8 from the Vienna Convention on the International Sale of Goods (CISG):

> '(1) For the purposes of this Convention, statements made by and other conduct of a party are to be interpreted according to his intent where the other party knew or could not have been unaware what that intent was.
> (2) If the preceding paragraph is not applicable, statements made by and other conduct of a party are to be interpreted according to the understanding that a reasonable person of the same kind as the other party would have had in the same circumstances.
> (3) In determining the intent of a party or the understanding a reasonable person would have had, due consideration is to be given to all relevant circumstances of

the case including the negotiations, any practices which the parties have established between themselves, usages and any subsequent conduct of the parties.'[7]

Paragraph one stipulates that the speaker's intention (i) will be taken under consideration only if the hearer has recognized it. Thus, (i) must equal (ii); otherwise, (i) will be dismissed. If, however, the hearer had no way to recognize the speaker's intention, paragraph two comes into play. It is precisely here that we make use of the idealization of (iii). Paragraph three is just a definition of context.

Now, let me recall the example in which David Kaplan pointed to a picture of Spiro Agnew when he wanted to refer to Rudolf Carnap. According to article 8, the solution would be as follows: if the hearers of Kaplan's words had been aware that for the last 10 years at this very same place a picture of Rudolf Carnap had been hanging, paragraph one would have been applicable. This would have resulted in Kaplan's intention to refer to and mean that Rudolf Carnap was respected. If, however the hearers had had no way of decoding Kaplan's intention, then, according to paragraph two, Kaplan would have been taken as referring to Spiro Agnew. Thus, in a pragmatic, epistemological theory, it is the idealized interpretation (iii) that is prevalent in the legal realm. Jeffrey Goldsworthy endorses a similar position: 'People can justifiably be bound by promises they appear to make because otherwise contracts would be unenforceable: parties could always claim later that they did not really intend to enter into them, and it would be impossible to prove that they did. (…) People are held responsible for what they appear to have said, regardless of what they may have intended to say. (…) We conceive of utterances as something essentially public, and not – like desires, pains or other mental states – as something essentially private of which we can have only indirect evidence.' (Goldsworthy 2005)

Analogously, article 60 of the PCC claims that:

'Subject to the exceptions provided for in the law, the intention of a person performing a legal act may be expressed by any behavior of that person which manifests his intention sufficiently, including the intent being expressed in electronic form (declaration of intent).'[8]

This provision clearly favors an externalist view of meaning. A sufficient manifestation of an intention is one that can be grasped by a hearer. Again, meaning collapses into (ii).

At first sight, article 65 paragraph two of the PCC seems to endorse an internalist view of language:

---

[7] See http://www.cisg.law.pace.edu/cisg/text/treaty.html.

[8] Art. 60 [Declaration of intent] Subject to the exceptions provided for in the law, the intention of a person performing a legal act may be expressed by any behavior of that person which manifests his intention sufficiently, including the intent being expressed in electronic form (declaration of intent).

'§ 1. A declaration of intent should be interpreted in view of the circumstances in which it is made as required by principles of community life and established custom.
§ 2. In contracts, the common intention of the parties and the aim of the contract should be examined rather than its literal meaning.'[9]

Yet an internalist reading of paragraph two is a mistaken deception. Commentaries on the PCC state that when interpreting contracts we usually have two competing interpretations: the subjective and the objective. The subjective interpretation is based on what the parties jointly declare as to the meaning of the provisions of their contract. If the parties are unanimous and there is a 'meeting of minds', the subjective interpretation prevails. However, if the parties are not unanimous, it is the objective interpretation that wins.[10] The objective interpretation is based on the literal meaning of the contractual provision and on reasoning about what an objective and reasonable hearer would have understood in the circumstances. Externalism wins again.[11,12] (Robaczyński 2014)

[9]Art. 65 [Interpretation] § 1. A declaration of intent should be interpreted in view of the circumstances in which it is made as required by principles of community life and established custom. § 2. In contracts, the common intention of the parties and the aim of the contract should be examined rather than its literal meaning.

[10] 'In non-standard cases, for example a discrepancy between a testament and its external manifestation, priority should be given to the manifestation of the will as the element which is subject to a standard and is an accessible source of information about the declaration of the will/intent.' [translated by IS] (Gwiazdomorski 1974).

[11] 'First priority is to be given to the genuine will of the parties. If it turns out however, that the parties did not ascribe the same meaning to their declaration of intent, we should proceed to the second phase, in which in an objective manner the meaning of the declaration is established, taking under consideration how the addressee of the declaration understood its sense and how he should understand it (see. A. Szpunar, W sprawie wykładni zobowiązania wekslowego [The interpretation of obligations arising out of exchange bills], PPH 1996, nr 4, s. 10). Similarly, P. Machnikowski states that the actions of the institution that applies the law undertaken to interpret the declaration of intent consist of two stages. First, the understanding of the parties is to be established, as well as whether both parties had a similar understanding (this is called the subjective interpretation and it consists more of establishing facts than interpreting). When it is not possible to establish a shared understanding by the parties, it is necessary to resort to the second stage, namely, the objective interpretation. According to P. Machnikowskiego, it is only in the second stage that we are facing interpretation.' (P. Machnikowski (in:) Kodeks cywilny [Civil Code]..., red. E. Gniewek, s. 155). This jurisprudence is backed by recent case law. In the ruling from the 13th of June 2012, II CSK 614/11, LEX nr 1231314, the Highest Court stated that: 'As far as the interpretation of declarations of intent on the basis of art. 65 k.c. is concerned, a hybrid method of interpretation is to be applied, based on the subjective and objective criterion, so as to aim to discover the real will of the parties. The text of a document and the linguistic rules of meaning constitute the basis for the interpretation of the declarations contained in them. We should also take into account, when interpreting concrete expressions, the context and the content relations between the text and the goal of the declaration. If the declarations are not clear, we should take into account the circumstances.' [translated by IS] (Robaczyński 2014).

[12] 'Art. 65 commits a kind of category mistake, conflating what is interpretation of linguistic utterances with the means by which it is facilitated. There is neither meaning nor interpretation without explicit or implicit reference to intentions of communicating agents. Such intentions are inferred

Article 133 of the BGB creates a very similar mistaken impression of internalism:

> 'Section 133, Interpretation of a declaration of intent: When a declaration of intent is interpreted, it is necessary to ascertain the true intention rather than adhering to the literal meaning of the declaration.'[13]

Commentaries on the aforementioned article reveal why the impression of internalism is mistaken. They state that the true intention needs to be externalized by the speaker; otherwise, it cannot count because we need to protect the trust and good will of our interlocutors. Thus, the 'true intention' counts only if a reasonable hearer can grasp it.[14]

Finally, articles 104 and 105 of the FCC adopt similar rules for the interpretation of legal declarations of intent:

> 'Art. 104 Proof of that intention shall result from an express declaration made both to the municipality of the place which one leaves and to that of the place where the domicile is transferred.
> Art. 105 Failing an express declaration, proof of intention shall depend on circumstances.'[15]

Both provisions pertain to the ascertaining of the domicile of a person. According to the FCC, a domicile requires the real fact of living in a place plus the intention of staying in this place. The intention is taken under consideration only if, according to article 104, the speaker makes an explicit declaration of his intent. In other words, she needs to externalize it with the use of linguistic conventions, otherwise such a '*reservatio mentalis*' does not count. Moreover, if there is no such explicit declaration, it is the circumstances—the context—that is decisive, and again external factors win the game.

on the basis of external evidence in which the basic role is played by the selection of precisely this or that linguistic means. The difference between more "textualist" (objective) and "intentionalist" (subjective) approaches to legal interpretation is actually in the scope in which other kinds of evidence is admissible and allowed to supplement or prevail over that basic and central piece of evidence.' (Pietrzykowski and Tobor 2010).

[13] § 133 Auslegung einer Willenserklärung: Bei der Auslegung einer Willenserklärung ist der wirkliche Wille zu erforschen und nicht an dem buchstäblichen Sinne des Ausdrucks zu haften.

[14] Meinung dazu, dass § 133 BGB auf dem Gebiet der empfangsbedürftigen Willenserklärung geradezu entgegen seinem Wortlaut verstanden werden muss. Grundsätzlich ist bei der Auslegung empfangsbedürftiger Willenserklärungen gerade nicht auf das subjektiv wirklich Gewollte, sondern auf die Verständnismöglichkeit des objektiven Empfängerhorizonts abzustellen. Maßgeblich ist also, wie der Empfänger die Erklärung bei objektiver Würdigung innerhalb des betroffenen Rechts- bzw. Personenkreises verstehen durfte. Dabei sind der Erklärungsakt selbst, aber auch alle weiteren Begleitumstände, wie z.B. vorangegangene Gespräche, Geschäftsbeziehungen oder Verkaufsprospekte in einem Gesamtkontext zu berücksichtigen. Source: http://bgb.kommentar.de/Buch-1/Abschnitt-3/Titel-2/Auslegung-einer-Willenserklaerung.

[15] Article 104 (code civil) La preuve de l'intention résultera d'une déclaration expresse, faite tant à la municipalité du lieu que l'on quittera, qu'à celle du lieu où on aura transféré son domicile. Art 105 A défaut de déclaration expresse, la preuve de l'intention dépendra des circonstances.

Additionally, the Polish doctrine of civil law has pronounced itself broadly on the subject. To understand the doctrine's claims, two notions must be introduced: the notion of a legal act and the notion of a legal declaration of intent. A legal act is an act performed by an agent of the system in order to achieve some legal consequences. For a legal act to occur, according to the standard claim, at least one declaration of intent is required (this is a necessary yet not always sufficient condition). A legal declaration of intent is a declaration of one's will to cause some legal consequences. This cannot be interpreted as a manifestation of a psychological will of the agent because there are cases in which there simply could not be such a will and yet the law acts (counterfactually) as if it were existent. This is the case with so-called 'deception' (art 83 of the PCC). The parties to a contract may deceive observers by making them believe that they are concluding a sales contract while in reality they are concluding a donation contract (for instance to avoid higher taxation). In such cases, the parties cannot have the intention/will to conclude a sales contract. Yet in some cases the PCC treats them as having the intention to conclude a faked contract. One of the reasons for such rules is the protection of the mutual trust of agents in a legal system. These cases show that internalism and psychological criteria are not decisive for the realm of law.[16] (Gwiazdomorski 1974)

One must be careful when analyzing the Polish civil law doctrine in philosophical terms because it tackles, for instance, the issue of non-existing legal acts. Yet this is not an ontological claim. A legal act is non-existent when there is no epistemological access to the outcome of rules that should be abided during its formation. Thus, the language of the civil law doctrine is an epistemological language. Since only the externalist can conflate the epistemological and ontological answer about meaning, the epistemological language of the civil law doctrine is another argument for its externalist character.[17] (Gizbert-Studnicki 1975)

The reason that legal texts have an external vision of meaning is probably the fact that epistemological access to intention may be impossible. Since theories of legal interpretation or of contract interpretation are practical theories, they must take into account facts about epistemology. They cannot remain strictly metaphysical:

---

[16] '(...) [I notice] the necessity of objectifying the notion of declaration of intent through defining it in the following way: "a declaration of intent is every behavior of a person", instead of defining it as "undertaken to achieve a legal goal", let's replace it with something like the following: "which implies – in virtue of the circumstances, the social rules and settled conventions – the will to declare the intent to achieve a concrete legal effect". In the above definition, the notion of declaration of intent is not subjective but objective because emphasis is put not on the internal will of the person making the declaration, but rather on how the behavior of this person is read "outside", i.e. to the person to whom this declaration is addressed. Alternatively, emphasis is put on whether the audience reads the behavior as not only the will to trigger a legal effect, but also the will to externalize intent to trigger legal effects through the very behavior undertaken.' [translated by IS] (Gwiazdomorski 1974).

[17] 'It is to be emphasized that when we talk about non-existent declarations, we do not have in mind the ontological meaning of the word "exist". A contrary opinion leads to contradiction or demands ontological assumptions that are either naive and idealistic, or difficult to accept [translated by IS].' (Gizbert-Studnicki 1975).

> In this traditional view, the "genuine will" of the parties is understood as contents of the actual mental states experienced by some natural persons. It is even unclear whose potential mental states should be decisive: those who actually drafted the contract, or those on behalf of whom it was concluded. Whoever it should be, in any case one would have to accept extremely strong assumptions concerning the scope and constitution of the propositional attitudes held by respective persons at the moment of contract formation. In order to provide in advance solutions to later interpretive problems, the contents of the mental states [of the persons concluding the contract – added by IS] would have to be much more comprehensive and precise than the language they used. We find such assumptions implausible. Research in cognitive psychology suggests that articulation of mental states makes them less blurred and fluctuating than they are before articulation. (Pietrzykowski and Tobor 2010)

Cognitive, epistemological views could also force us to question even sincere answers to questions about one's mental state:

> (…) cognitive research reveals that there is no neutral recollection of one's own past mental states. The contents of our so-called episodic memory is constantly infused by later experiences, information and impressions (…) (Pietrzykowski and Tobor 2010)

Analogously, Stephen Neale concedes that even a pragmatic (in his sense) theory of everyday conversation has a lot to do with the idealization of the objective hearer and with 'linguistic meaning', which is conventionalized and deeply external:

> A pragmatic theory concerns itself with the sorts of information and types of cognitive states and processes involved when interpreters form hypotheses about what speakers mean. The information in question includes information about linguistic meaning – which the Gricean sees as constitutively determined by conventions explained in terms of regularities in speaker meaning – and a whole lot more. (Neale 2016)

Thus, an epistemological theory must encompass a substantial number of external factors. The Gricean theory of the CP, maxims and implicatures can be read as a strictly pragmatic, epistemological theory. By contrast, Grice's theory of meaning is a metaphysical theory. Here, as we shall see in a moment, he is a strong internalist. For this reason, for him the speaker's intention was a necessary constituent of an implicature. However, I will argue that in the context of law the Gricean theory of implicatures can be read as independent from his view on meaning. In other words, in the legal context, it is possible to substitute an internal intention understood as a subjective mental state with external, public cues found in the context.

Thus, my point is that, as far as the legal case is concerned, even if one disagrees with Grice on his theory of meaning, one can still fully endorse his theory of CP, maxims and implicatures without being incoherent.

I have already argued in chapters one and two that I am sympathetic with the Gricean theory of pragmatics (with important modifications), both in standard conversation and as a counterfactual basis for the strategic framework. By contrast, while in standard conversation there may be various reasons to endorse the Gricean internalist project concerning meaning, I believe in the legal realm the Gricean theory of meaning must be rejected. An externalist account is necessary.

Let me now discuss the Gricean theory of meaning, the other internalist and externalist approaches, and why in the legal case we need a metaphysical externalism of meaning.

5.3 The Gricean Theory of Meaning

To understand Grice's metaphysical considerations of meaning, one must be aware of one crucial assumption. Grice analyzes transparent exchanges or communication in the strictest sense. This means that this is a communication in which every agent is trustworthy and responsible. A communication that involves as an interlocutor a 'creature who takes adequate trouble to make sure that what he is trying to get the other creature to believe is in fact the case, and who is not careless, negligent or rash.' (Grice 1975) This transparency and trustworthiness are taken as conditions that enable language to develop. They are similar to this evolutionary need to cooperate in order to survive. Note that this assumption could not be made in the legal realm, which is descriptively inherently strategic, deceptive and manipulative[18] (only normative idealizations claim the contrary, but they are simply idealizations).

Grice first outlined his theory in an article entitled 'Meaning'. Next, over the years and because of heated discussions with, among others, Schiffer, Grice modified his theory in 'Meaning revisited'. Both texts are included in his book 'Studies in the way of words'. Note that the text 'Meaning' is in a section entitled 'Semantics and Metaphysics'. This seems yet another argument for the thesis that it is possible to modify Grice's theory so as to separate his theory of meaning and his theory of pragmatics (and treat them as independent). Meaning is a metaphysical question, not an epistemological one.

Grice created the notion of meaning$_{NN}$, which is an abbreviation for 'non-natural' meaning contrasted with natural meaning. The latter is supposed to be biological, spontaneous and necessary. If a policeman stops a car by blocking the road, he naturally means that he wants the car to stop. If a child burns himself or herself and emits a spontaneous scream, he naturally means that he is in pain. However, if a policeman stops a car by waving his hand or, if the child screams so anyone can recognize that he is in pain, then his or her meaning is non-natural and is labeled meaning$_{NN}$ (Grice 1989). This notion has three principal characteristics:

(1) "A meant$_{NN}$ something by x" is (roughly) equivalent to "A intended the utterance of x to produce some effect in an audience by means of the recognition of his intention"; and we may add that to ask what A meant is to ask for a specification of the intended effect (though, of course, it may not always be possible to get a straight answer involving a "that" clause, for example, "a belief that…").

[18] Or at least, such is the communication between the parties to a dispute. The exchange between legislatures and courts is mostly strategic and probably much less deceptive and manipulative.

(2) "x meant something" is (roughly) equivalent to "Somebody $meant_{NN}$ something by x." Here again there will be cases in which this will not require work. I feel inclined to say that (as regards traffic lights) the change to red $meant_{NN}$ that the traffic was to stop; but it would be very unnatural to say, "Somebody (e.g. the Corporation) $meant_{NN}$ by the red-light change that the traffic was to stop". ***Nevertheless, there seems to be some sort of reference to somebody's intentions.***

(3) "x $means_{NN}$ (timeless) that so-and-so" might at first shot be equated with some statement or disjunction of statements about what "people" vaguely intend (with qualifications about "recognition") to effect by x. [emphasis mine] (Grice 1989)

In a nutshell, the central idea is that the audience has to recognize the speaker's communicative intention. That is, the audience must recognize what belief the speaker wants to induce in his audience. Moreover, the audience needs to recognize this belief in virtue of the recognition of the speaker's intention to make his audience recognize his belief. Consequently, the speaker needs to want to make his audience believe what he intends to communicate and the audience needs to believe it because the speaker intends her to believe it. In 'Meaning revisited' Grice labels this a 'make-believe game' (Grice 1989). The game is about not only the audience's recognition of the speaker's communicative intentions, but also about the audience's recognition of the fact that the speaker intends his audience to believe what he is communicating.

5.4 More Internal Projects

In the previous section I argued that Grice started with a strong internalist account of meaning. Many have followed him in this metaphysical decision. Here are a few examples of speaker-oriented metaphysical claims about meaning[19]:

> (…) indexical expressions must be evaluated with respect to what I have called the intended context of interpretation, i.e., with respect to a context providing the co-ordinates intended by the speaker as semantically relevant. (Predelli 1998)

According to Predelli, metaphysically speaking, only the elements of context encompassed by the speaker's intention count. Another definition that is still strongly internalist, especially as it gives an internalist account of 'speaker's expectations', is presented by Neale:

> What U means by uttering X is determined solely by U's communicative intentions; but of course the formation of genuine communicative intentions by U is constrained by U's expectations: U cannot be said to utter X M-intending A to ϕ if U thinks that there is very little or no hope that U's production of X will result in A ϕ-ing. (Neale 1992)

Note that this constraint through expectations is internalist because expectations are the speaker's beliefs about the context. The external context plays only a weak etiological role: it only indirectly influences the formation of the speaker's beliefs

[19] I owe the selection of examples to Palle Leth, who gave a presentation on the subject at the Institut Jean Nicod in 2016.

about context, which have a direct influence on the formation of the speaker's communicative intentions. Consequently, on this account, what constitutively determines the speaker's meaning is only the speaker's communicative intention. The speaker's meaning is only partially constituted by the context. This result is controversial because it entails that a speaker can never be wrong about what he has said. Stephen Neale often invokes, in his lectures, the following example: Even if a speaker claims that he meant 'dog' by saying 'cat' and the rest of the world (about 7 billion people) claim that he meant 'cat' by saying 'cat', the speaker cannot be wrong about his own speaker meaning. For Neale, speaker meaning and expression meaning are two distinct matters of interest. Such a theory is heavily counterintuitive, but this is the price Neale pays for his theory being ontologically light. Neale does not need to postulate any ontologically dubious entities because they all reduce to the speaker's intention.

Finally, the counter-intuitive divergence of speaker meaning and expression meaning[20] led theorists such as King to form hybrid accounts of meaning. Such accounts claim that both internal and external factors constitute meaning; they give a hybrid answer to the metaphysical question:

> (…) the value of a use of a demonstrative in a context is that the object o that meets the conditions 1) the speaker intends o to be the value and 2) a competent, attentive, reasonable hearer would take o to be the object that the speaker intends to be the value. (King 2014)

Such an approach is supposed to render more intuitive results. However, it needs to face issues such as the standard of reasonableness of the hearer. It is unclear who or what is supposed to fix this standard in a context.

Thus, the common point of the quoted content is a tendency to qualify the intentional approach by some external factors (for instance, objective hearers etc.). There seems to be a spectrum between a completely free intentional account and an external framework that completely neglects intentions. Since both extremes are unacceptable, the answer lies somewhere in between. Meaning and reference is probably a matter of striking a balance between the two. But, if it is a matter of degree, where exactly is the line? Because of the difficulty in answering this question, some theorists choose the external account. As Marcin Matczak argues '(…) the meaning-constituting factor is thus not outside language in the realm of the speaker, their mind, or our representation of their mind. Rather it is inside language, in its syntax and in its semantics.' (Matczak 2016, forthcoming)

[20]This has been nicely summarized by John Perry: 'We are pretty clear about what he intended to say, and what he was understood as saying. But what did he say?' (Perry 2009).

5.5 More External Projects

The metaphysical question about what facts constitute or determine meaning and reference can also be answered in an external fashion. External theories are hearer centered. They claim that the constitutive, decisive factors when deciding upon meaning are linguistic conventions (whatever their nature), literal meaning, lexicon, expression meaning etc. Everything that is a potential cue available to a reasonable hearer in the circumstances is the object of interest of externalism. Everything which is not available to a hearer yet is encompassed by the speaker's intention is irrelevant for answering the question on what meaning really is.

Note that externalism is a claim about meaning after the formation of conventions. No externalist denies that we need intentions in the formation of a language. We need them to have signs. Any object can be the token of a sign only if it is used with the intention to convey something through the sign. The externalist will accept that a primary intention of ascribing meaning to a sign is needed. However, the externalist will claim that the content of conventions, once they are settled, is decisive and constitutive for meaning. Thus, if you recall Kaplan's example, an externalist will take Kaplan to mean Spiro Agnew through his utterance of 'that'.

Consider the examples of externalist stances[21]:

> What the speaker says, strictly speaking, and thus his reference, is determined by the cues available to the addressee. (Wettstein 1984)

This definition would be quite non-controversial if it were treated as an answer to the epistemic question of Neale's pragmatics. Even Grice would have probably agreed that since we cannot read the speaker's mind, we must calculate on the basis of cues. By contrast, as an answer to the metaphysical question (CQ), this is a strong externalist claim. Similarly:

> (…) the referent is the object spatio-temporally related to the speaker in the way specified by the aforementioned rule of pointing. (McGinn 1981)

Taken as a metaphysical claim, McGinn's idea is heavily ontologically committed. It presupposes the existence (in some form or other) of at least objects and rules. A somewhat similar but more moderate account is the 'accessibility criteria' view:

> We can say that the referent of a demonstrative is the object of an all-things-considered judgment in which the things to be considered are the accessibility criteria, and what has to be determined is which object, if any, adequately and best satisfies those criteria. (Gauker 2008)

This view is more moderate because if the speaker's communicative intention satisfies the accessibility criteria (because for instance the context is rich and clear enough), then, indirectly, this intention can be taken into account in the all-things-considered judgment.

---

[21] Again, I owe the selection of definitions to Palle Leth.

Let us now come back to McGinn's observation that the rule of pointing plays a crucial role in externalist theories. A very interesting and powerful externalist account is provided by the philosophy developed by Saul Kripke and Hilary Putnam. Very roughly, the idea is that meaning is usually constituted by a baptism which takes the form of pointing to an object and pronouncing its name. Later other members of the linguistic community also employ the name of the object and this creates a chain of uses that is started by the baptism. Thus, reference and meaning are defined in terms of causal chains. This theory was devised to explain mainly proper names (for instance 'John' or 'Jack') and natural kinds (for instance 'gold' or 'water')[22] (Kripke 1998; Putnam 2015).

The above theory was one of the inspirations for Ruth Millikan's account of meaning:

> Semantic externalism advocates the idea of meaning that is autonomous of individual users of a language, be they speaker or recipient. Meaning evolves in the process of the repeatable co-occurrence of words (sentences) and states of affairs. A name co-occurs with a person, a noun co-occurs with a thing, a predicate co-occurs with a given attribute. The co-occurrence can be physical (words and things or qualities are present at the same time and place), or of a historical–causal nature (as in Kripke-Putnam semantics, in which our current reference extends back to the first use of the word). As a result of this co-occurrence, historical chains of usages come into existence – Millikan calls them "lineages". (Matczak 2016, forthcoming; Millikan 2005)

Thus, Millikan bases her theory on three notions. First, the notion of a 'lineage' defined above; second, the notion of a 'stabilizing function'; and third, the notion of a 'proper function'. 'The stabilizing function means that irrespective of a particular user's intention, a word refers to a state of affairs to which it referred in the past. What defines the reference is the link between the word and the state of affairs typical to it; the link has been constituted by a critical mass of cases in which users use this word to refer to that state of affairs. In this way a public language emerges which consists of the history of usages and a relatively stable semantic link between the words and the reality [context – added by IS] that constitutes meaning. Individual intentions are far from central to this process.' (Matczak 2016, forthcoming)

The third notion of 'proper function' is most crucial because this is what meaning really is on Millikan's account: signs 'are copied by the members of a linguistic community because they work: they help their users in achieving their vital purposes and so are reproduced, creating a historical chain of usages. These chains are sets of tokens of a particular sign, used many times for a similar purpose. This purpose or the reason why a sign is useful and is reproduced is this sign's "proper function": the function the sign performs in a particular linguistic community. In the

[22] 'A second approach to meaning, referred to as K–P semantics (from the names of Saul Kripke and Hilary Putnam), breaks with the intentionalist concept of meaning and adopts the causal conception of reference, which assumes, as Putnam writes, that "meaning ain't in the head". In search for meaning, K–P semantics resort not to the intention of the speaker, but to the social practice of using concrete names, which, due to a long tradition of standard uses of certain expressions, decides to which objects and situations, in a non-linguistic reality, the words pronounced or written by a person refer.' [translated by IS] (Matczak 2007).

pragmatic framework, the proper function equates with the meaning of the sign.' (Matczak 2016, forthcoming)

In theoretical frameworks such as Millikan's, intention again ceases to be a crucial element of the theory of meaning: 'meaning is a product of relations in the world, not the relations within someone's mind: through a process of use, recognition and re-use, some relations become semantic relations, and others not. In terms of an interpreter's work, to determine the meaning of a sign is not to determine the intention of an individual user, but rather to determine the sign's proper function. The meaning does not depend on an individual user's intention or their mental states but is created by the long-lasting practice of a community that keeps reproducing the signs in order to influence their environment. As a consequence, the meaning becomes not only autonomous from an individual intention, but sometimes even conflicts with it.' (Matczak 2016, forthcoming)

Let us know concentrate on the theory of meaning that is needed in legal discourse.

5.6 A Theory of Meaning for Legal Discourse

5.6.1 Grice on the Meaning of Law

Let us again have a look at the Gricean definition:

(1) "A meant$_{NN}$ something by x" is (roughly) equivalent to "A intended the utterance of x to produce some effect in an audience by means of the recognition of his intention"; and we may add that to ask what A meant is to ask for a specification of the intended effect (though, of course, it may not always be possible to get a straight answer involving a 'that' clause, for example, "a belief that…").

(2) "x meant something" is (roughly) equivalent to "Somebody meant$_{NN}$ something by x." Here again there will be cases in which this will not require work. **I feel inclined to say that (as regards traffic lights) the change to red meant$_{NN}$ that the traffic was to stop; but it would be very unnatural to say, "Somebody (e.g. the Corporation) meant$_{NN}$ by the red-light change that the traffic was to stop".** ***Nevertheless, there seems to be some sort of reference to somebody's intentions.*** [emphasis mine]

(3) "x means$_{NN}$ (timeless) that so-and-so" might at first shot be equated with some statement or disjunction of statements about what "people" vaguely intend (with qualifications about "recognition") to effect by x. (Grice 1989)

In the bolded fragment in point (2) of the definition, Grice points out that in such cases as traffic lights, something different is going on because there are no standard, human, communicative intentions involved. Even if we imagine an autocratic or authoritarian regime where a single person—a king or a dictator—pronounces laws and thus a human intention is always involved (no need to speak of collective or institutional intentions of a legislative entity), Grice would not apply his theory of meaning$_{NN}$ to interpreting the laws of the dictator:

In certain linguistic cases we ask the utterer afterwards about his intention, and in a few of these cases (the very difficult ones, such as a philosopher being asked to explain the mean-

> ing of an unclear passage in one of his works), the answer is based not on what he remembers, but is more like a decision about how what he said is to be taken. I cannot find a non-linguistic parallel here; however, the case is so **special** that it seems not to contribute a vital difference. [emphasis mine] (Grice 1989)

Grice's reflection above seems to support the thesis that some cases (such as the legal one) are so special that they need to be treated separately as they are independent of any theory of 'everyday' meaning. However, since the Gricean account of pragmatics is independent of his theory of meaning, it could hypothetically apply to both natural language and legal cases.

I have stated that linguistic exchanges within the realm of law can be deceptive. What I meant was that manipulative behavior of the kind Marmor describes can occur: 'cases in which a speaker asserts something true while deliberately trying to implicate something that he knows to be false'. Recall Smith, the philosophy doctor who presents himself as a doctor *tout court* in a hospital (Marmor 2014). By contrast, Grice clearly excludes deceptive behavior from his theory of meaning:

> (…) We suppose that creature Y not only recognizes that the behavior is voluntary on the part of X, but also recognizes that X intends Y to recognize his behavior as voluntary. That is, we have now undermined the idea that this is a straightforward piece of deception. Deceiving consists in trying to get a creature to accept certain things as signs of something or other without knowing that this is a faked case. Here, however, we would have a sort of perverse faked case in which something is faked, but at the same time a clear indication is put in that the faking has been done. (Grice 1989)

On the basis of the excerpt above, it is clear that Grice would accept that deceptive cases need separate treatment because they are not what he calls communication.

Finally, in 'Meaning revisited' Grice is arguing for a flexible account of communication. His claim is roughly the following: since it is a fact that speakers often use linguistic conventions loosely in context, we need to accept that bare expression meaning is too stiff for communication. Thus, speakers often require hearers to make an approximation of what the speaker means. For instance, if you claim that a table is round, you probably do not mean that it is exactly, geometrically round. Interestingly, he emphasizes that in the legal case, the approximation may go much further:

> it is not my business on this occasion to suggest exactly, or in any detail, what the demands for approach or approximation might be. I will only say that (…) they ought to be ones which justify us in deeming certain cases to satisfy a given ideal even though they do not, in fact, strictly speaking exemplify it; just as in Oxford on one occasion, there was difficulty between an incoming provost and a college rule that dogs were not allowed in college: the governing body passed a resolution deeming the new provost's dog to be a cat. I suspect crucially we do a lot of deeming, though perhaps not always in such an entertaining fashion. (Grice 1989)

This seems to suggest that the meaning of law can have not only very little to do with human intentions, but also it can play with conventions. The latter can be simply changed by a legal rule itself.

To sum up, I will claim that the Gricean theory of meaning that relies on the speaker's intention is inapplicable to the legal realm. You could argue that since for Grice the speaker's intention was a necessary component of an implicature, the theory of implicatures does not apply to the legal realm either. I believe this is not the case. I want to claim that we can replace the speaker's intention with external, contextual cues. If this is correct, then it is possible to treat the Gricean theory of meaning and the modified version of the Gricean theory of implicatures as two distinct theories. If this is also correct, then even if you are an externalist about meaning you can still accept the theory of implicatures in the legal realm.

This is because the classic Gricean theory of meaning and the modified account of the Gricean implicature theory are now supposed to answer two distinct questions—CQ and EQ:

> (CQ – constitutive determination) In virtue of what facts does someone, S, mean whatever he or she means by performing something, x, on a given occasion?
>
> (EQ – epistemic determination) What sorts of information, what principles, and what types of cognitive states and processes are involved in the (typically spontaneous) arrival in the mind of an interpreter of a (typically resilient) conclusion about what S means by performing x on that occasion? (Neale 2016)

Independently of whether you answer CQ in an internalist or externalist manner, you can answer EQ with the modified Gricean CP, maxims and modified implicatures. Conflating the metaphysical and epistemological question (and answer)—at least in the legal realm—is therefore a mistake that leads to substantial confusion.

Let me now explain the nature of the modification. The alteration of the CP and the maxims have already been described in the previous chapters as the strategic framework, which consists of a strategic principle and second-order strategic maxims. For this reason, I will now concentrate on explaining what needs to be substituted for the notion of intention in the concept of implicature. The claim is that empirical evidence suggests that sometimes even when there is no intention, there is an implicature. Consider two examples: the 'spill the beans' example and the cancellation example.

First, consider the following situation—Jane asks Jack, her lover:

3. Jane: Whose wedding ring is this?
4. Jack: It's mine.
5. Obviously, he had no intention to implicate that he is married. He just spilt the beans. Yet the implicature that he is married is already 'out there'. Any reasonable hearer would have grasped it.

The second example is a more general observation. There is a reason that we cancel implicatures: we do it because we have no intention of implicating something, yet we know that what we have said gives enough evidence for rational hearers to decode an implicature. Thus, we feel obliged to cancel the implicature, which is already out there because of what we have said.[23]

[23] Francesca Poggi notes that: '(…) generalized implicatures are always produced, except in special

I hope that these two cases show that even in natural language, even though intention of the speaker is not present, the hearer grasps implicatures. The latter constructs these implicatures out of available external, namely contextual, cues. Note that the worry of delimiting between implicatures and presuppositions does not occur here because a presupposition follows both from the sentence and from the negation of a sentence. If you say, 'the king of France is bald' or 'the king of France is not bald', both sentences presuppose that there is a king of France. By contrast, the implicature follows only from Jack's positive answer to Jill's answer, 'it's mine'. There would be no implicature that Jack is married from the answer 'it is not mine'. A similar observation was made by Francesca Poggi:

> (…) When the speaker's intention does not coincide with what she should have implicated on the basis of the maxims and the CP, i.e. when a speaker implicates something she did not intend to implicate or does not implicate something she intended to implicate, communication is flawed because in everyday conversations we normally assume that our speakers follow the CP. The speaker's intention is therefore relevant for the success of communication. It is, on the other hand, irrelevant for the production of implicatures: they come into being even when they were not intended by the speaker, and this is exactly the cause of interpretive misunderstandings. Here, I'm not arguing that this thesis was endorsed by Grice: on the contrary, I'm arguing that this is the correct way to represent the production of the implicatum, and more the communicative process in general.[24] (Poggi 2016)

Note that even if in natural language you can ask your interlocutor for clarifications, in the legal realm you cannot do so. For this reason, it seems even more reasonable to say that in the legal realm we can only speak of objectively manifested intentions that constitute meaning. A similar approach is adopted by Jeffrey Goldsworthy in his paper entitled 'Moderate versus strong intentionalism: Knapp and Michaels revisited' (Goldsworthy 2005).

Let me now try to further argue why the theory of meaning of law needs to be external.

5.6.2 *The Meaning of Legal Texts Is External*

A striking majority of scholars believe that the meaning of law is external. Moreover, as I shall argue, internalists about the meaning of law are in fact externalists in disguise. Even the strongest possible internalist about everyday language such as

circumstances, and they are certainly cancellable: however, if the context does not prevent them, and if the speaker does not cancel them, they are produced regardless of the speaker's intention, that is to say that if the speaker does not intend them, nevertheless the recipient grasps them correctly (while the speaker is wrong and cause the communication failure).' (Poggi 2016).

[24] Jeffrey Goldsworthy makes a similar observation: 'People can intend to say or imply something but fail to do so, and conversely, they can say or imply something they did not intend. If we are told that we have misunderstood someone's utterance, we often defend ourselves by replying, "I now realize what she meant to say, but it's not what she did say". Or "He may not have intended to say that, but he did"' (Goldsworthy 2005).

Stephen Neale agrees with the externalist view of the meaning of law. Let me now summarize his views on meaning in everyday communication, and then his views on communication in the legal case.

Neale claims that intentions are constitutive (in the ontological sense) of the speaker's meaning. He claims that it is in virtue of facts about the speaker's communicative intentions that S means something by an act on a given occasion. He distinguishes between determination in the strong and weak sense. Determination in the strong sense is ontological (constitutive). Consequently, the speaker's meaning is constituted by intentions in the strong sense. However, intentions (and thus meaning) are determined in a weak (non-ontological, epistemological) sense by etiological, causal facts.

The problem is that when a legislature enacts a statute, there is no individual phenomenological state that could be labeled communicative intention. We tend to speak about collective, institutional intentions, but this is something different from phenomenological mental states. Consequently, meaning in law cannot be constitutively determined by a human intention understood as a phenomenological mental state.

Thus, it must be constituted by some external factors, for instance facts about the legislative procedure or the epistemology of the judges that are carrying out the interpretive process. These facts in turn will be shaped by the contextual cues (contextual evidence) available to the judges.[25]

The result is agreement between the internalist and externalist about the theory of meaning in law. In other words, there are four possible stances:

(I.) Internalism about meaning in natural language and internalism about meaning in legal language
(II.) Internalism about meaning in natural language and externalism about meaning in legal language
(III.) Externalism about meaning in natural language and externalism about meaning in legal language
(IV.) Externalism about meaning in natural language and internalism about meaning in legal language

The first stance is controversial and I will discuss it in the next sub-chapter. I will argue that internalist theories of the meaning of law eventually collapse into a version of externalism. Moreover, no theorist seriously endorses the last stance (IV). If the choice is between (II) and (III), the asset of the externalist is that she has a universal theory about both everyday language and the language of law. By contrast, the internalist will need two distinct theories. Now, you may claim that universal theories are always better just because they are simpler. That may be true; however, every human being that has any contact with the legal system seems to have the intuition that there is something different going on in the legal case. The internalist is in a better position to capture this intuition with his twofold theory of meaning.

[25] This view was presented by Stephen Neale during a seminar on meaning at the University of Genova in April 2016.

Recall David Kaplan pointing to the picture behind him. In the realm of law, there will be no dispute as to what he meant. He must have meant Spiro Agnew because no cues enabled his hearers to recognize that he meant Rudolf Carnap (this holds on the assumption that his hearers were unaware that previously a picture of Carnap had been hanging where Kaplan pointed).

You may object to this by claiming that the above is true only of contract law (recall article 8 of the CISG). By contrast, you may say that if one is an intentionalist about statutory interpretation,[26] then one can be an internalist about legal meaning (and even endorse (I)). I believe this reasoning is misguided. When we look closer at the intentionalist arguments, they claim that meaning in law is determined constitutively by facts and evidence about (collective) institutional intentions in the form of legislative records of debates and draft texts, social campaigns, the aims of the majority party, the context at the time of legislation etc. They never invoke even a phenomenological intention. They break with any kind of psychological views (Tobor 2013).

Jeffrey Goldsworthy also notices the importance of external factors in the law. For this reason, he labels his view 'moderate intentionalism'. In the terminology I have introduced in this chapter, this also is a version of externalism about meaning. Goldsworthy claims that

> For a text to mean what its author intended it to mean, it is necessary that its intended audience be capable of ascertaining its intended meaning. This requires that the audience have access to persuasive evidence of that meaning, provided partly by the conventional meaning of the text and partly by other clues of the author's intention, such as the context in which it was written. If the audience does not have access to such evidence, then not only will the author's attempt to communicate his intention fail, but the text will not mean what he intended it to mean. And that is to say that his intention is neither sufficient for, nor identical to, the meaning of the text.[27] (Goldsworthy 2005)

Goldsworthy defines utterance meaning as 'what the speaker's meaning ***appears to be***, given all the evidence that is readily available to his intended audience, which may include the sentence meaning of the utterance and other clues such as its context.' [emphasis mine] (Goldsworthy 2005) The point is that what the speaker's meaning appears to be is not the speaker's meaning itself. The above argument can be strengthened by the fact that collective, group intentions such as legislative intentions simply cannot be reduced to an individual intention, which is the source of the speaker's meaning in the Gricean sense.

Thus, when interpreters attribute intentions to entities, they are aware that this is some kind of a metaphor, social construct or even fiction. Consequently, they are not so naive as to claim that these are real human intentions. The internalist theory of

---

[26] The same applies for one sort of originalist view about constitutional interpretation, namely the originalist who speaks about an original intention. There is a second variety of originalists, such as justice Antonin Scalia, who speak about original public meaning (Gizbert-Studnicki 2012).

[27] Goldsworthy accepts a broad range of possible available evidence. In other words, the evidence is not limited to linguistic conventions: 'what is essential to meaning are "clues" or "signals" of the speaker's intentions, whether those clues consist of his apparent use of conventions or something else.' (Goldsworthy 2005).

law is hardly possible; however, there can be rational and sensible disputes over which external factors need to be taken into account (Scalia and Gutmann 2001). As Matczak argues

> in enacting a new law, the lawmaker includes into the legal language the words that have been used before, with their histories – their lineages. The existing lineages and the proper functions of the words used make language autonomous from the lawmaker. (…) the lawmaker's situation does not differ much from that of the interpreter. Neither of them can impact the meaning of particular words by his or her individual understanding. In order to make the lawmaker's use a crucial factor in defining the meaning, there must be something special in this use: it must be in some sense a milestone use which changes the way the public language is used. In the historical chain of usages, such milestone moments do not happen often, if at all. (…) Legal interpretation should therefore by necessity involve tracing how a particular term has been used in a particular linguistic community. (Matczak 2016, forthcoming)

Slocum holds a similar view:

> The relevant context is not the particular statute itself but, rather, the long history of legislative use of such clauses and of courts interpreting them more narrowly than their literal meanings would indicate. (Slocum 2016)

In opposition to intentionalists are textualists (in statutory interpretation). They claim that legislative records can be neglected, and we should instead look at the context and conventions at the time of the interpretation of the legal rule. Finally, purposivists will ignore all this and claim that only the purpose of the law counts. Crucially, note that all the interpretive options make use of external factors when answering the question about which factors constitutively (ontologically) determine the meaning of law.[28] This also seems to be Goldsworthy's position:

> (…) the courts seek to give effect to the objective meaning of a statute which is informed both by the linguistic conventions that determine literal meanings, and by other evidence of the legislature's intention, provided that it is readily available to the statute's intended audience. That other evidence can include common sense understandings of the legislature's probable purposes and intentions, the historical circumstances in which the statute was enacted, and (to a limited extent) legislative history. (Goldsworthy 2005)

---

[28] Zygmunt Tobor claims to be a moderate intentionalist about legal interpretation, but this does not mean that he would not agree with the claim laid in this chapter. This is because he defines moderate intentionalism in a way that is defined as moderate externalism in this chapter. Thus, this is just a terminological discussion. Nevertheless, there is agreement on the fact that institutional intentions are not psychological but constructive. There is also agreement on the fact that the debates between intentionalists and textualists are debates about the scope of evidence of the legislature's intention that can be taken into account. It is also a debate about whether we can take into account the idealized view of legislative intentions in a context (the answer to the question 'what should be the intentions' rather than the answer to the question 'what were the intentions'): 'A sensible use of the notion of 'legislative intention' happens when intention is understood as an institutional rather than psychological notion. The proponents of both stances consider an example in which a participant of a marriage ceremony states afterwards that his or her 'yes' was a joke. Both theorists are concordant that the marriage is valid, but they justify it in a different way. For the 'moderate theorist' this follows from the lack of evidence that it was a joke. By contrast, the 'radical theorist' claims that it follows from non-linguistic reasons that have nothing in common with the relation between intention and meaning.' [translated by IS] (Tobor 2013).

Let me now proceed to a discussion of the metaphysical nature of legislative intentions. I will claim that their nature imposes an externalist view of the meaning of law.

5.6.3 *Institutional Intentions Are Not Reducible to Collective Intentionality*

We tend to take a lot of elements of our social reality for granted. Yet 'money, language, property, marriage, government, universities, cocktail parties, lawyers, presidents of the United States etc.' exist in part only because we think they exist (Searle 1999). Consequently, we need a distinction between brute facts which do not depict this contingency, and institutional facts. This subchapter is an attempt to formulate a definition of institutional facts, specifically of legislative intentions.

One possibility is to claim that institutional facts are a subcategory of social facts. I will claim that this idea is misguided. John Searle defines social facts as 'any facts involving two or more agents who have collective intentionality. So, for example, animals hunting together, birds cooperating in building a nest, and presumably social insects such as ants and bees, manifest collective intentionality and thus have social facts.' (Searle 1999)

The key notion in the above definition is 'collective intentionality'. What does this mysterious phrase stand for? Collective intentionality requires for its existence (yet is not reducible to) a set of individual intentions of a special kind. Searle gives the following reason for the irreducibility of collective intentions to a set of individual standard intentions:

> Contrast an orchestra performing a symphony with the individual members of the symphony playing their parts in isolation. Even if by chance the individual members were all rehearsing their parts in a way that happened to be synchronized, so that it sounded like a symphony, there is still a crucial difference between the intentionality of collective cooperative behavior and individual behavior. (Searle 1999)

Yet what is this special kind of individual intention that leads to collective intentionality? One possible answer is that this is an individual intention combined with 'mutual belief'. However, the problem is that we are left with another mysterious and ontologically dubious notion of precisely 'mutual belief'. For this reason, Searle suggests a different solution:

> I think the whole approach, which attempts to reduce collective intentionality to individual intentionality plus mutual belief, is confused. (…) the requirement that all intentionality be in the heads on individual agents (…) does not require that all intentionality be expressed in the first person singular. (Searle 1999)

In other words, intentionality of individual agents can always take the form of 'we intend', 'we believe' etc.

Thus, the idea is that collective intentionality is based on 'we intentions' of individuals. These 'we intentions' are intertwined with 'I intentions':

> (…) if I have a "we intention", I must also have an "I intention", because if I am intentionally doing something as part of our doing something, then I must intend to do my part. And in order to intend to do my part, I must intend that I do something that is part of our doing something. (Searle 1999)

Legislatures generate social facts based on collective intentionality of the above kind. Richard Ekins formulates a similar view as Searle on the necessity of intertwining the 'I intention' and the 'we intention'. He defines the 'I intention' in the following words:

> Each legislator forms the intention "I intend that we legislate by means of the relevant set of procedures, in which a majority vote for a complete statutory proposal on the third reading counts as the legislature enacting the proposal" (Ekins 2012).

Ekins labels the 'we intention' a 'standing intention', which he defines as a reasoned plan to act collectively:

> The assembly's standing intention is its plan to adopt particular plans, which is to say its plan for how to legislate on particular occasions (…) However, the standing intention is more than the custom and practice alone, because one must grasp the reason for these procedures, the end to which they are ordered. (Ekins 2012)

Nevertheless, collective intentionality is neither necessary nor sufficient for the existence of institutional facts. Additionally, institutional facts such as the legislative intention do not reduce to collective intentionality—something extra is needed. Moreover, there are institutional facts that are not even partly constituted by any collective intentionality.

Christian List describes 'collective intentionality' as 'joint agency', and 'institutional facts' such as legislatures as 'group agents'. He argues that

> it is important to distinguish the phenomenon of group agency from the related phenomenon of joint agency. We speak of joint agency whenever two or more individuals engage in some joint action. For example, they go for a walk together, carry a piano downstairs together, or undertake some common project. Clearly, some shared or joint intentions (or intentions that are suitably collectively directed) need to be present among the participants in order to make joint actions possible. (…) Two or more individuals who engage in a joint action do not necessarily bring into existence a group agent. We can make sense of joint actions without ascribing a single "center" of belief, desire, and agency to the group in its entirety. It is sufficient for a joint action that the bearers of the underlying intentions are individuals; no group-level intentional states are needed. Of course, there may be joint actions within the context of a group agent. The practical mechanisms of forming a group agent may often include shared or joint intentions among the individual members. But joint agency is neither sufficient, nor (from purely logical perspective) even necessary, for group agency. (List 2018)

Thus, there remains the question about what constitutes institutional intentions. If we accept List's claim, then collective intentionality is not a satisfactory answer because there can be group agency without joint actions. Institutional intentions need to be explained through a different notion. The second hypothesis I would like to analyze is the claim that institutional facts are constituted by a set of special rules. We speak of institutional intentions when we ascribe to some entities an intention on the basis of some more or less formalized rules. In other words, we agree to some rules and we agree to treat as intentions whatever outcome those rules produce. For this reason, an utterance of the form 'the parliament intended so and so' can be treated as a form of ellipsis.[29] What is subject to ellipsis is precisely the set of rules, or the procedure that makes it the case that the outcome of this procedure is treated as an institutional intention.[30] (Studnicki 1971)

Crucially, when the institutional intention is the intention of a collective body, it cannot be reduced to a sum of individual intentions (even those of the 'we intend' kind). There are at least three arguments for this thesis: the intransitivity argument, Arrow's impossibility theorem and Condorcet's paradox.

The transitivity relation states that if p is identical to p′ and p′ is identical to p″, then p is identical to p″. The intransitivity argument claims that even if a local governmental body is constituted by the same group of people as a fishermen's club, this does not entail the identity of the two collective bodies. The decisions rendered by the local government will not be the decisions of the fishermen's club and vice versa. Thus, there is nothing psychological in institutional intentions—the individual intentions of the voters are irrelevant.[31] (Studnicki 1971)

Second, Arrow's impossibility theorem states that there is no way of turning individual preferences into collective preferences whilst simultaneously satisfying some rational criteria of decision taking. Timothy Grinsell describes these criteria in a simplified manner: 'The first of five such rules is Unrestricted Domain: the voters should be able to rank the available alternatives in any way they like. Second, the aggregation procedure should obey Unanimity: if everyone in the society strictly prefers alternative a to alternative b, society as a whole should also prefer alternative a. Third, the choice between any two alternatives should be governed by the voters' relative preference between those two alternatives (as opposed to a preference with respect to a third alternative, for instance). This rule is called Independence of Irrelevant Alternatives. Fourth, no voter should be a dictator (non-dictatorship). Finally, the result of the aggregation procedure should be a non-cycling ordering of preferences (Ordering).' (Grinsell forthcoming) Even if each and every of the criteria is rational, useful and should be respected, there is no possibility of respecting all of them at once (Arrow 1978).

---

[29] 'Claims of the form "collective k prefers alternative a_i from alternative a_k", proclaimed without resorting to a concrete procedure, are elliptical claims (…) semantic rules of natural language allow the interpretation of such claims as shortcuts for claims encompassing the resorting to some not explicitly indicated procedure' [translated by IS] (Studnicki 1971).

[30] F. Studnicki has the intuition that the empirical language we use to describe institutional intention is inadequate. We need a different one, which he labels 'normative language'. This could be treated as agreement with the claim that we need a different theory of meaning for the language of the law: 'The specific character of institutional bodies makes it impossible to characterize them with the language we use to describe empirical objects.' [Translated by IS] (Studnicki 1971).

[31] '(…) the processing of a definite set of individual decisions, especially a set, formed in the second stage of the final decision, which on the basis of a relevant procedure are ascribed to the collective body. Such processing is a formal operation without any psychological content.' [Translated by IS] (Studnicki 1971).

Table 5.1 The Condorcet's paradox (Studnicki 1971)

	Voter I	Voter II	Voter III
First preference	a	b	c
Second preference	b	c	a
Third preference	c	a	b

Third, there is Condorcet's paradox, also referred to in the literature as 'cycling' (Grinsell forthcoming). Imagine the following in Table 5.1: at least three voters, I, II and III, can choose between at least three options (decisions) a, b and c. Voter I prefers a to b and b to c. Voter II prefers b to c and c to a. Voter III prefers c to a and a to b:

On the basis of the above you can claim that option a is preferred to option b by the collectivity of voters (since voters I and III show this preference). You can also claim that the collective prefers option b to option c, since voters I and II show this preference. Consequently, you would probably like to claim on the basis of the transitive relation that decision a is preferred to decision c. Yet this is clearly not the case (Studnicki 1971).

All the three arguments lead to the conclusion that speaking of collective preferences must be a kind of ellipsis as to the kind of procedure that determines the preference (Studnicki 1971). This procedure is a set of rules. In other words, it is the set of rules which is constitutive of the institutional fact:

> Constitutive rules also regulate, but they do more than regulate; they constitute the very activity they regulate (…). The distinction between brute facts and institutional facts (…) can only be fully explained in terms of constitutive rules, because institutional facts only exist within a system of such rules. (Searle 1999)

Searle claims that these rules have the logical form 'X counts as Y in C', where C is a symbol for a context. Consequently, lifting your arm will count as voting for an option in a legislative environment (Searle 1999).

Richard Ekins also shares the view that institutional facts are not reducible to a set of individual intentionality of any kind. Moreover, they are not reducible to the intentions of the majority in a legislative body:

> My approach departs from those accounts of legislative intent in which scholars aim to reduce the legislature's intention, somehow, to that of some subset of the legislators. (…) I do not accept the sharp distinction that Manning makes between objectified intent, which is what a reasonable reader concludes was intended, and actual or subjective intent, which is what a majority of legislators wanted. He has no good reason to assume that actual, subjective legislative intent must be the shared preference of the majority (Ekins 2012)

According to Ekins, both the legislative majority and the minority share the intent to act on a reasoned plan. This is the minimal content that their intentions have in common. Moreover, this content makes it the case that the plan achieved on the basis of rules of voting will not be reducible to ideas of the pivotal legislative majority:

> The legislative intent in any particular act is the plan on which the legislature acts, not some summation of each legislator's reasoning in voting for or against the particular statutory

> proposal, none of which is open to other legislators or understood by any of them to be the object of joint action. It is the plan or proposal that is held in common by all legislators and which explains the joint action. The legislative minority does not trouble my account. The legislator in the minority shares the unanimous interlocking intention to legislate in accordance with procedures that include majority voting, from which arises the group's standing intention to that effect. (Ekins 2012)

The above view entails that even though Ekins labels himself a supporter of intentionalism, he accepts the externalist intuition about the meaning of legal text. He seems an externalist in disguise. Consider his statement:

> It is true that a bill cannot be enacted without the support of pivotal legislators and this means that those legislators have capacity to frame the content of the bill. ***It does not follow that the bill means what those legislators agree it shall mean***, for they must put the bill that they frame before the other legislators as a proposal for their joint action. [emphasis mine] (Ekins 2012)

To sum up, institutional facts seem to be constituted by a set of rules. The outcome of the rules is the content of an institutional intention. This content is constituted by external factors rather than any kind of psychological state.

5.6.4 The Functionalist Account of Institutional Intentions

I hope to have established in the previous subchapter that institutional intentions are not reducible to any kind of psychological individual mental states. However, does this automatically mean that we must have a different account of individual and institutional intentions? Not necessarily. The theory labeled functionalism claims that mental states can be defined in terms of their functions. This entails that they do not need to be realized by human brains. Any other kind of 'hardware' that can perform the functions is appropriate: 'Functionalism about agency, in very rough terms, is the view that what makes a system an agent – and what generates its intentional states – is nothing heavily metaphysically loaded, but simply the way the system functions, internally and externally, including in relation to its environment.' (List 2018) Thus, a functionalist could refute psychological intentions yet still claim that individual and institutional intentions are alike. On this account, individual and group agents are not qualitatively different. The fact that they may have different perceptual sensitivity is not treated as indicative of any important difference: 'Just as we humans are sensitive to sounds at certain frequencies but not to sounds outside that range, so a group agent may be perceptually sensitive to some environmental features but not to others.' (List 2018)

The principal reproach to functionalism about individual agents is the claim that it cannot account for qualia. Qualia are conscious, phenomenal states. This idea was introduced by Thomas Nagel in his article 'What is it like to be a bat?' (Nagel 1974) Roughly, if one is not a bat, one will never know what it is like to be a bat. Take another example: until you are not in pain, you do not know how it is to feel pain. Thus, the mere function of a mental state leaves out something important.

Now, you can claim that group agents do not have qualia, so this is not a problem for a functionalist account of them. However, the very idea of functionalism is to make the individual and group agency alike. Yet qualia make us come to the exactly opposite conclusion—individual and group agency are different. An individual agent has qualia while a group agent does not. Consequently, the two types of agents need different treatment:

> One could argue that an important difference in ultimate moral significance between individuals and groups lies precisely in their difference with respect to consciousness. Specifically, one might say that a necessary condition that an agent must satisfy in order to be of non-derivative moral significance is a capacity for phenomenal consciousness. Humans and other primates clearly have that capacity, while group agents do not – or at least not to any non-negligible extent. (…) In our book on group agency, Philip Pettit and I [C. List] asserted a normative asymmetry between individuals and groups. We argued that while group agents should be held responsible for their corporate actions, they should not be given the same rights as individuals, and they should be subject to especially strict checks and controls. (List 2018)

Yet the functionalist that dreams of a universal theory of individual and group agency does not have to give up this easily. There is a version of functionalism called eliminativism which claims that qualia are just an illusion and we do not need to explain them in the theories we build (Chalmers 1997). An eliminativist could claim that individual and group agency is alike. However, on an eliminativist account of a group agent such as the legislature, the only thing that exists is the text that it issues. Consequently, the only possible constitutive elements of the meaning of this text are external elements. Thus, this project also collapses into an external account of the meaning of the law. The absence of qualia removes the last barrier for the externalist:

> Let me close by returning to my original question: what is it like to be a group agent? Although my argument is tentative and conditional, it seems that the answer may well be (close to) nothing. (List 2018)

5.6.5 *Externalism in Disguise*

There are three arguments used by internalists in the debate. The first argument is quantitative. It claims that since people so often use the term 'legislative intention', there must be something substantial behind it. The second argument claims that we cannot create a coherent account of legislative errors without a substantial account of legislative intentions. The third argument claims that the mechanism of cycling (or Condorcet's paradox) is analogous to the mechanism of multicriterial vague terms used in everyday conversation and thus does not preclude the existence of legislative intentions (just as it does not preclude individual intentions).

Moving to the first argument, its proponents claim that 'Congress intends' or 'the legislature meant' have appeared in legal opinions at a frequency of about 60,000 times per decade for the last two decades. Even those normally hostile to reliance on legislative intent use these locutions.' (Grinsell forthcoming; Solan 2010) I do not believe that such a claim is indicative of anything. The fact that some expression appears frequently in a corpus cannot be straightforward evidence for the ontological nature of the issue at stake. The fact that we use an expression does not mean that it has to correspond to anything that objectively exists (independently of the language we use). These expressions can be just metaphors or parts of a 'folk theory', or just a way of speaking 'as if' there were something behind it (a fiction). Language uses expressions which do not correspond to anything in the world, yet we use them; for instance, concepts such as Santa Claus etc.

The second argument pertains to legislative errors. It claims that if courts reject some interpretations as absurd and claim that 'the legislator could not have intended so and so', legislative intentions must be something irreducible to the external factors available to interpreters (Grinsell forthcoming). Yet again this might be just a way of speaking. The erroneous content is often derived by the judge through interpretation on the basis of external evidence. This is very often the most easily accessible evidence, which is literal meaning (whatever its definition). Nothing precludes the judge from claiming that this content is absurd with respect to the judge's preferred definition of rationality. Consequently, the interpreter can use other available external evidence if this choice can be backed by inter-subjective reasons. There is nothing internal in this treatment of legislative error.

The third argument dismissed cycling as analogous to vagueness of multicriterial adjectives. For cycling to occur, it is sufficient to have some criteria and alternatives, not necessarily voters or proposals. Consequently, when an individual makes a decision that involves criteria and alternatives, her decision and her individual intent may suffer from the same kind of cycling objections as legislative intent. Consider the example:

> Imagine, (…) that your business partner has given you instructions to buy a "nice" car for your business. (…) A "nice" car is a car that ranks highly on the criteria your partner cares (equally) about: fuel efficiency, price, and comfort. There are three cars, or alternatives, to choose from: the Ford, the Chevy, and the Chrysler. The rankings of the cars according to the criteria are as follows in
>
> Table 5.2:
>
> (…) On the weak Arrowian assumptions, you are likely to cycle in your decision-making, preferring the Ford to the Chevy (on the basis of fuel efficiency and comfort), the Chevy to the Chrysler (on the basis of fuel efficiency and price), and the Chrysler to the Ford (on the basis of price and comfort). The result is paralysis by indecision. (Grinsell forthcoming)

Thus, when you use adjectives such as 'nice', your utterance is subject to vagueness that is the result of the same intransitivity that underlies legislative cycling:

Table 5.2 Can individual decisions cycle? (Grinsell forthcoming)

	Fuel efficiency	Price	Comfort
First best	Ford	Chevy	Chrysler
Second best	Chevy	Chrysler	Ford
Third best	Chrysler	Ford	Chevy

> Vagueness is the individual-level analog to legislative cycling. At bottom, both vagueness and cycling are instances of intransitivity and at bottom, this intransitivity has the same source: a decision procedure that takes into account multiple criteria and many alternatives. If individual decision-making is subject to the same public choice problems as collective decision-making, then the notions of "individual intent" and "legislative intent" – the intent behind the decision made – stand or fall together. (Grinsell forthcoming)

The problem with this reasoning is, I believe, that there is a crucial difference between individual decisions and legislative decisions. When you take an individual decision, you usually have a ranking of the criteria (here fuel efficiency, price and comfort). Consequently, you decide which criterion is the most important for you and you make the decision on the basis of this criterion. Your preference is then satisfied. By contrast, this move is not possible in the legislative context. This is because, in a legislature, the above criteria consist of voters. Each voter is a criterion. While making a decision, the preferences of a voter (for instance the majority party) overrule the preferences of other voters. Consequently, the preferences of other voters are neglected. Now this is precisely a threat to democracy since it entails a reduction of the democratic decision-making process to the preferences of one voter (or a dominant sub-group of voters). If one wants to build a theory of democratic legislative intent, then cycling is a serious objection that can make it impossible. No such problem arises with an individual who can simply decide on which criterion he prefers.

The conclusion that looms out of the above considerations is that even authors that claim to be proponents of legislative intentions (and internalists) are in fact externalists in disguise. I use the term externalists just as it is used in the philosophy of language and in the way I defined it at the outset of the chapter. Consider Ekins' statement:

> What is open to them [interpreters] may, at the risk of confusion, be said to be objective, because the content of the proposal turns on how it is reasonably to be understood. Yet the joint intention to act on that proposal is an intention that truly arises out of the interlocking intentions of all legislators and, to that extent, is fully actual and subjective. The distinction purports to open up a gap between what the legislators jointly do and what interpreters say that they intended to do. However, the object of legislative deliberation is a proposal that is transparent to legislators and the community, so that **what interpreters infer the legislature intended to do should be what was open to and thus chosen by the legislators**. [emphasis mine] (Ekins 2012)

Thus, by conflating the content inferred by interpreters on the basis of external evidence and the content of the legislative intention, Ekins places himself on the externalist side of the debate.

You could ask why all these considerations of institutional ontology are in a chapter about linguistic meaning. John Searle put the link neatly:

> I believe that language is the fundamental human institution in the sense that other institutions, such as money, government, private property, marriage, and games, require language, or at least language-like forms of symbolism, in a way that language does not require the other institutions for its existence. (Searle 1999)

Consequently, if language and linguistic rules are primary to institutions, then the latter are at least partly constituted by the former. As a result, a decision on the nature of meaning of legal language is a decision on the (constitutive) nature of the institutions.

To sum up, in this chapter I have been arguing for an externalist account of meaning of legal texts. I have also argued that the Gricean theory of implicatures can be treated as an epistemological theory independent of Grice's internalist views on meaning. If this is the case, then we can speak of implicatures while having externalist views on meaning. Since for the externalist it is the evidence available to a hearer—such as conventions or context—that constitutively determines meaning, we can speak of the legislator conversationally implicating some content. This is because such an implicature is formed if the external evidence leads the hearer to the conclusion that there was an implicature. Take the example provided by Richard Ekins:

> The assembly over time is like a succession of princes, each of whom should act to change the law as he thinks warranted, having considered the existing law and the importance of legal stability. The legislature should form and enact workable plans of action, which requires at the very least avoiding contradiction. This requirement of rational legislative agency supports the practical conclusion that the legislature repeals ***by implication*** (earlier) existing legal propositions inconsistent with its present (latest) choice. (Ekins 2012)

I believe that the implication mentioned is precisely the following conversational implicature:

(I.) 'All former claims on the subject are repealed by the present ones'.

This is because this content passes all tests for implicature. As I have argued in the previous chapters, an implicature must be cancelable, calculable and reinforceable. (I.) passes the test for cancelability because the legislator could always enact a provision of the form 'all former statutes regulating subject x remain in force'. This happens in practice when, for instance, intertemporal matters are at stake. (I.) passes the test of calculability through the following reasoning of the interpreter: On the basis of the second maxim of quantity (say no more than you must) and the maxim of relation, the legislature states how it would like to regulate a subject and does not need to add that it cancels former contradictory regulative solutions. On the basis of the maxim of manner, it does not need to formulate the redundant observation that 'all former claims on the subject are superseded by the present ones'. Finally, (I.) is reinforceable because there could be an article explicitly stating that 'The provisions of this statute supersede all former statutes regulating the present subject'.

Moreover, since the results of the three tests described above depend on evidence available to the interpreter, there could always be a context in which one could find evidence both backing up the above implicature as well as just the opposite implicature. For instance, imagine a context in which the new statute contains solution x, which is contradictory to the former solution y. Consequently, x and y cannot both be simultaneously enforced. Additionally, when the new statute was voted on, a social campaign claimed that its purpose was not to replace but to amend former defective solutions contained in statute y. In such a case, one could argue both ways.

First, it is possible to argue that the legislator implicated that the new statute supersedes the former statute because solutions a and y contradict one another. Second, one could argue that the new statute does not supersede the former one but—because of the social campaign—the contrary is true as it is supposed to supplement the former statute and the former statute remains in force. I believe that the decision upon what the legislature has implicated will be taken on the basis of the strategic framework. The judge will choose the implicature that best fits his immediate goal in reasoning. In other words, he will choose the implicature that is concordant with his moral or political reasons that incline him to solution A rather than solution B. Implicatures are just linguistic tools for achieving one's argumentative goals.

5.7 Conclusion

In the present chapter I hope to have shown that every theorist of language needs to answer two questions separately:

> (CQ – constitutive determination) In virtue of what facts does someone, S, mean whatever he or she means by performing something, x, on a given occasion?
>
> (EQ – epistemic determination) What sorts of information, what principles, and what types of cognitive states and processes are involved in the (typically spontaneous) arrival in the mind of an interpreter of a (typically resilient) conclusion about what S means by performing x on that occasion? (Neale 2016)

Conflating the answers to these two questions results in a philosophical mess. Paul Grice gave an internalist answer to CQ. He claimed that the speaker's meaning is constituted by the speaker's intentions. By contrast, his pragmatic theory of communicated meaning (the CP and maxims), if modified, can be considered in separation from his views on meaning, at least in the context of law. Moreover, an answer to EQ does not require a strong internalist approach to meaning. The answers to the two questions are independent in the sense that you can be either an internalist or an externalist about meaning and still endorse the Gricean answer to the epistemological question without being incoherent.

Let me now summarize the answer to the two questions is concerning the legal language that I tried to give in the first part of this study. My answer to CQ is that meaning in law is determined (ontologically constituted) by external factors. My answer to EQ is more complex. J. Goldsworthy notes that

> (…) the meaning of an utterance is the meaning which evidence readily available to its intended audience suggests it was intended to mean. An arguably counterintuitive consequence of this thesis is that *an utterance may have* ***more than one meaning****, because different evidence of the speaker's intended meaning may be available to different members of his intended audience*. [emphasis mine] (Goldsworthy 2005)

Thus, we need a mechanism that explains how the choice from among the available meanings is made during interpretation. The following strategic framework must be applied to explain the (epistemic) selectivity of pragmatic phenomena in the law. Strategic speech is **parasitic upon** cooperative speech. Consequently, strategic speech seems to be based on a different 'strategic' principle:

I. **Strategic principle (SP): assume that the speech is cooperative, infer all the implicatures and then apply the second-order strategic maxims to the inferred implicatures (anticipate which implicatures your hearer/speaker will choose/ignore).**

This principle is precisified in the following second-order maxims:

1. The strategic maxim—pursue your goal (independently of your interlocutor's ultimate goal).
2. The selectivity maxim—Deny implicated content that does not conform to your goal.
   a. Maxim of selectivity for the speaker: deny the implicated content formed on the basis of standard maxims if it does not conform to your goal (admit only the implicatures you want to admit)
   b. Maxim of selectivity for the hearer: take into account only the content that conforms with your goal (hear only what you want to hear)
3. The anticipation maxim—anticipate the goal of your interlocutor and anticipate what content he may wish to deny
4. The persuasion maxim—model your strategic contribution so as to convince the hearer to join your goal.

To sum up, the entire strategic framework can be summarized in one super-maxim (based on the strategic principle):

- **The strategic maxim—pursue your goal by selecting conforming implicatures.**

The classic Gricean epistemological theory faces two problems. First, there are theories that postulate that the four maxims (quantity, quality, relation and manner) can be reduced to two maxims. As I argued in the second chapter, I believe this is a useful reduction. I just do not think that psychological theories are of much use to an interpretive theory or the philosophy of law. This is because we need a mechanism that explains how we give reasons for choosing one interpretation over another in a conscious way. We do not need an account of semi-conscious processes. Second, the classic Gricean notion of 'what is said' does not explain the multitude of pragmatic enrichments made by speakers. For this reason, I have proposed modifying his notion of 'what is said' according to neo-Gricean theories and applying to this the strategic framework so as to get an explanation of what is going in the legal realm.

References

Arrow KJ (1978) Social choice and individual values, 2nd edn, 9. printing. Yale University Press, New Haven

Chalmers DJ (1997) The conscious mind: in search of a fundamental theory, 1. issued as an Oxford University Press paperback. Oxford University Press, New York

Ekins R (2012) The nature of legislative intent, 1st edn. Oxford University Press, Oxford

Gauker C (2008) Zero tolerance for pragmatics. Synthese 165:359–371. https://doi.org/10.1007/s11229-007-9189-2

Gizbert-Studnicki T (1975) O nieważnych czynnościach prawnych w świetle koncepcji czynności konwencjonalnych [Invalid legal acts in light of the concept of conventional acts]. pp 70–82

Gizbert-Studnicki T (2012) Oryginalizm i living constitutionalism a koncepcja państwa prawnego [Originalism, living-constitutionalism and the concept of the rule of law]. In: Kardas P, Wróbel W, Sroka T (eds) Państwo prawa i prawo karne: Księga jubileuszowa Profesora Andrzeja Zolla. Wolters Kluwer, Warszawa

Goldsworthy J (2005) Moderate versus strong intentionalism: Knapp and Michaels revisited. 42:669

Grice P (1975) Logic and conversation. In: Cole P, Morgan J (eds) Syntax and semantics. Academic Press, New York

Grice HP (1989) Studies in the way of words. Harvard University Press, Cambridge

Grinsell T (forthcoming) Linguistics and legislative intent

Gwiazdomorski J (1974) Próba korektury pojęcia czynności prawnej [An attempt to reformulate the notion of legal action]. In: Zeszyty Naukowe Uniwersytetu Jagiellońskiego, Prace z Wynalazczcości i ochrony własności intelektualnej

Kaplan D (1979) Dthat. In: Uehling, Wettstein (eds) Contemporary perspectives in the philosophy of language, pp 383–400

King JC (2014) Speaker intentions in context: speaker intentions in context. Noûs 48:219–237. https://doi.org/10.1111/j.1468-0068.2012.00857.x

Kripke SA (1998) Naming and necessity. Blackwell Publishers, Oxford

List C (2018) What is it like to be a group agent? Noûs 52:295–319. https://doi.org/10.1111/nous.12162

Marmor A (2014) The language of law, 1st edn. Oxford University Press, Oxford

Matczak M (2007) Summa iniuria: o błędzie formalizmu w stosowaniu prawa [On the mistake of formalism in applying the law]. Wyd. 1. Wydawn.Nauk. "Scholar", Warszawa

Matczak M (2016) Does legal interpretation need Paul Grice? Polish J Philos 10(1):67–87

Matczak M (forthcoming) A theory that beats the theory? Lineages, the growth of signs and dynamic legal interpretation

McGinn C (1981) The mechanism of reference. Synthese 49:157–186. https://doi.org/10.1007/BF01064297

Millikan RG (2005) Language: a biological model. Clarendon Press; Oxford University Press, Oxford; New York

Montminy M (2010) Context and communication: a defense of intentionalism. J Pragmat 42:2910–2918. https://doi.org/10.1016/j.pragma.2010.06.010

Nagel T (1974) What is it like to be a bat? Philos Revue 83:435. https://doi.org/10.2307/2183914

Neale S (1992) Paul Grice and the philosophy of language. Linguis Philos 15:509–559. https://doi.org/10.1007/BF00630629

Neale S (2005) Pragmatism and binding. In: Szabó ZG (ed) Semantics vs. pragmatics. Clarendon Press; Oxford University Press, Oxford: New York

Neale S (2016) Silent reference. In: Ostertag G (ed) Meanings and other things. Themes from the work of Stephen Schiffer. Oxford University Press

Perry J (2009) Directing intentions. In: Almog J, Leonardi P (eds) The philosophy of David Kaplan. Oxford University Press

Pietrzykowski T, Tobor Z (2010) Does a theory of contractual interpretation rest on a mistake? In: Heiderhoff B, Żmij G (eds) Interpretation in Polish, German and European Private Law. Sellier. European Law Publishers, München

Poggi F (2016) Grice, the law and the linguistic special case thesis. In: Capone A, Poggi F (eds) Pragmatics and law: philosophical perspectives

Predelli S (1998) I am not here now. Analysis 58:107–115. https://doi.org/10.1111/1467-8284.00110

Putnam H (2015) The meaning of "meaning". In: Pessin A, Goldberg S (eds) The Twin earth chronicles: twenty years of reflection on Hilary Putnam's "The meaning of 'meaning'"

Robaczyński W (2014) Komentarz do art.65 Kodeksu cywilnego [Commentary to article 65 of the Polish Civil Code]. In: Kodeks Cywilny. Komentarz. Część Ogólna, Lex 2014. Wolters Kluwer Polska

Scalia A, Gutmann A (2001) A matter of interpretation federal courts and the law. Princeton University Press, Princeton

Searle JR (1999) Mind, language, and society: philosophy in the real world, 1. paperb. ed. Basic Books, New York

Slocum BG (2016) Conversational implicatures and legal texts: conversational implicatures and legal texts. Ratio Juris 29:23–43. https://doi.org/10.1111/raju.12114

Solan L (2010) The language of statutes laws and their interpretation. University of Chicago Press, Chicago

Studnicki F (1971) O decyzjach kolektywnych [On collective decisions]. Państwo Prawo 266–274

Tobor Z (2013) W poszukiwaniu intencji prawodawcy [Searching for legislative intentions]. Lex, Warszawa

Wettstein HK (1984) How to bridge the gap between meaning and reference. Synthese 58:63–84. https://doi.org/10.1007/BF00485362

Chapter 6
The Exchange Between Legislature and Courts: Examples of Strategic Behavior from the Polish Legal System

6.1 Introduction

The previous chapters focus on two matters: first, abstract considerations of pragmatic mechanisms in the legal realm; second, examples most broadly discussed in the literature of 'law and language' (examples from common law systems). By contrast, this chapter aims to provide concrete examples from a continental law system, specifically the Polish legal system. These examples come from the two main branches of legal enterprise: civil and criminal law. In the present considerations I will try to argue that decisions taken by courts can be explained with the strategic principle and the second-order strategic maxims described in the previous chapters.

Before proceeding to the examples, a few words must be said about why the immediate goals of judicial hearers may sometimes be divergent with the goals of the legislature. This statement does not mean that there is no loosely understood common principal goal between them. This very general goal could be, for instance, ensuring democracy, the effective functioning of a society, social order etc. Nevertheless, when one looks closely at the immediate goals of the legislature and the judiciary, one discovers that these goals are often slightly divergent in the sense that, for instance, the legislature must consider more global policy goals, while courts work on a case-by-case basis. This entails that what can seem just or good on a global or impersonal scale may not be such in the particular, concrete context of a specific case. Thus, it is the job of judges to ensure that their ruling has a content they find just and good. Now, if the context is indeterminate and there are a few possible implicatures/pragmatic enrichments that can be strategically selected, a court might be interested in choosing an implicature that might not conform to, for instance, the goal that a statute was meant to achieve. Imagine a context in which a social campaign precedes the enactment of a statute. This campaign aims to communicate to the broad public that the statute is meant to achieve goal X. The judge might be aware that interpretation Y conforms to goal X. However, she may also

I. Skoczeń, *Implicatures within Legal Language*, Law and Philosophy Library 127, https://doi.org/10.1007/978-3-030-12532-5_6

find that interpretation Y leads to unjust results in the concrete case at hand. In such circumstances, the strategic, immediate goal of the judge is to ignore the pragmatic elements of the context that leads to interpretation Y and selectively select the elements of the context that lead to interpretation Z—an interpretation that in the eyes of the judge leads to just results.

6.2 Criminal Law

The Polish criminal code dates from 1997. As every such continental-European code, it contains a catalogue of descriptions of offences. The descriptions are of two kinds (other kinds are usually a mix of those two); First, they can be descriptions of an action undertaken by a subject. These are called 'formal' or 'no effect' offences. To convict someone for such an offence it is sufficient to prove that he undertook the action described by the legal text. It is not necessary that the action causes any effects in the world. By contrast, 'material' or 'effect' offenses are merely descriptions of effects in the world that can be caused by various actions. To convict someone for an 'effect' offense, it is necessary to prove a causal link between the action of the agent and the effect. The only literal element of the articles that indicates the necessity of establishing the causal link is the verb. For instance, article 148 paragraph 1 of the Polish Criminal Code states that:

> 'Whoever kills a man is subject to imprisonment not shorter than 8 years [up to 15 years on the basis of article 32], or 25 years of imprisonment or life imprisonment.[1]'

The article describes merely the effect of an action that is a deed of a person. The necessity of a causal link is inferred from the verb 'kills'. Consequently, the provision is fairly uncontroversially enriched to:

'Whoever kills a man [in some way or other such that this action causes the death], is subject to imprisonment not shorter than 8 years [up to 15 years on the basis of article 32], or 25 years of imprisonment or life imprisonment'. The basis for this is the meaning of the verb 'kills'.

Now, this is where the problem starts because we now have to define the verb 'cause'. The notion of a causal chain is both practically and philosophically controversial. Moreover, there is no rule in the code that provides a definition of a causal chain or a set of criteria that need to be fulfilled to establish a causal chain. Judges and scholars pragmatically supply both the definitions and the criteria, which they label for 'the objective ascription of effect' (Wróbel and Zoll 2010).

The verb 'cause' is taken to mean an 'information or energy link between the action and the effect' (Wróbel and Zoll 2010). Exceptions are material or effect crimes that are not caused by an action of the agent, but rather by the agent failing

[1] Art. 148. § 1. Whoever kills a man is subject to imprisonment for a period not shorter than 8 years [up to 15 years on the basis of article 32], 25 years or life imprisonment.

to undertake an action that he was legally obliged to undertake. In such situations, the judicial considerations boil down to answering one question. This involves imagining that the agent undertook the action and verifying whether his action would have broken the causal chain that led to the criminal effect. For instance, had the agent called an ambulance, the death of the victim could have been avoided.

Let us now leave this exception aside and come back to the definition of the verb 'cause' taken as 'the flow of an information or energy between the action and the effect'. This definition is problematic, especially when distinctions between intentional and unintentional material (or 'effect') offenses are at stake because, while the definition works for intentional crimes, it creates controversy with crimes committed unintentionally. To make a decision about the latter, the strategic framework seems vital. Let me illustrate this with an example of a famous case referred to as the 'case of the burning angel'.[2]

The facts were the following: during a school theatre performance, a 17-year-old girl dressed as an angel was severely burned. Her costume and 'wings', which were made of synthetic fabric, cotton wool and cardboard, caught fire. The burns were life-threatening (30–35 % of her skin surface was burned) and the girl went to hospital. The source of the flames were little candles carried by all the pupils dressed as angels. The fire started when the girl was walking with her colleagues through the audience towards the stage. The plan prepared by the teachers was such that the candles would be lit only once the teens were already on stage. However, the teens lit the candles before entering the stage. The teachers were accused of 'exposing humans to immediate danger of severe injury or loss of life' (art 160 paragraphs 2 and 3 of the Polish Criminal Code), 'causing severe bodily injury of the girl' (article 156 paragraph 2 of the Polish Criminal Code) and 'creating a high risk of a fire at school (article 164 paragraph 2 of the Polish Criminal Code)'. All the three judicial instances ultimately ruled that the teachers were innocent (Małecki 2013).

Nevertheless, does this decision not seem counterintuitive on the basis of the theoretical framework mentioned above? After all, the causal chain of an informational or energetic character was in place. The costumes, candles and the entire event was planned and organized by the teachers at school. The judges pointed out that since the teachers' actions were unintentional in the sense that those actions were not intended to cause the fire, paragraphs two and three of article 160 of the Polish Criminal Code were applicable:

[2]Ruling from the 15th of February 2012 II KK 193/11 http://www.sn.pl/sites/orzecznictwo/Orzeczenia2/II%20KK%20193-11-1.pdf.

Article 160

1. Whoever exposes a human being to an immediate danger of loss of life or severe injury can be subject to up to 3 years of imprisonment.
2. If the offender was supposed to guard the person subject to danger, the imprisonment can last from 3 months to 5 years.
3. If the offender acts unintentionally, she can be subject to a fine, a restriction of freedom or imprisonment up to 1 year. (…)[3]

We have established that the first paragraph of the discussed rule should be understood as:

> Whoever exposes a human being to [**in some way such that this action causes**] an immediate danger of loss of life or severe injury can be subject to up to three years of imprisonment. [emphasis mine]

However, the problem was not paragraph one of article 160, but paragraph three. This rule describes an unintentional offence. Since there is no intention of the offender to cause the effects, the negative moral assessment of his deeds is much more controversial than when his deeds were intentional. On this basis some judges argued that to compensate for the lack of a negative moral assessment, the risk or danger caused needs to be very high, and the level of probability of the effect occurring needs to be substantially elevated. Moreover, some basic and important safety rules must be violated (Małecki 2013).

Recall Asgeirsson's distinction which claims that judges are usually faced with two types of difficulties: the decision on whether to enrich or stick to the literal meaning, or the decision on what the content of the enrichment should be (the possibilities are constrained by context) (Asgeirsson 2016). In the discussed case, the question was of the first type. Namely, whether to enrich (or stick to the literal meaning) paragraph three in the manner below:

> If the offender acts unintentionally [**and the action significantly increases the risk of the effect occurring**], she can be subject to a fine, a restriction of freedom or imprisonment up to one year. [emphasis mine]

Mikołaj Małecki points to the fact that there was nothing in the text or in the context of the enactment that could clearly indicate that the legislature 'intended' such enrichment. Thus, the argumentation is instead based on an abstract, moral or political policy goal of the legislature to differentiate between intentional and unintentional offences. On the one hand, one can argue that the legislature could be

[3]Art. 160 § 1. Whoever exposes a human being to [in any way that causes—author's note] an immediate danger of loss of life, a serious bodily injury, or a serious impairment of health shall be subject to the penalty of deprivation of liberty for up to 3 years. § 2. If the perpetrator has a duty to take care of the person exposed to danger, he shall be subject to the penalty of the deprivation of liberty for a term of between 3 months and 5 years. § 3. If the perpetrator of an act specified in §1 or 2 acts unintentionally he shall be subject to a fine, the penalty of restriction of liberty or the penalty of deprivation of liberty for up to 1 year. § 4. A perpetrator who voluntarily averted the impending danger shall not be subject to the penalty for the offence specified in § 1–3. § 5. The prosecution of the offence specified in § 3 shall occur if the injured person files a motion.

ascribed the enrichment because it clearly differentiates intentional and unintentional offences in numerous provisions of the Polish criminal code. The differentiation is especially visible in the facts that penalties are lower for unintentional crimes. On the other hand, if the differentiating is already done by the criterion of the level of penalties, then why introduce some further criteria (such as the high probability of the effect occurring given the action undertaken)?[4] (Małecki 2013).

In terms of the theory sketched in the present study, on the basis of the elements of the context that we dispose of, two contradictory types of pragmatic reasoning can be carried out. First, recall the rule referred to as either the 'first Gricean sub-maxim of quantity' or the 'Q principle': 'make your contribution as informative as is required for the current purposes of the exchange', or 'say as much as you (truthfully and relevantly) can'; this corresponds to the heuristic 'what isn't said isn't the case' (which in turn corresponds to the canon 'expressio unius est exclusio alterius') (Carston 2013). On the basis of this reasoning, if the legislature explicitly differentiated intentional and unintentional crimes with the levels of punishment, no further unexpressed differentiations would be possible.

Now recall the second rule referred to as either the 'second Gricean sub-maxim of quantity' or the 'R principle': 'do not make your contribution more informative than is required', or 'say no more than you must', both of which correspond to the heuristic 'What is simply/briefly described is the stereotypical or normal (default) instance' (which in turn corresponds to the canon 'eiusdem generis') (Carston 2013). On the basis of such reasoning, if the legislature distinguished the intentional and unintentional crimes by the levels of punishment, introducing a further criterion for the same distinction is legitimate because the goal of the further criterion being introduced is analogous to the explicit differentiation inscribed in paragraph three of article 160 of the Polish criminal code. The goal is to take into account the lack of negative moral assessment of deeds committed unintentionally.

---

[4] 'the legislator must answer whether a certain type of causing or allowing of effect occurring is prohibited under the risk of punishment, in virtue of its typical social detriment, that licenses the penalization of an action without considering the context of a concrete case. Broadly speaking, a penalized action needs to be typically blameworthy [which means that there needs to be a broad agreement on its blameworthiness]. Could an attempt to establish legislative intentions about the construction of "material types of crimes" be successful? Are there clear statutory or non-statutory criteria that enable warranted conclusions on the subject? One might wonder whether the present penal code, which licenses the claim that only an effect (of an unintentional crime), together with a substantial increase of risk for the protected legal good, is "blameworthy" independently of the context of the case at stake. Non-statutory argumentation (moral or political rationalizations) seems unclear. The search for such criteria is doomed to be arbitrary (independently of its merits). The Highest Court stated that the "blameworthiness of effect of unintentional crime type" has to be 'qualified' (important, blatant). Let us emphasize that in comparison to intentional crimes, unintentional ones have a lower penalty (for example: at least 8 years of imprisonment in the case of murder, from art. 148 § 1 of the penal code and at most 5 years of imprisonment for unintentionally causing death, from art. 155 of the penal code). You could counter-argue – and this has grounds in the statute – that the abstract blameworthiness of causing "effect" has been differentiated at the level of punishment, rather than at the level of substantial criteria of effect type crimes.' [Translated by IS] (Małecki 2013).

Consequently, the context allows two contradictory types of pragmatic reasoning to be drawn, but a decision needs to be taken. This is where the strategic framework needs to be applied. In other words, since the judges have identified all the possible pragmatic interpretations on the basis of the neo-Gricean theories, they now need to choose the one that conforms to their goal. This is done through the strategic principle described in the previous chapters, which states that:

I. *Strategic principle (SP)*: assume that the speech is cooperative, infer all the implicatures/enrichments and then apply the second-order strategic maxims to the inferred implicatures (anticipate which implicatures your hearer/speaker will choose/ignore).

Recall that the second-order maxims boil down to one rule:

- *The strategic maxim*: pursue your goal by selecting conforming implicatures.

As they mentioned in their ruling, the reason the judges reached such a decision in the burning angel case was natural justice. This meant taking under consideration some facts of the case. For instance, the fact that the teachers thought that the candles would be lit by the teens only once they were on the stage, or the fact that candles are not unusual in Polish schools. Christmas theatre performances with candles and people dressed as angels are also not unusual. Finally, it is not a standard consequence (even in an inductive sense) of giving a candle to a 17 or 18-year-old that the teen gets such severe bodily injury. People of this age are cautious with open fire and are fully aware of the dangers associated with it. The probability of such a severe injury is very low and, in the circumstances, it could have been hard to predict. As an effect, the requirements of article 160 paragraph three, in its enriched version, were not fulfilled and the rule could not be applied (Małecki 2013).

Jeffrey Goldsworthy emphasizes the fact that in such cases the judges should clearly admit that they are acting creatively—they are adding some content to the legal rule. They should admit that what they are doing is no longer an interpretation, but some kind of construction (Goldsworthy 1994).

Małecki notices that the case was part of a broader discussion concerning the interpretation of some rules in the criminal code which regulate the so-called 'objective ascriptions of effect' to agents. Thus, there is widespread and openly admitted permission for judges to act actively in the matter. Lower courts follow higher courts in their reasoning because the language of the current code is indeterminate as far as this issue is concerned (Małecki 2013). For this reason, the ascription of effects requires pragmatic considerations from courts at every reprise. However, since enacting new rules may take time and decisions are necessary, judges must resort to strategic pragmatics. Interestingly, some scholars have argued against the enactment of clear rules of the objective ascription of effect. They claim that the matter involves an extremely complex philosophical and scientific discussion which asks questions but provides no broadly agreed upon answer. Consequently, if scholars that minutely analyze the issue have no clues for answers, then a fortiori the legislator has no chance of formulating an effective regulation,[5] see (Giezek and Kaczmarek 2013).

Nevertheless, even if one calls this kind of judicial reasoning 'activism', one must admit that it is constrained by context, including the so-called 'co-text' which is constituted by other rules included in the Polish criminal code and other statutory material. Let us now move on to further examples from a different branch of Polish law: civil law.

6.3 Civil Law

6.3.1 Incapacitation

A recent example of strategic behavior in civil law is the Supreme Court's decision number III CZP 38/16 from the 28th of September 2016 on whether a motion for incapacitation can be filed by a to-be-incapacitated person. Article 545 paragraph one of the Polish code of civil procedure states that:

'A motion for incapacitation can be filed by:

1. the spouse of the person that is to be incapacitated
2. close relatives and siblings
3. a legal representative'[6]

Another rule of the code provides explicitly that a prosecutor can also file such a motion. The enumeration above does not list the person that is to be incapacitated as entitled to file a motion for herself. Taken literally the list seems exhaustive. However, did the legislator really 'intend' it to be exhaustive? Can the to-be-incapacitated person file a motion herself? Before attempting to answer this question, let me say a few words about the history of the rule and the history of the judges interpreting the rule, as these facts form vital contextual elements for the present considerations.

---

[5] 'Is it the legislator that is supposed to settle unfinished scientific disputes and discussions which do not provide a translation of the jurisprudential criteria of "objective ascription of effect" to statutory language? A worry arises, confirmed by the effect of the work of the "Komisja Kodyfikacyjna" (commission for the writing of legal codes), that it is currently an unfeasible task to give a precise wording of these criteria in the penal code that is free of inconsistencies (which usually have to be erased thanks to the intuition and common sense of a judge). Our skepticism is greater when we notice that even the proponents of a statutory regulation of a "normative" basis for the "ascription of effect", (...), disagree on whether the planned regulation should take into account all the criteria, or, rather, only some of them.' [Translated by IS] (Giezek and Kaczmarek 2013).

[6] Art. 545. § 1. Wniosek o ubezwłasnowolnienie może zgłosić: (1) małżonek osoby, której dotyczy wniosek o ubezwłasnowolnienie; (2) jej krewni w linii prostej oraz rodzeństwo; (3) jej przedstawiciel ustawowy.

In the 1960s, this provision was interpreted by courts as non-exhaustive (7th June 1965, II CR 148/65, OSN 1966/2/30)—the person concerned could file a motion for herself. Note that 1965 was the year of the enactment of the code of civil procedure. Consequently, some facts from the legislative procedure might have suggested that this was the 'intended' interpretation. Later the courts started to interpret the provision as exhaustive. This was probably due to the fear that this could provide an instrument for avoiding debts. Moreover, an already incapacitated person could not file a motion to repeal or modify the incapacitation. In 2007 the Polish constitutional court ruled that the lack of possibility for an incapacitated person to file a motion to repeal or modify her own incapacitation was unconstitutional. As a consequence, in 2007 the legislature enacted a new provision in the code of civil procedure. Yet, filing a motion for one's own incapacitation was still not possible.

The Supreme Court decided to change the trend. The main motive was situations in which the persons listed in points one to three of article 545 paragraph one are lacking and the prosecutor delays his motion. In such cases, the to-be-incapacitated person is left helpless and risks financial losses. This mainly concerns persons with a severe handicap.[7] For this reason, the court decided to enrich the provision to the form below:

'A motion for incapacitation can be filed by:

1. the spouse of the person that is to be incapacitated
2. close relatives and siblings
3. a legal representative
4. [the person that is to be incapacitated]'

Let us now try to explain step-by-step the decision of the Supreme Court with the theory sketched in the present study, namely the strategic framework. Recall again the two contradictory canons of construction. First, *expressio unius est exclusio alterius*. On the basis of this, the list needs to be exhaustive, so the enrichment is [and no other person]. There are at least two reasons for this interpretation: the settled case law and the risk of people avoiding debts by incapacitating themselves in the eyes of the law. Second, the *eiusdem generis* canon points to the opposite interpretation: the to-be-incapacitated person is equally (or even more) informed of her own situation as the persons listed in points one to three. A good policy argument for this interpretation is the decision of the constitutional tribunal from 2007 and the necessity to protect persons with a handicap.

Since the Supreme Court's goal was to develop the protection of handicapped persons and form a case law in accordance with the constitutional tribunal, it chose to uphold the second possible implicature, namely that the list is not exhaustive. This way the court allowed persons that want to be incapacitated to file a motion for themselves. Again, this is a case in which different elements of the context can point to different enrichments. Strategic behavior is needed to make a decision.

[7] See http://www.kancelaria.lex.pl/czytaj/-/artykul/sn-wniosek-o-ubezwlasnowolnienie-moze-zlozyc-takze-osoba-ktora-ma-byc-ubezwlasnowolniona.

6.3.2 *Oral Wills*

Another example of enrichment from the civil law system are rules concerning oral wills. Consider article 952 paragraph one of the Polish civil code:

> 'If imminent death of the testator is expected or, if due to extraordinary circumstances, it is not possible or very difficult for a will to be made in ordinary form, the testator may declare his final wishes orally in the simultaneous presence of at least three witnesses.'[8]

The interpretive question that has concerned judges for decades was whether an expectation of imminent death needs to be merely subjective, merely objective or both. In 1992, the Supreme Court ruled that subjective expectation is sufficient (III CZP 135/91). However, both preceding and subsequent case law indicated that both the subjective and objective expectations are necessary (in 1952 C 1321/52, in 1958 I CR 512/58, In 1974 III CRN 5/74 and in 1974 III CRN 118/74).

An interesting opinion of the Supreme Court on the question is a case in which a person made an oral will before committing suicide in 2003 (III CK 7/02). The court made the decision that the rule must be enriched to:

> If the imminent death of the testator is [**both subjectively and objectively**] expected or, if due to extraordinary circumstances, it is not possible or very difficult for a will to be made in ordinary form, the testator may declare his final wishes orally in the simultaneous presence of at least three witnesses.

Objective means foreseeable by competent medical staff. Since suicide was predictable only subjectively in the circumstances, the oral will was not valid. Again, in these cases cooperative pragmatic rules gave rise to two contradictory enrichments: either the subjective expectation suffices or both subjective and objective expectations are needed. The court applied the strategic framework to the two possibilities.

6.4 Conclusions

Since the cases discussed in the literature concerning the question of whether the Gricean framework can be applied to the legal realm are mostly those from common law systems (with the exception of cases provided in, for instance, the article 'Law and conversational implicatures' (Poggi 2011)), this chapter aimed to provide more examples from a continental system, namely the Polish legal system. The more

---

[8] Art. 952. § 1. Jeżeli istnieje obawa rychłej śmierci spadkodawcy albo jeżeli wskutek szczególnych okoliczności zachowanie zwykłej formy testamentu jest niemożliwe lub bardzo utrudnione, spadkodawca może oświadczyć ostatnią wolę ustnie przy jednoczesnej obecności co najmniej trzech świadków.

general aim was to emphasize the fact that strategic inferences take place regardless of the type of system, the legal culture or the branch of law discussed.

As far as criminal law was concerned, I summarized the case of the 'burning angel', which dealt with the question of whether to enrich the provision on non-intentional causing of a criminal effect. The possible content of the enrichment arising from the context would require the non-intentional action to cause a very high risk of the effect occurring.

As far as civil law was concerned, I described two interesting cases of strategic enrichment. The first case concerned treating an enumeration as non-exhaustive. This move enabled a person interested in incapacitating herself to file a motion to a court. The policy goal in this case was to protect handicapped persons. Second, the requirements concerning an oral testament were discussed. The court chose the enrichment of the provision so as to require an expectation of imminent death that would be more than just the subjective feeling of the person making the will.

References

Asgeirsson H (2016) On the possibility of non-literal legislative speech. In: Capone A, Poggi F (eds) Pragmatics and law: philosophical perspectives. Springer, Berlin

Carston R (2013) Legal texts and canons of construction: a view from current pragmatic theory. In: Freeman MDA, Smith F (eds) Law and language, 1st edn. Oxford University Press, Oxford

Giezek JW, Kaczmarek T (2013) Przeciwko ustawowej regulacji kryteriów obiektywnego przypisania skutku [Against legal rules on criteria of the objective ascription of effect]. Państwo Prawo 5:79–92

Goldsworthy J (1994) Implications in language, law and the constitution. In: Lindell G, Zines L (eds) Future directions in Australian constitutional law: essays in honour of Professor Leslie Zines. Federation Press in association with the Centre for International and Public Law and the Law Faculty, Australian National University, Sydney

Małecki M (2013) Z problematyki obiektywnego przypisania skutku (przypadek płonącego anioła) [The problem of the objective ascription of effect (the case of the burning angel)]. Czasopismo Prawa Karnego i Nauk Penalnych XVII

Poggi F (2011) Law and conversational implicatures. Int J Semiotics Law - Revue internationale de Sémiotique juridique 24:21–40. https://doi.org/10.1007/s11196-010-9201-x

Wróbel W, Zoll A (2010) Polskie prawo karne: część ogólna [Polish Criminal Law: general part]. Społeczny Instytut Wydawniczy Znak, Kraków

Chapter 7
General Conclusions

In the present study I hope to have built an analytical theory that provides an explanation of the mechanisms behind the linguistic exchange between the legislatures and courts. The idea is that the classic Gricean version of the implicature theory is inapplicable to the legal realm because it is not possible to claim that in the legal realm the Cooperative Principle, as defined by Paul Grice, is in force. Moreover, the content and number of maxims as defined by Grice seem inapplicable to the legal situation. Finally, Grice's internalist theory of meaning does not fit the legal picture. However, it is possible to modify the Gricean picture so as to view Grice's theory of meaning and Grice's theory of implicature as an answer to various philosophical questions. Namely, the first answers the metaphysical question and the second answers the epistemic question. For this reason, one can coherently dispute the theory of implicatures without using the Gricean theory of meaning.

The legal situation is a type of strategic speech. Thus, it requires a two-step procedure. The first step is a counterfactual assumption of the cooperative principle in force and the inference of all possible implicatures and pragmatic enrichments on the basis of available external cues. This inference need not be based on the number and content of maxims that Grice postulated. Quite the contrary, in the legal realm the maxims can be replaced with, for instance, canons of construction or Horn's Q and R principles and corresponding heuristics (for instance, 'say as much as you can' or 'say no more than you must'). Just as in Relevance Theory, reducing Gricean maxims to a single principle of relevance does not seem to be an adequate solution because it would exclude the linguistically counterintuitive outcomes of courts' decisions. Since it is a fact that judicial decisions can run counter to the technically defined linguistic relevance, a different explanation is necessary.

The second step involves applying a second-order strategic framework to the inferred possible pragmatic enrichments and implicatures. Strategic speech is *parasitic upon* cooperative speech. Consequently, strategic speech seems to be based on a different 'strategic' principle:

I. Skoczeń, *Implicatures within Legal Language*, Law and Philosophy Library 127, https://doi.org/10.1007/978-3-030-12532-5_7

I. **Strategic principle (SP): assume that the speech is cooperative, infer all the implicatures/enrichments and then apply the second-order strategic maxims to the inferred implicatures/enrichments (anticipate which implicatures your hearer/speaker will choose/ignore).**

This principle is precisified in the following second-order maxims:

1. The strategic maxim—pursue your goal (independently of your interlocutor's ultimate goal).
2. The selectivity maxim—deny implicated/enriched content that does not conform to your goal.
    a. Maxim of selectivity for the speaker: deny the implicated/enriched content formed on the basis of standard maxims if it does not conform to your goal (admit only the implicatures/enrichments you want to admit)
    b. Maxim of selectivity for the hearer: take into account only the content that conforms to your goal (hear only what you want to hear)
3. The anticipation maxim—anticipate the goal of your interlocutor and anticipate what content he may wish to deny.
4. The persuasion maxim—model your strategic contribution so as to convince the hearer to join your goal.

This entire strategic framework can be summarized in one super-maxim (based on the strategic principle):

- **The strategic maxim—pursue your goal by selecting conforming implicatures/enrichments.**

The above framework requires an external theory of meaning. Thus, the claim is that while an internalist theory of meaning can be explanatorily valuable for everyday linguistic exchanges, in the realm of law an external framework is needed.

Note that the strategic framework applies not only to strong pragmatic effects such as conversational implicatures, but also to pragmatic developments of the logical form of the proposition uttered; these are referred to as pragmatic enrichments.

The present study concentrated on a limited amount of linguistic exchanges within the realm of law. Namely, it concentrated on the exchange between the legislatures and courts. However, the plethora of linguistic occurrences is much broader and encompasses exchanges such as:

1. An exchange within a legislative body
2. An exchange between a court and parties
3. An exchange between parties
4. Contracts and other legal declarations of intent

It could be that these exchanges are subject to analogous strategic interactions, but an exact analysis remains necessary and could be the subject of further investigations.

The manufacturer's authorised representative in the EU is Springer Nature Customer Service Centre GmbH, Europaplatz 3, 69115 Heidelberg, Germany. If you have any concerns regarding our products, please contact ProductSafety@springernature.com

Printed and bound by CPI Group (UK) Ltd, Croydon, CR0 4YY
30/09/2026
02225513-0019